# China's Digital Presence in the Asia-Pacific

China's Digital Presence in the Asia-Pacific

Culture, Technology and Platforms

Michael Keane, Haiqing Yu, Elaine Jing Zhao
and Susan Leong

ANTHEM PRESS

Anthem Press
An imprint of Wimbledon Publishing Company
www.anthempress.com

This edition first published in UK and USA 2022
by ANTHEM PRESS
75–76 Blackfriars Road, London SE1 8HA, UK
or PO Box 9779, London SW19 7ZG, UK
and
244 Madison Ave #116, New York, NY 10016, USA

First published in the UK and USA by Anthem Press in 2021

Copyright © Michael Keane, Haiqing Yu, Elaine Jing Zhao, Susan Leong 2022

The authors assert the moral right to be identified as the authors of this work.

All rights reserved. Without limiting the rights under copyright reserved above, no part of this publication may be reproduced, stored or introduced into a retrieval system, or transmitted, in any form or by any means (electronic, mechanical, photocopying, recording or otherwise), without the prior written permission of both the copyright owner and the above publisher of this book.

British Library Cataloguing-in-Publication Data
A catalogue record for this book is available from the British Library.

ISBN-13: 978-1-83998-567-6 (Pbk)
ISBN-10: 1-83998-567-4 (Pbk)

This title is also available as an e-book.

CONTENTS

List of Tables   vii
List of Abbreviations   ix
Acknowledgements   xi

Introduction: A Giant Awakening?   1

PART 1   China's '+' Long Game

1. Culture +   13
2. Industry +   31
3. Internet +   47
4. Platform +   67

PART 2   The Asia-Pacific as a Chinese Cultural Landing Pad

5. Assessing the Evidence   85
6. East Asia: Hong Kong and Taiwan   101
7. South East Asia: Singapore and Malaysia   119
8. Oceania: Australia and New Zealand   135
9. From Cultural Presence to Innovative Nation   155

Appendix: Survey Conducted from August to December 2019   163
Notes   169
Index   195

TABLES

1.1	China's cultural services trade deficit 1997–2005	17
2.1	Cultural innovation timeline	36
3.1	From Internet + to Intelligent +	56
4.1	China's digital companies IPO valuations	75

ABBREVIATIONS

AI	artificial intelligence
API	application programming interface
BAT	Baidu Alibaba Tencent
BMD	ByteDance Meituan-Dianping Didi Chuxing
BRI	Belt and Road Initiative
CAC	Cyberspace Administration of China
CCP	Chinese Communist Party
CCTV	China Central Television
CEPA	Closer Economic Partnership Agreement
CFO	chief financial officer
CNNIC	China Internet Network Information Centre
CPPCC	Chinese Peoples' Political Consultative Conference
CRI	China Radio International
DFTZ	Digital Free Trade Zone
ECFA	Economic Cooperation Framework Agreement
ETZs	economic and technology zones
EWTP	electronic World Trade Platform
FinTech	financial technology
FYP	Five-Year Plans
GFC	Great Firewall of China
HKSAR or Hong Kong SAR	Hong Kong Special Autonomous Region
ICT	information and communication technology
IoT	Internet of Things
IPO	initial public offering
IPR	intellectual property rights
MIC25	Made in China 2025
MIIT	Ministry of Industry and Information Technology
MoC	Ministry of Culture
MPT	Ministry of Posts and Telecommunication
NZIFF	New Zealand International Film Festival

O2O	offline to online
ODM	original design manufacturing
OEM	original equipment manufacturing
OTT	over-the-top
PGC	professionally generated content
PRC	Peoples Republic of China
R&D	research and development
SAIC	State Administration of Industry and Commerce
SAPPRFT	State Administration of Press Publication Radio Film and Television
SARFT	State Administration of Radio Film and Television
SBS	Special Broadcasting Service
SIIO	State Internet Information Office
VR	virtual reality
WTO	World Trade Organization

ACKNOWLEDGEMENTS

The authors would like to acknowledge funding from the Australian Research Council Discovery Project scheme DP170102176: Digital China: From Cultural Presence to Innovative Nation.

The authors would like to particularly express thanks to Huan Wu who provided invaluable and timely assistance in research during the course of this project, as well as making important intellectual contributions.

The authors would also like to acknowledge the contribution of Brian Yecies to the project as well as Jack Jie Yang at the University of Wollongong. We would like to extend our thanks to all the interviewees for their generosity in sharing their views. Along the way a number of colleagues and PhD students made contributions and suggestions to our work-in-progress and we thank them for this. They include (in no particular order) Anthony Fung, Chen Guo, Guanhua Su, Qing Wang, Xinyang Zhao, Yao Cao, Shanshan Liu, Qian Gong, Denis Leonov, and Liwen Li.

The authors would like to thank Megan Greiving at Anthem Press and Anthem Editorial Team in Newgen.

We have used the *hanyu pinyin* system for Chinese terms. With regard to family names we place the family name first for scholars and commentators working within China and publishing mostly in Chinese. Chinese scholars writing in English outside China are represented by their names as they are listed in their English-language outputs.

INTRODUCTION: A GIANT AWAKENING?

Napoleon Bonaparte, emperor of France, is said to have called China a sleeping giant. While the veracity of the quote attributed to Napoleon sometime in the dying embers of the eighteenth century is open to question, its relevance to China's global presence is emblematic of the state of geopolitics in the early twenty-first century. Up until the 1980s people in China were living under a planned political system, a system that has since become increasingly capitalist. It's a cliché to say that the impact of China is everywhere you look. Ask anyone in the developed world where most of their consumer goods come from. In the developing world too, China's presence is ubiquitous.

Many commentators have pondered the exact significance of President Xi Jinping's Chinese Dream, unveiled to the masses in 2012. Does Xi's dreamscape allude to an awakening or is it just a convenient riposte to the American Dream? After all, why can't Chinese people dream of a good life, of becoming successful, of being famous? Throughout China, media promotes positive slogans: 'a community of shared future', 'positive energy' and the 'great rejuvenation'. The last of these is probably most pertinent. Is the Dream a metaphor for a utopian future, a great rejuvenation?

The proclivity to see the Chinese nation as a rising technological power informs global strategy and global business. The Chinese government is advancing its interests abroad, expanding the economy. China's reach is extended by infrastructure projects and digital connectivity. As the strategist Parag Khanna maintains, somewhat hyperbolically, 'Connectivity is destiny [...] Infrastructure is like a nervous system connecting all parts of the planetary body; capital and code are the blood cells flowing through it.'[1] Indeed, such a description accords well with Chinese metaphysics. China's destiny is to be great once again: the time has arrived, at least that is the sentiment fermenting in Beijing.

This book explores China's digital presence in relation to its cultural influence. The focus is the Asia-Pacific, a region that is most proximate to the People's Republic of China, where one finds the settled existence of the

Chinese diaspora and where many people connect with, consume and share Chinese media and cultural products. Chinese culture has deep roots in some of the nation-states of the Asia-Pacific and this legacy plays to China's national advantage as its digital empire expands. China has acquired technological prowess over the past 30 years and Chinese graduates from Western institutions have returned home to join the national cause. Moreover, a great deal of the investment driving Chinese high-technology ventures comes from East and Southeast Asia.[2]

The research for this book was conducted from 2017 to 2019, before the events that unfolded in 2020 that led to security bans on TikTok in the United States and India, along with many other Chinese social media apps. Notwithstanding the complications of the political jostling by Donald Trump and allegations against China, our primary findings remain valid, particularly our contention that Chinese digital start-ups and platforms are more attuned to the rules of international financial capitalism than the dictates of the party-state.

In this study we investigate six locations in the Asia-Pacific where Chinese cultural influence is very evident.[3] Four of the locations – Hong Kong, Taiwan, Singapore and Malaysia – have sizeable Chinese-speaking communities. Hong Kong and Taiwan are geographically proximate to the mainland and are designated Chinese territories according to the PRC government. Singapore and Malaysia are liberal democratic in terms of institutions and governance structures. They are closer than Hong Kong and Taiwan to the Eurasian region, the so-called Belt and Road Initiative (BRI), where China is expanding its influence and where authoritarianism is in favour among several nation-states.[4] While Australia and New Zealand are Anglophone nations, Chinese migration has changed the social fabric 'down under' over the past few decades. In Australia and New Zealand, moreover, the term 'Chinese influence' has become extremely politically charged.

We identify three orienting themes – culture, technology and platforms – as a framework to organize the chapters. Throughout the book the symbol '+' (plus) signifies the inevitable convergence of the three themes. The symbol '+' (positivity) is also a reflection of the dominant political discourse in China, scripted by Chinese President Xi Jinping. China's planners, system builders, digital entrepreneurs and grassroots practitioners see digital technology as a positive force. After all, the media's role has been, and continues to be, the promotion of 'positive energy' (*zheng nengliang*).

The first of our aims is to analyse Beijing's changing policies towards the governance of internet technologies; the second is to show how the global image of China is changing; and the third is to examine how China's image is understood in the Asia-Pacific region. Of course, what the image of China represents in the twenty-first century is open to dispute according to one's global geographical and cultural positioning. A factory worker in the US Midwest Rust Belt would no doubt be resentful of China's rise; likewise, in the southern states of the United States Trump's invective against unfair Chinese trade practice has exploited racist stereotypes. In Silicon Valley and Hollywood, meanwhile, a different picture of the future emerges. China has drawn technological know-how from the disruptive start-up culture of northern California and has sought to emulate the creative entertainment media culture of southern California. In Singapore and Malaysia, we notice a hybrid Chinese identity among people who have migrated from the PRC to start new lives and those that have lived in the Southeast Asian region for several generations.

China's attempts to move its culture into global markets has not been without challenges. While global audiences are attuned to Hollywood, the centre of media production is shifting. In recent years many East Asian practitioners in film, television and animation, particularly from Hong Kong and Taiwan, have moved their projects to the mainland,[5] hoping to cash in on what Michael Curtin has termed the 'world's biggest audience'.[6] The magnetic pull of the mainland is part of a larger geopolitical narrative. But while the PRC may be flexing its muscles as a global superpower, the nation's culture is not receiving accolades that are dispensed on the world stage. The Asia-Pacific presents an opportunity. The key questions we ask are, Can China's visionary entrepreneurs, innovators, film-makers, writers and artists change perceptions of China in the Asia-Pacific? And is digital technology strengthening China's cultural power?

In 2014, the World Economic Forum summer meeting convened in the northern city of Tianjin. It was here that Premier Li Keqiang announced a new development slogan, 'Mass entrepreneurship, mass innovation' (*dazhong chuangye, wanzhong chuangxin*), that would stimulate start-up enterprises.[7] In a few months the campaign was elevated to Internet + (*hulianwang jia*). The objectives of Internet + are by now well known, although it is useful to repeat the official line: 'to integrate mobile Internet, cloud computing big data, and the Internet of Things with modern manufacturing, to encourage the healthy development of e-commerce, industrial networks, and Internet banking, and to get Internet-based companies to increase their presence in the international market'.[8] According to this vision, advanced digital technology will transform China, moving the economy to ever-dizzying heights. Premier Li's intervention took place at Chaihuo, translated literally as 'firewood', a popular Shenzhen makerspace. Shenzhen now has hundreds of makerspaces; in fact, it probably has more incubators, accelerators, fab labs and co-working spaces per population than any other city in the world.[9]

In 1996, China's commercial internet service was launched. Prior to this, the nascent technology was viewed as a mechanism for scholars and scientists to share information. But disruption is inevitably part of development. The government has erected firewalls to stop unwanted foreign ideas, although such restrictions have hindered rather than stopped the flow. The newly formed Cyberspace Administration of China (CAC) has threatened to close down all virtual private networks (VPNs), which according to some estimates are used by up to 20 per cent of the population, including business enterprises that deal with international investors.[10] Since 2014, the Chinese government through the aegis of the CAC has organized a World Internet Conference in the picturesque town of Wuzhen, outside Shanghai; in 2017 CEOs from Apple and Google were invited. While advocating an open internet to promote the digital economy, the government mandates internet sovereignty, essentially to restrict peoples' access to information that is deemed unhealthy, too foreign or dangerous to the national interest. In other words, it advocates positive disruption for the development of the digital economy but steers away from disruption-as-social dissent. The internet therefore has a role to play in the popularization of the Chinese Dream, at least the part of the dream that speaks to the idea of a great rejuvenation.

In 2000, only 1.8 per cent of the Chinese population was online.[11] With the burgeoning commercial internet services, hundreds of millions of Chinese people rushed to purchase smart phones and tablets, most seeing no need for a computer, or even email. By the end of the first decade of the new millennium, internet penetration had climbed to 34 per cent of the population, a total of 516 million people. The number now exceeds 900 million. In 2014, start-up fever took hold in coastal cities like Shenzhen, Hangzhou, Shanghai and Beijing and the previous decade's focus on creative clusters turned to incubators and makerspaces.[12] In the government's 2015 Work Report the term 'innovation' featured 14 times, compared with only three the previous year. Masses of young Chinese were aspiring to be digital entrepreneurs rather than engineers of the soul. This digital transformation has happened at breakneck speed. Regional governments, mayors and many venture capitalists have been quick to accept the vision that China is becoming an artificial intelligence (AI) superpower.[13]

Seizing the power of the internet and using this borderless medium to reinvigorate culture is ambitious and not without challenges. China's national image has been tarnished by what many in the West see as a repressive approach to the expression of ideas, especially when it affects citizens that are less enamoured with the Chinese Dream. However, the Asia-Pacific presents Chinese digital platforms with some competitive advantages. First, Chinese (Mandarin, Cantonese and other dialects) is widely spoken. Second, China is not a foreign or exotic place (many people have resettled from the PRC in the region). Third, much of the investment in China's technological future is coming from the Asia-Pacific.

For over two decades now, researchers have focused on the political, economic and social impacts of the internet *in* and *on* China, offering multileveled, multifaceted and multidisciplinary analyses.[14] Research has investigated political control, online activism and cultures of contention. Studies have had three main foci: the internet and democratization or liberalization in China; the rapid uptake of digital economy and platforms, including e-commerce, social networking, online video and streaming within China; and internet technologies as a means of entry for Western corporations into the large Chinese market. The first, representing the dominant approach, in terms of both numbers and citations, views the internet as a site of contestation. This approach is represented in critiques of its political economy; sociocultural space; control and surveillance; e-governance; as well as the identification of digital, rural, local and urban divides.[15] Interest in the transformative impact of digital technology in China has considered digital infrastructures and capitalization, and the 'platformization' of Chinese society.[16]

Discussions on legal and regulatory issues concerning the Chinese online space have included intellectual property and *shanzhai* culture, consumer rights protection, social media and user experience.[17] A growing body of work has emerged on online philanthropy, cyber security, digital clusters, cloud computing, smart cities, makerspaces and digital payment systems.[18] When it comes to internet culture, scholarship on celebrity (*wang hong*) influencers and social media in China has been growing.[19]

Yet, despite some recent work, the overwhelming focus has been on the internet *within* China.[20] This book argues that the internet and digital platforms are contributing not only to enhancing China's economic productivity and connectivity but also to its presence and influence in the world. This is despite suspicions and disputes over Made-in-China digital technologies and companies. The 'two cultures' (the sciences and the humanities) find their connecting point in the internet. The internet is undoubtedly making China, the nation, more innovative.

China's tech companies are providing new solutions for smart cities, allowing would-be entrepreneurs to access credit. Chinese people are augmenting their realities, connecting to the world, streaming their lives online, making and sharing short videos, buying and selling online. At the other end of the scale, technology has obvious negative implications, not the least being the rise of the surveillance state and the so-called social credit system.[21] The rise of 'digital capitalism'[22] in China brings negative externalities, including exploitation of workers and reinforcing digital inequalities.[23] We recognise the significance of these themes, among others, associated with digital China, but have instead focused on Chinese transnational digital companies and their growing pains in the Asia Pacific.

Chapter outline

This study is divided into two parts: the four chapters in the first part draw on the + formula, now widely used in government discourse to celebrate China's digital industry emergence. Part two identifies the Asia-Pacific region as a landing pad for Chinese cultural and media content and shows how consumers and users in Hong Kong, Taiwan, Singapore, Malaysia, Australia and New Zealand are adapting to the widespread availability of Chinese print media and social media apps. The findings on consumption and attitudes towards Chinese culture are drawn from online surveys and focus groups.

PART 1: CHINA'S '+' LONG GAME

Chapter 1: Culture +

In the opening chapter we question the intrinsic value of Chinese culture, that is, its significance and resilience within the PRC and across the Chinese diaspora as well as its legacy relationship with tradition and civilization. While Chinese culture is increasingly globalizing, language remains a key barrier to understanding. China therefore needs 'to tell its stories well', according to the government. Challenges have come in 'waves', not just from the West but also from East Asia, notably South Korea and Japan. China's cultural trade deficit in professional media content services remains a cause for concern. The solution is technological according to many observers in China. We look at the increasing integration of culture and technology, manifest in makerspaces, virtual reality projects, social media apps and online communities. The term culture + signifies that culture (including ideology) must be bootstrapped to industry and technology. Other '+'s' advanced in this formula include culture + technology, culture + tourism, culture + finance, culture + sports, culture + manufacturing, culture + medicine and culture + agriculture. Finally, the chapter considers cultural soft power and the validity of this normative concept in a digital age.

Chapter 2: Industry +

In this chapter we describe how culture was industrialized in China, following the nation's accession to the World Trade Organization (WTO) in 2001, when the 'going out' strategy also came into play, culminating in the expectation that culture would become a pillar industry in the 13th Five-Year Plan. We look at how cultural and creative industries have scaled up during the 2000s in response to government subvention and how certain regions of China have invested in media culture, for instance, film and animation bases, software parks, theme parks and technology processing parks. The chapter outlines the evolution of China as a services economy and an innovative nation, a theme introduced in 2006 by Premier Wen Jiabao. The rhetoric has now shifted from 'Made in China' (the world factory) to 'Created in China' (the world laboratory). This ambition has led to a significant change of business operational models in the era of networked communication and changes in regulatory policy.

Chapter 3: Internet +

In this chapter we provide a condensed framework of development in China's telecommunications and internet industries from the late 1980s, which culminated in the Internet + initiative (proposed in the 2015 government Work Report). We note policy reports and industry responses to Internet + and 'Intelligent +' (proposed in the 2019 government Work Report). We show why the internet industry and emerging technologies such as AI, machine learning and robotics are pivotal in transforming China's economy. We critically examine the advent of technology-led industry upgrading, the rise of China's internet content industries, new modes of content production and their sociocultural implications with a focus on digital champions such as Baidu, Alibaba and Tencent. The chapter considers the impact of digitalization on the Chinese economy and society, as well as the 'social +' model of business and social engagement.

Chapter 4: Platform +

This chapter considers the unprecedented rise of digital platforms in China, which are lauded as a new generation of national champions and which promote public–private diplomacy within the 'going out' initiative. The term 'platform +' not only incorporates notions of network, big data and algorithms but also implies new modes of cultural production, distribution and consumption, that is, the infrastructure of digital empire. We look at academic, industry and policy discourses on the platform economy and discuss how China's digital platforms chart out an ambitious empire building project from China to the Asia-Pacific. The examination of these platforms' incursion into new territories involves expansion of both cultural and technological infrastructure. We examine how different platforms approach overseas markets and their evolving relationships with political and market players both at home and abroad.

PART 2: THE ASIA-PACIFIC AS A CHINESE CULTURAL LANDING PAD

Chapter 5: Assessing the Evidence

This chapter interrogates the question of how effective China's cultural power is in the era of digital platforms. China's cultural and creative industries have for some time been embroiled in debates about validity of data: How do Chinese agencies collect data, for instance, on consumption of film, television and artefacts? How does this data compare with global statistics? In many instances there have been criticisms of inflation of data, while on the other hand data has been deliberately downplayed. In a development state, however, data is crucial. The fascination with data has resulted in a mini-industry of publishing called Blue Books, which are industry reports that provide advice to government and guidelines to business. In this chapter we examine existing evidence and consider new ways of assessing China's reputational effect in the world more broadly, and specifically in the Asia-Pacific.

Chapter 6: East Asia: Hong Kong and Taiwan

In this chapter we examine the role of Hong Kong SAR and Taiwan in China's digital rejuvenation. As Hong Kong is increasingly integrated with the Chinese economy as part of the Greater Bay Area Project (Shenzhen-Macau-Kong Kong-Guangzhou), it has witnessed a 'culture of disappearance'. Creative and technical workers have moved to the mainland and political tensions have increased. Taiwan has long played a role in mainland China's rising power, economically and culturally. Leading businesses in both territories have tapped into the mainland market for its low-cost labour and production as well as exploiting under-addressed consumer demand. But there is also wariness about the future. The chapter identifies governance challenges and analyses how digital platforms are circumventing existing regulations to establish their presence. Case studies of iQiyi and LeTV (LeEco) shed light on how digital platforms mobilize local partnerships. Another rising star we investigate is TikTok. In the final section we look at changing user attitudes in Hong Kong and Taiwan towards Chinese online platforms.

Chapter 7: South East Asia: Singapore and Malaysia

In market terms, neither Singapore nor Malaysia is as crucial or large as any of the other nations already mentioned. Yet, culturally, these two Southeast Asian nations are significant. First, both are young nations with histories as former colonies of a Western nation; second, they have ethnic Chinese populations that are economically dominant but who may not identify strongly with contemporary China, its values or its national objectives; third, both nations are demographically multicultural and have come some way towards establishing their own national identities. The realities of economics, the size of China's market, the depth of Chinese corporations' pockets and the tide of Chinese technological products suggest that the integration of culture and technology will increase China's economic presence in Singapore and Malaysia. However, cultural power is another matter. Findings from fieldwork suggest that tangible technological products from Chinese brands such as mobile phones, computers and air purifiers are welcomed, while video games, messaging platforms and media content have had a mixed reception and have not been readily accepted unless they have been indigenized or used for instrumental reasons.

Chapter 8: Oceania: Australia and New Zealand

Australia and New Zealand are home to many native Chinese speakers, mostly mandarin but also Cantonese and other dialects. Australia and New Zealand are also Anglo-spheres, examples of predominantly English-speaking Western territories. The challenge here is to understand how Chinese culture fares in such territories and how Chinese platforms are performing. We note evidence of pockets of Chinese cultural production, aided by resources from the PRC. We consider Chinese print and digital media forays into Australia and some unsuccessful attempts by Australian media entrepreneurs to position themselves in the PRC. We then look at Chinese film co-productions with Australia and New Zealand, and we show examples of television location shooting. The chapter also draws on a study of reception of Chinese film in New Zealand that shows an increase in distribution of made-in-PRC films through theatres in Auckland and Wellington but a corresponding decrease in the distribution of Chinese independent cinema. Drawing on survey data, reports and interviews, we calculate the effectiveness of Chinese media on both analogue and digital platforms.

Chapter 9: From Cultural Presence to Innovative Nation

The final chapter reconsiders the question of how effective China's cultural power is likely to become in the era of digital platforms and recommendation algorithms. A theatre of war during the period of China's great 'People's Revolution', the Asia-Pacific is now part of a new Cold War between the forces of Western liberalism and an emboldened power, the PRC. Indeed, the rise of China and its global ambitions have caused tension among its rivals and partners alike. President Xi Jinping extols the benefits of globalization even while Western nations erect physical and logistical barriers to entry, as exemplified in the case of Huawei.[24] Drawing on the discussions in the previous three chapters, the chapter reviews challenges faced by Chinese digital platforms as they navigate a path into the Asia-Pacific and beyond.

PART 1

CHINA'S '+' LONG GAME

Chapter 1

CULTURE +

Chinese culture is often misunderstood. According to China's leaders and many commentators, the nation and its people are misrepresented in foreign media. The Chinese government has for this reason embarked on a grand plan to engage in a 'discourse war' (*huayuzhan*).[1] China should 'tell its stories well', proclaims its paramount leader, Xi Jinping. Such a plan ties in with the rise of China as a global power. However, the nature of Chinese culture, particularly its frequent allusions to history and dynastic struggles, hinders dissemination of media and cultural products outside the PRC. Meanwhile, China's near neighbours Japan and South Korea have infused elements of Western modernity into popular culture; their cultural products resonate with the idea of 'cool' soft power. Compared with mainland China, these East Asian nations were quick to see the advantages of combining culture and technology.

This chapter begins by briefly considering the nature of Chinese culture, both inside and outside the PRC, including state-endorsed traditional models of 'culture as civilization' and reactions to the tidal forces of regional audiovisual culture. We consider the popularity of East Asian pop culture in the PRC since the late 1990s. The next section, 'Waves of discontent', describes how foreign media imports precipitated government policies in the early 2000s aimed at rectifying a 'cultural trade deficit'. Following this, the discussion turns to the role of technology in peoples' lives, the increasing availability of digital cultural goods and services and the emergence of so-called digital champions in the cultural sphere. Section three considers 'culture +', a framework proposed by Chinese think tank academics and embraced by Beijing's cultural bureaucrats. This leads to the question of how the integration of culture and technology might expand Chinese cultural exports and elevate China's 'discursive' influence. The penultimate section offers a brief evaluation of such efforts through the framework of 'cultural soft power' in which we problematize the notion of influence, while remaining cognizant of the fact that 'influencers' now abound online. Soft power, while a flawed concept, at least allows us to understand how states act to manage national image.

Culture in flux

China, the so-called Middle Kingdom, an entity writ large in global history, is often characterized as enjoying an unbroken glorious civilization; its soft power, at least within the PRC, is defined by enduring traditional values. Chinese culture is mysterious, spectacular, exotic, ambiguous and ordinary at the same time. The Beijing 2008 Olympics Opening ceremony and the 2010 Shanghai Expo are held up as exemplars of the nation's 'cultural soft power'.[2] The sight of 2008 musicians drumming in perfect unison at the Olympic Opening ceremony in Beijing was seen by many foreign observers as exotic artistry of the highest order. Others saw an excessively regimented display of strident nationalism and authoritarianism.

Culture and civilization are used interchangeably in Chinese cultural policy, with the latter term, civilization, indicating something essential and permanent. The dominant cultural grouping in China is Han, a majority with regard to its population size and political influence. Within the PRC Han culture is often equated with Chinese culture at the cost of erasing the diverse cultures and traditions of ethnic minorities mostly living in the peripheries of the nation. By way of comparison, Western culture and civilization have globalized and have infused disparate ideologies within their (mostly) diverse multicultural societies, particularly in the twentieth century.

Western media have carried messages of a free society, where individualism feeds innovation. 'Traditional culture' carries very little meaning in most modern Western societies. When used as an adjective, for instance, traditional values, traditional morality or traditional authority, the word suggests something outdated and irrelevant. Whereas China looks to history for answers, celebrating sages and past glories, the West looks at the present. The film celebrities Brad Pitt, Tom Hanks and Angelina Jolie are known globally. Over the past two decades US movies have connected with audiences internationally. The reach of Hollywood movies into China has had a dual effect on China's media industries; first, in the eyes of many it has eroded the credibility of China's audiovisual culture, which is resolutely political, subject to strict control and thematically backward looking; second, it has provided an impetus for China's media industries and Chinese film directors and TV producers to adapt to the times and to make more universal stories about modern life. In responding to these challenges, Chinese audiovisual culture has refreshed its formats and genres, borrowed ideas from Hollywood and absorbed talent from East Asia. China now has a dynamic media production sector and is pulling other nations into its orbit.

How much China needs to borrow or copy from the West is a point of some disputation, and even consternation. Whereas the impact of Western technology is a relatively recent thread in the history of Chinese civilization, the story of cultural borrowing is a long one. The Silk Roads of history provided a bridge for the exchange of ideas between the East and West. The Venetian adventurer Marco Polo was reputed to have spent time in China during the Yuan dynasty (1279–1368). Certainly, there were Jesuit monks in the emperors' courts and libraries of the Ming and Qing dynasties, and they did bring technological know-how, but it wasn't until the late Qing dynasty that the force of Western technological power was felt in China. The Opium Wars of the mid-nineteenth century (1839–60) had shown how far China had fallen behind. The term 'sick man of Asia' was used derogatively to show the gap, even between China and Japan.

At the end of the nineteenth century Chinese reformers had come up with the adage 'Western learning for practical application, Chinese learning for substance' (*xixue wei yong, zhongxue wei ti*). The so-called self-strengthening movement of the time was shortened to *tiyong*. According to Wang Gungwu, China's reformers saw technology as a kind of methodology without understanding the ideas that underpinned it, ideas that would ultimately challenge their own civilization. In the Chinese view, their own philosophical tradition was fundamental and essential – providing the systemic *ti*. But behind the industrial capital and powerful technology of the West – described as the functional *yong* – were powerful financial systems.[3] Following the demise of the *tiyong* appeal to self-strengthening, the New Culture Movement began to sweep through China's coastal cities. Many were critical of the nation's inability to innovate. Some, like the great early twentieth-century writer Lu Xun, advocated deliberate cultural borrowing as a bridge to develop China.[4] The New Culture renaissance was short-lived and China plunged into civil war followed by revolutionary struggles. China's thought leaders assimilated elements of Western Marxism, purged feudal elements of Confucianism and under the leadership of Mao Zedong set about liberating the nation. Cultural propaganda provided the masses with basic knowledge of the normative trajectory by which they might become pure political subjects. In accordance with Marxist–Leninist doctrines, cultural works were viewed by the CCP primarily as the superstructure – educational texts which reflected and guided social reality. In effect, ideology had now become the 'fundamental' *ti*.

Insofar as the Leninist 'theory of reflection' provided a cultural road map for the nation, it was imperative that what was reflected was the so-called socialist viewpoint. The coordinates were mapped as contradictions and relationships: good communists/bad reactionaries, advanced culture/backward culture, organic peasant/professional intellectual, political content/artistic value and an array of exemplary or typical characters were promoted to show why this was the correct trajectory for China. Prior to the 1980s, centrally organized cultural bureaux coordinated and monitored cultural and artistic activities. The function of cultural bureaucracy, apart from directing and organizing activities, was to inculcate a political consciousness among the masses. In this scheme of things cultural workers viewed themselves as cogs in the wheel of the machinery of the state. This reached its apex in the Cultural Revolution (1966–76) when cultural workers were charged with the responsibility of overthrowing feudal forms of culture and replacing these with approved ideological formats such as revolutionary model operas (*yang ban xi*). If cultural workers were screws and cogs, progress was calibrated in the struggle against oppression, a theme revisited in the 2017 film *Youth* directed by Feng Xiaogang, about the privileged lives of members of a revolutionary cultural troupe.

When the Cultural Revolution ended with the death of Mao and the overthrow of the Gang of Four in 1976, China emerged from its seclusion. Culture was heavily insulated from global market forces and it would take two more decades before cultural industries were conceptualized as part of China's modernization project. Technology and the internet, specifically, would eventually become key elements of China's cultural renaissance, as we will discover in Chapters 3 and 4. The questions we need to consider is: how far can Chinese culture travel without losing its uniqueness? And is technology the great enabler?

Waves of discontent

The Australian novelist, translator and cultural commentator Linda Jaivin is well credentialed to offer a definition of Chinese culture. Jaivin has lived and worked in China and has written extensively about cultural encounters with China from afar. Jaivin says that the character-based tonal language that underpins the rich Chinese literary, artistic and philosophical heritage presents a barrier to comprehension. Chinese is a hard language to learn. From a linguistic perspective alone, it is difficult for China's culture to become globally recognized. Unsurprisingly, the English-speaking world at large is not China literate. However, Jaivin believes that the Chinese government's official depiction of Chinese culture doesn't represent the cultural heterogeneity of 1.4 billion people.[5] So, what is Chinese culture today? Jaivin suggests:

> Chinese culture is many things. It is Peking opera and Beijing punk. It is ancient classics and internet slang. It can be historical, retro,

Table 1.1 China's cultural services trade deficit 1997–2005 (adapted by authors from Li Wuwei, 'The Challenges of China's Culture "Going to the World"')

In USD	1997	2001	2004	2005
Export trade: volume of cultural products	$22.861 billion	$28.845 billion	$50.143 million	$61.360 million
Export trade: volume of cultural services	$303 million	$415 million	$1.126 billion	$1.367 billion
Import trade: volume of cultural services	$828 million	$2.246 billion	$5.371 billion	$6.190 billion

Source: Wuwei Li, 'The Challenges of China's Culture "Going to the World"', in *The Handbook of China's Cultural and Creative Industries*, ed. Michael Keane (Cheltenham, Edward Elgar, 2016), 116–28 (123).

contemporary, highbrow, popular, propagandist or rebellious, and may originate on the mainland, or in Taiwan, Hong Kong or the Chinese diaspora.[6]

Chinese culture obviously has a different flavouring depending on where one is physically situated. Northeast (*dongbei*) culture is different in many ways from southern Guangdong where Cantonese is mostly spoken. Southwest and Northwest China are infused with minority cultures: the Tibetan, Uighur, Zhuang, Hui, Dai, Yi, among others.[7] In the Chinese diaspora, moreover, there are many contending versions of Chinese culture as well as a great deal of commonality. Beijing promotes an official version, more opera than punk, more classical than slang. Beijing's cultural officials are intent on enhancing the reputation of its official version of Chinese culture in and beyond Chinese-language markets.

In the early 2000s, government cultural officials proclaimed that China's cultural forces needed to strike back against the waves of foreign media content popular among Chinese youth. In 2005, four years after joining the World Trade Organization, China's cultural trade deficit in audiovisual services became news.[8] See Table 1.1.

The problem for China's cultural officials was not the export of cultural commodities so much as cultural services. China does export its culture in large numbers. It has a large surplus in cultural trade, but this is dominated by tangible goods: artworks, jewellery and games, and increasingly electronic games. While trade numbers include the cultural and expressive arts, for instance, performing arts and martial arts, as well as press and publications, in 2013, tangible goods accounted for 83 per cent of exports. Processing of cultural products for others, including non-Chinese businesses (such as toys, games), took up 40 per cent of the total. In the same year the export of cultural services reached US$5.13 billion, five times the total of 2005 but the deficit in film and TV industries had jumped. In 2009, it was US$200 million but four years later the figure was US$600 million. The considered advice to government from within its own think tanks is 'to strive to build a cultural brand with international reputation and influence', something that has proved a great challenge.[9]

Although the Chinese government's hard line on censorship and protection of local content slowed down the number of imported products coming into China in the mid-2000s, the nation's film and television industries were struggling to export. Chinese films did better internationally. Fifth-generation filmmakers, including Zhang Yimou, Chen Kaige, Tian Zhuangzhuang, achieved a degree of respect and recognition in the 1980s and 1990s but it wasn't until the success of *Crouching Tiger, Hidden Dragon* in 2000 that Chinese cinema achieved a measure of popular success. *Crouching Tiger, Hidden Dragon* was in fact directed by Ang Lee (Li An), a Taiwanese who graduated in film production from New York University. As we discuss in later chapters, Chinese films do achieve significant box office success outside the PRC among Chinese-speaking communities, but aside from the films of Ang Lee and a few independent auteur directors they rarely garner major international accolades. Although hundreds of feature films are produced annually in China, many are propaganda works that never make it to mainstream theatres. Success in the home market, moreover, does not equate to success abroad; and critical success abroad, as we will see later, does not necessarily translate into economic success at home.

In the 1980s and 1990s, Chinese audiovisual media with the exception of dynastic costume television dramas such as *The Three Kingdoms* (1994), *The Water Margin* (1998), *The Dream of the Red Chamber* (1986) and *Journey to the West* (1988) had made few inroads into global or even regional markets.[10] China's comparative advantage in overseas sales comes from adaptations of classics of Chinese popular literature as well as an ever-expanding slate of historical serials about emperors, eunuchs and court intrigues. The main markets for TV serials in the past have been Taiwan and Hong Kong; other markets, roughly in order of sales volume, include Singapore, Malaysia, Japan, Korea, the United States, Indonesia and Thailand.[11] In 2003, however, China's revenue from serial drama exports to its core markets in Taiwan, Hong Kong and South East Asia began to be hit by the popularity of South Korean dramas.

From the mid-1990s, the trendiness of media products of Japan and South Korea, in addition to the already popular audiovisual content of Hong Kong SAR and Taiwan, had generated widespread appreciation for these nations' (and regions') culture.[12] These positive evaluations of China's smaller neighbours reflected poorly on audiovisual content produced in the PRC, which was invariably propaganda-heavy and formulaic. The attractiveness of East Asian content – in particular TV drama, manga, anime and games, combined with the greater technical sophistication of East Asian producers and artists, generated a flow-on effect, often characterized by scholars as a 'wave'. The influence of East Asian audiovisual within the region led to numerous invitations to film-makers, movie stars, singers, musicians and technicians to work on co-production projects with the PRC and to feature in PRC film and television shows.[13] The tide of East Asian popular culture had the effect of breaking down the dams, dykes and (fire)walls erected to privilege national culture in China. Korean pop culture, which blended visually attractive actors and clever content, had not only washed away China's markets but instilled a sense of despair within China about its over-reliance on historical dramas.

The belief that Chinese culture should, and could, go global assumed critical importance. The solution as always was to create a raft of policies. Acutely aware of these regional waves and the global reputation of Hollywood content, the Chinese government and provincial and city governments provided incentives to mainland media producers, including free rent for studio space, tax holidays and access to cheap labour, while endeavouring to restrict the kinds of foreign content that could be accessed within China. Regulation also had a positive effect. As Wendy Su notes, the controlled introduction of international blockbusters after 1994 had served as a means to build domestic audiences and encourage investment and new technologies in film production. Profits were siphoned into politically correct 'main melody' films, which were heavy on propaganda and which the state believed might counter foreign influence.[14]

China's 'Cultural Industry Rejuvenation Plan' (*wenhua chanye zhenxing guihua*) was issued on 22 July 2009; this was an indication that the government would actively support cultural enterprises to invest in and run businesses abroad as well as participate in cultural activities that contribute to the development of cultural trade. Then in May 2012, the Central Propaganda Department head Liu Yunshan spoke about the importance of promoting the competitiveness of Chinese national culture on the global stage, a theme that was later picked by Xi Jinping, whose own prescription, as we have mentioned previously, is that China 'must tell its stories well'.[15]

Indeed, China has many stories that should be told. But for Chinese audiovisual content to effectively 'go out' a number of obstacles needed to be overcome. Yingchi Chu describes one key obstacle: many in the international community don't know how to read Chinese audiovisual culture.[16] As we observed in our research, audience expectations of Chinese culture among non-Chinese, what Chinese people like to refer to as 'foreigners' (*laowai*), fall into certain 'horizons of expectation', either an orientalist mode of reception or a view that Chinese culture, particularly its media, is politically flawed. Some people have little understanding of the cultural nuances that attract Chinese audiences. When it comes to cross-cultural exchange there is often cognitive dissonance. Chu cites the example of Zhang Yimou whose early films were banned in China for depicting the nation's poverty, its simple folk and decadent sensuality. Western critics often read these films differently, showering Zhang with accolades. However, these accolades have not translated into commercial success, nor has the strategy of using Hollywood A-listers in Chinese films. Zhang's later films, particularly *The Flowers of War* with Christian Bale and *The Great Wall* with Matt Damon, have failed the audience test in the West.

While Made-in-China cinema struggled to make a significant impression in the foreign box office, mostly due to a lack of visibility and its reliance on historical epics, greater acceptance of Chinese content was meanwhile taking place online. As we discuss in more detail in Chapter 3, the circuit breaker was the commercial internet, which arrived in China in 1996. In the years leading up to China's accession to the World Trade Organization (WTO) in 2001, the internet was not central to the plans of China's cultural reformers, aside from concerted efforts by officials to monitor its influence by erecting firewalls. Discussion of technological convergence was also largely confined to small groups of media scholars. Telecommunications infrastructure, on the other hand, was connecting people all over the country; for instance, internet data centres had sprung up offering space for servers and bandwidth for users prior to the arrival of big tech.[17] Mobile phones soon became smart, allowing cultural content to be widely accessed and shared.

Chinese overseas communities were avid audiences of history. The number of internet users in China increased from 120,000 in 1996 to 137 million in 2006,[18] driving the culture of downloading and sharing. International media content also became more accessible within China, initially as pirated DVDs and VCDs,[19] then as free downloads on BitTorrent China sites.[20] Although there was a notable demand for foreign content, including South Korean film and TV drama, user-generated content was also flooding the internet with little concern for copyright. The internet had become an incubator of creativity.

Added to the 1.4 billion people living in the PRC is a diaspora made up of overseas students and persons with Chinese heritage, numbering between 30 and 50 million (depending on sources), who by the early 2000s were able to access content online. As Keane has argued, while the 1990s was a decade in which the Chinese authorities sought to disconnect Chinese audiences from foreign content by taking down offending satellite networks in Guangdong province, the 2000s saw a rush to connect as hundreds of millions acquired the internet and smart phones.[21] By the second decade, Chinese platforms began to link up with overseas Chinese communities. Professional content providers such as Vue, Viki and even Netflix could offer new options: documentaries, sports and news combined with the best entertainment shows from China's satellite TV stations.

Chinese culture was reconnecting with overseas Chinese, many of whom had adopted Western viewing habits. Overseas audiences could revaluate Made-in-China content, especially newer offerings of commercial film and reality TV, which compared to those of the 1980s and 1990s were more professional. The potential of digital technology to reconnect China with its diaspora validates Michael Curtin's argument made as early as 2007: 'Although dispersed across vast stretches of Asia and around the world, this audience is now connected for the very first time via the intricate matrix of digital and satellite media.'[22] China's culture going-out strategy was enhanced by investment in Hollywood film studios. In 2016, the Wanda Group had acquired Legendary Pictures.[23] Wanda's investments also included acquisition of the movie theatre exhibition chains AMC Theatre Multiplex in North America (2012), followed by Hoyts in Australia (2015), Odeon and UCI in Europe (2016) and the Carmike cinema chain in the United States (2016). In April 2017, soon after purchasing Legendary Pictures, CEO Wang Jianlin was reprimanded by the government for his excessive overseas debt, especially on acquiring foreign cultural acquisitions, and was forced to sell off many of his assets.

The overseas production of reality TV shows and films, meanwhile, had led to a visible Chinese production presence outside the PRC, occasionally making the entertainment news overseas. Co-productions with foreign partners, including the United States, were adding to the quota of talent coming into the PRC.[24] The key point here is skills transfer, notably creatives from South Korea and Hong Kong moving to China. The same kind of creative know-how transfers that occurred in the film industry occurred with TV formats.[25] Overseas filming of reality TV shows like *Where Are We Going, Dad?* (*baba qu na'er?*), *Running Man* (*benpao ba*) and *If You Are the One* (*feicheng wurao*) helped to justify the claim that China's media was going out. Somewhat ironically, the above reality TV shows were copies of foreign programmes, the first two being Korean. In fact, a large part of the mini-renaissance of Made in PR China content was due to the influence of the region. The development of China's pan-Asian strategy has therefore largely been a consequence of East Asian media success in China.

During the early 2000s, as discussed above, the dominant development theme in cultural policy circles was the cultural industries, the leadership's attempt to fortify the nation against the onset of globalization, most notably the forces of Hollywood, often portrayed as 'wolves at the door'.[26] Films like *Transformers* (2007) and *Avatar* (2010) were an advertisement for the creative power of Hollywood. Youthful audiences in China were drawn to genres like science fiction and fantasy, which offer a contemporary appeal to the senses and which actually speak of the power of technology. It would be a decade, however, before the solution of technology as a carrier of content to the world came to the attention of cultural bureaucrats in Beijing. In the so-called great rejuvenation of the Chinese nation, the country's cultural ambassadors – artists, film-makers, celebrities and entrepreneurs – are now assisted by the forces of China's internet technology companies whose platforms are connecting people in unprecedented ways. Technology promises many things for China. But significantly, it now plays a key role in China's soft power, a theme that we will discuss later in this chapter.

The changing role of technology

China is seeking to recharge its economic model and change its national image. China today is far different from the past and much different from stereotypes that are perpetuated in much of the Western media. While China is a developing country according to the WTO, in many parts of China people feel modern. The nation's own media is changing the narrative. The sharing economy, big data, artificial intelligence, the Internet of Things and an ever-expanding repertoire of online affordances available to consumers have become hot topics over the past decade. Technological progress is front-page news. The China Central Television (CCTV) evening bulletin has replaced stories about the productivity of people's manual labour, once a symbol of shared national growth, with news of labour-saving machines. Robot toys and drones can be found in shopping centres along with virtual reality (VR) amusement arcades. Mass innovation spaces, co-working spaces and fab labs appear in the proximity of university campuses.

Technology has transformed large parts of the Chinese economy – from commerce, finance, health care, to cultural industries and transportation. In May 2015, soon after Premier Li Keqiang launched a digital blueprint called Internet + (see Chapter 3), the government announced Made in China 2025, an ambitious plan to revolutionize China's manufacturing base using so-called 'intelligent technology'. As we discuss in Chapter 2, over the past two decades China has acquired expertise in science and technology that it had lacked in the past. Expertise has also moved to China from the West, mostly returning graduates of Western universities but also entrepreneurs hoping to ride the new wave of technological innovation. A sense of confidence is building.

E-commerce is powering entrepreneurs in the countryside, providing new ways of getting goods to consumers. Culture is undergoing makeovers at the same time. A decade ago, tourists visiting Shenzhen, the city where Li Keqiang unveiled Internet +, would have been surprised to see reconstituted foreign culture – a miniaturized Eiffel Tower in a theme park called Window on the World and Van Gogh masterpieces for sale at the Dafen Oil Painting Village, as well as an almost full-scale replica of the Swiss ski resort Interlaken. By the mid-2000s, the city had achieved the dubious honour of being named the birthplace of *shanzhai*, a form of grassroots technology design that produces cheap knock-off products for millions of Chinese consumers. Shanzhai phones proliferated, capitalizing on lax intellectual property enforcement and a willingness among Chinese consumers to purchase cheap versions of international products. Once a place where copy culture was seen as retarding China's ambitions to become an innovative nation, Shenzhen is now a centrepiece of China's 13th Five-Year Plan (2016–20). It promotes itself as the centre of the Greater Bay project, a development plan that seeks to replicate Silicon Valley.

Internet celebrities and corporate high-flyers have joined the mission to rejuvenate Chinese culture. The former CEO of Alibaba, Jack Ma (Ma Yun), is known to parade his cultural tastes; in 2018 he confounded audiences with his clumsy skills at martial arts (*gongfu*); at other times he has paraded grotesquely as a Chinese Michael Jackson clone at Alibaba conferences and performed a musical duet with the Chinese songstress, Faye Wang.[27] In the internet age these displays of chutzpah are available for all to view on the video platform Youku, owned by Alibaba.com.

The role of technology in shaping China's future is supported by the eminent Taiwanese venture capitalist Kai-fu Lee who claims that China is on track to become an AI superpower.[28] Having represented Google's business ambitions in China, Lee has a distinctive view on the differences between the two AI superpowers, the United States and China. Of course, Lee's boosterish commentary about China needs to be contextualized due to his position as an industry insider and a confidante of the Chinese leadership. One of the key reasons why China will become an AI superpower, Lee says, is that people in China are happy to release their data to the big tech companies whose algorithms are getting exponentially stronger. Of course, people in the PRC have far less recourse to data protection. Online services in China, mostly provided on Android platforms, require data permissions, as well as real names and phone numbers. As the COVID-19 outbreak has shown people in China have no choice but to opt in to surveillance. Without access to online services people would be excluded from China's modernization project. It is the scalability of the data of the masses, combined with the widespread acceptance of a digital lifestyle that makes the difference.

The massive growth in users of video platforms such as iQiyi, Youku Tudou, WeChat, ByteDance and Tencent Video is clear evidence of the cultural power of digital technology. These are in fact cultural technologies. Many have expressed a new-found optimism that technology will take China's ideas to the world and accelerate the nation's quest to rejuvenate. Many agree that China's cultural presence should expand globally, a mission described as 'going out' (*zou chuqu*). Indeed, the main advantage of Chinese digital platforms, apart from the fact that they allow people to create and share stories, is that Chinese websites, apps and online booking services are accessible globally; they are already global. Many, like WeChat, Didi and Alipay, are recognizable in cities in the Asia-Pacific. Their predominantly Made-in-China content is easily downloadable, thanks to advances in digital compression technologies.

Digitalization liberates a great deal content, much of it amateur and much of it uncensored. Digital images have the capacity to multiply and disseminate themselves, almost virally. The diversity of images of China circulating online *outside* the PRC is more heterogeneous and transgressive than within, although this is not to deny the reality that a great deal of online content within China is fast moving, aesthetically pleasing and creative. A positive sign of the broader dissemination of Chinese culture globally, moreover, is that there are few political restrictions outside China, that is, outside the Great Firewall. Within the PRC the internet is heavily policed for content that might challenge the legitimacy of the government; for instance, the Chinese government's intractability on issues relating to Tibet, Hong Kong, Taiwan and the South China Sea.

Culture +: Integrating culture and technology

In response to the challenges, cultural ministry spokespersons and party-affiliated academics have become disposed to refer to the value-adding proposition Culture +. Along with a number of other plusses, like Internet + and Intelligent +, this signifies an integration of fields of endeavour. Integration (*ronghe*) is a power terminology in policy documents and government-funded reports. In March 2014, the Chinese State Council issued 'Several Opinions on Promoting the Integration and Development of Culture and Creativity, Design Services and Related Services', which at that time was the first such integration policy to impact the cultural and creative industries.[29] Cultural and creative industries were set to be further transformed and upgraded (*zhuanxing shengji*), another favoured policy term.

For those working within cultural policy domains, however, the operational principle is Culture +. Fan Zhou, a professor at the Communication University of China who is a consultant to the national government's Five-Year Economic Plans, offers a definition in his account of the history of China's cultural industries from 1978 to 2018: Fan says that Culture + 'is the wide-ranging integration of fields of culture and the national economy, precipitating more comprehensive, deeper and more multi-layered innovations, which through the promotion of industrial transformation, upgrading and optimization, stimulates the vitality of industrial development and endogenous forces'.[30]

To illustrate Culture +, Fan nominates innovations that have impacted on the development of China's cultural industries. The internet, he says, has diversified cultural industry formats. He identifies the *wanghong* (or influencer) economy, live streaming, mobile e-sports and the IP economy. Fan also attributes Culture + with the power of a new cultural content ecosystem, combined with the sharing and the platform economies. Accordingly, he maintains that China's emergence as a cultural power is dependent on technology. In his book, ostensibly a policy manual for party officials, he identifies several industrial domains in which culture acts as a driver of convergence: these are culture + technology, culture + tourism, culture + finance, culture + sports, culture + manufacturing, culture + medicine and culture + agriculture. The argument put forward by Fan is that the internet facilitates the transmission of creative content to consumers faster, cheaper and more effectively; it also promotes user-generated content and improves the design of creative products and the quality of service through online data collection; for instance, users' experience. As we see in later chapters, China's tech leaders had come to the same conclusion, albeit with the terminology Internet +.

Essentially, while the Culture + proposition is about the convergent power of technology, it is ideologically grounded. Culture remains largely the superstructure (as it was under Maoism). The internet is part of the economic base. Yet the separation is less evident than prescribed in Marxist theory. The base is becoming more than just infrastructural. Integration is impacting on these two distinctive components of Marxist political doctrine. In debates originating in the 1950s in the UK, this became known as the 'two cultures', the separation of the humanities and the sciences.[31] In more recent times Scott Lash and Celia Lury have suggested that these once distinct domains have come closer together and that cultural products are everywhere.[32] Another way of expressing this relationship is that meanings are increasingly embodied in 'things' rather than just in the output of cultural workers. In accepting the

Culture + proposition, the cultural and creative industries in China today provide myriad 'cultural characteristics' (*wenhua tese*) that will drive the economy forward, that is, according to cultural officials. Diversity is represented in a multitude of subcultures: these range from official minorities (*shaoshu minzu*) who perform for tourists to more groups and individuals that represent tech-savvy youthful generations, including online influencers, some of which threaten to disrupt mainstream culture.

Prior to the coinage of Culture + and Internet +, scholars had advocated the integration of technological innovation and cultural creativity. The most important contributor to this debate was Prof Li Wuwei, a senior economist in the Shanghai Academy of Social Sciences and formerly the vice-chair of the National Committee of the Chinese Peoples' Political Consultative Conference (CPPCC). Li had written about the economic logic of value adding since 2002, at a time when cultural bureaucrats in Beijing were more intent on ensuring 'cultural security' (*wenhua anquan*), erecting quotas, barriers and firewalls to foreign content. Li's seniority (he was also vice-chair of the Revolutionary Kuomintang) allowed him the freedom to promote the globalizing concept of the creative industries, which, as he wrote in 2009, 'are a combination of science and technology, culture, industry and the market'.[33]

What Culture + actually entails beyond the development rhetoric and political sloganeering emanating from the corridors of power in Beijing, however, is open to debate, but there is broad agreement that digital technology is contributing vitality to China's cultural and creative industries and that this vitality underpins China's cultural expansion globally. Another way of saying this, following Lash and Lury, is that digital culture has infused everyday life with an excess of the symbolic. Couldry and Hepp use the description 'deep mediatization' to illustrate the ubiquity of the data revolution. They say that 'It is important also to see the various stages of mediatization in a transcultural perspective, which means grasping the multiple forms that mediatization has taken over its long duration in various sites across the world.'[34] Indeed, once fed a strict diet of propaganda, Chinese people now enjoy a heavily mediatized lifestyle, one that is defined by an embrace of online connectivity. Propaganda still persists of course, but it is spiced with variety and is more online than ever. The lifestyle of choice includes sharing cultural videos, memes and patriotic messages with distant friends and relatives. Chinese internet companies, accordingly, are cognizant not just of the commercial value of the peoples' data but recognize the monetary value of the youthful audiences' yearnings for appealing audiovisual content. The term 'content is king' still applies in a congested Chinese internet space, albeit one that is riddled with fake news and rumours, as it is in the West. While getting the attention of users is paramount, however, engaging with them is the next challenge.

Cultural soft power

In 1989, a US political scientist, Joseph Nye Jnr, developed a concept called soft power to explain why some nations' ideas are more attractive globally. Nye's soft power model is a resource-based approach,[35] that is, according to Nye a nation's soft power 'rests on' three resources: its culture (in places where it is attractive to others), its political values (when it lives up to them at home and abroad) and its foreign policies (when they are seen as legitimate and having moral authority).[36] Nye has had very little to say directly about representational media, echoing Marshall McLuhan's focus on the medium rather than the message. Significantly, it is the representational aspects of Chinese media that have led to failure in many parts of the world and among foreigners.

Soft power made its way into discussions of China's media and culture in the early 2000s, largely as a result of the inter-regional success of East Asian pop culture. The uptake of this Western term was not immediate. China already had developed its own power matrix called 'comprehensive national power' (*zonghe guoli*), and 'cultural power' was one part of this equation.[37] The Chinese variant in time came to be referred to as 'cultural soft power' (*wenhua ruanshili*), which as the name suggests prioritizes cultural influence. By the time Xi Jinping ascended to power, the term 'cultural empowerment' (*wenhua qiangguo*) had gained prominence over 'cultural soft power', at least in the lexicon of party documents.

Public diplomacy is the basis of many of China's soft power initiatives and cultural diplomacy is part of that package. In the cultural field Chinese public diplomacy has been led by state-owned media with CCTV-9 and CCTV News (rebranded as CGTN since 2016), CRI (China Radio International) and Xinhua News Agency as the flagships. Their existence as government-funded highly controlled media organizations (*shiye*) is a limiting factor in China's effort to tell its stories well. Despite the Chinese government's 'abiding faith in the ability of international broadcasting to shape the global conversation about China'[38] and the capacity of broadcast footprint to reach far and wide, its exercise of cultural power is ultimately measured by 'the capacity to influence the thinking and thus the behaviour of others, whether around matters of cultural consumption or international alliances'.[39] How influential CGTN is remains a moot point. Indeed, as a 2009 survey showed, CCTV-9 (formerly known as CCTV International), then available in many parts of the world and in multiple languages, struggled to get significant audience reach even among the Chinese diaspora.[40]

While China's presence in the world is hard to ignore, it is much harder to reliably assess cultural influence. Soft power has methodological limitations, which we discuss in some detail in Chapter 5. For now, suffice it to say that most soft power metrics are predicated on data that can be gleaned from available secondary sources, rather than assessing the degree of engagement among users; for instance, using qualitative methods. Soft power, moreover, assesses reputational effects from a variety of categorizations, many of which have little to do with media.

In the light of these misgivings about measurement, is 'cultural soft power' a valid approach to understanding China's influence? Can China's media deliver the results? James Watson and Anne Hill argue that 'The actual effects of media on audiences, so far as it can be ascertained, are arguably less than the *perceived* effect.'[41] Of course, advertising exists because people can be persuaded to purchase commodities. Propaganda continues to be produced because of its perceived effect and influencers cash in on peoples' gullibility to market products. While a great deal of media scholarship is concerned with the effects of audiovisual texts, it is difficult to really gauge how these texts effect behaviour.[42] We might be better off asking the question: What do people actually do with media texts? Aside from actual streaming and downloading content, people browse, search, create, share and comment.[43] We might then ask: What platform, channels, affordances and devices do people use, when do they use them, how often and why? In other words, what are the social, practical and political contexts of media use?

Matching behavioural practice with media reception requires a different kind of analysis, for instance, in line with the algorithmic pattern matching of consumers by media companies, we should ask: Does reception lead the viewer to seek out more of the same content or to share with friends? After the mid-1990s, for instance, it was observed that East Asian media were having behavioural effects on audience beyond reception; there was an observable increase in consumption of Korean and Japanese fashion and food as well as an increase in tourism numbers. As well, one can use box office returns and celebrity news as proxies of cultural influence, when this makes world headlines. Then there is evidence of the growing international reputation of key opinion leaders like Jack Ma, arguably China's leading influencer outside China (with apologies to Xi Jinping). Sharing, commenting, paying for and downloading content moreover are perhaps the best indicators in our digital world. Such online activity, as well as its limitations, is discussed in later chapters.

Concluding remarks: Digital dreaming

This chapter has shown the intrinsic value of Chinese culture, that is, its significance and resilience within the People's Republic of China and across the Chinese diaspora. Today the terminology soft power is used by many observers as a barometer of national popularity. Aside from pandas and green tea, however, many persons outside the Chinese mainland harbour negative stereotypes of China, and sometimes these views are generated by anti-Chinese political forces worldwide. The chapter has considered the nation's media ambition beyond the mainland, including the harder task of winning the hearts and minds of non-Chinese audiences, essentially adding new converts. The irrepressible rise of East Asian popular culture and its online presence has led to more concerted efforts to modernize China's culture. Culture + is thus used as formula by policy makers and academics within China, along with other '+' formulations, to promote China's cultural foundations, ideologies and to make the case for taking Chinese ideas and models of governance to the world. The term 'culture +' therefore signifies that culture must be bootstrapped to industry and technology.

As many have noted, China's extraordinary influence on the global stage is due to its economic power, not its cultural authority. While China's culture within China is extraordinarily heterogeneous, echoing Linda Jaivin's definition, content that goes to the world has to bear the weight of political expectation. The problem is that China's political ideology and its reversion to a more authoritarian style of governance under Xi Jinping than his predecessors is out of sync with the pluralism of other great nations. Authoritarianism and soft power are not natural bedfellows, which is why China fares poorly on global soft power comparisons such as the Portland 30, where it barely makes the list, coming in at 27. The rise of China as a digital power, however, seems to offer a glimmer of hope in renovating its national soft power.

The challenging aspect of Xi's great rejuvenation project, however, is that the global understandings of China conspire against widespread reception of its rich culture, for instance, Chinese culture has little traction among people with little knowledge of Chinese history and society, as we will illustrate in the chapters of Part 2. Yet South Korea, a small nation by area and population in North-East Asia, won Academy Award Oscars for Best Picture (*The Parasite*), Best Director (Boon Jong-ho), Best original Screenplay and Best Foreign Language Film in 2020, and Korea's language and culture are far more marginal globally than the PRC's. If China is telling its stories well, why is the world not responding? One recent analysis of China's soft power concludes: 'China appears no closer to solving the fundamental problem of how to cultivate an association with the kinds of political values that resonate positively beyond its borders and overcome the deep-seated suspicions of authoritarian states held by people in liberal democracies.'[44]

In the following chapter we turn to look at the emergence of cultural and creative industries in China, the rise of the digital economy and their eventual digitization. China's digital platforms have already claimed the kudos of national champions. The question is not how far they reach but rather how deep they reach.

Chapter 2

INDUSTRY +

If culture is the superstructure of society according to Marxism-Leninism, industry is the concrete manifestation of economic policy, at least under a planned system. The socialist planned economy championed by Mao Zedong in the 1950s and 1960s began to be phased out in 1979 when Deng Xiaoping assumed leadership and introduced his economic reforms. The results transformed the nation and the lives of Chinese people. China now has a domestic market of over a billion consumers; its double-digit economic growth from 1978 to 2011 saw the emergence of thousands of millionaires. China is an industrial behemoth. Its global economic presence is made visible by the brand recognition of 'Made in China'. Its infrastructural muscle is felt in neighbouring nations through the Belt and Road Initiative (BRI). Its economy moreover represents a curious hybrid of state planning and cut-throat market entrepreneurialism.

China's internet industries have gathered momentum over the past decade. Their founders and CEOs frequently feature on the evening national CCTV news. Policy makers and officials seek out their opinions. China's film industries have also seen millionaire high-flyers, names like Zhang Yimou, Feng Xiaogang and Fan Bingbing. Their work has won recognition outside the mainland, albeit without scaling the commanding heights of Oscar success. Since the late 1990s, China's popular entertainment media has taken on a more international look: its formats and genres are recognizable worldwide.[1] E-sport and games industries have reached dizzying heights of mass participation[2] while social media use is ubiquitous, even among older demographics.[3]

The Chinese government recognizes the importance of making money from its cultural resources, although the proposition that media production could be commercialized and still serve the state's goals took a long time to come to fruition. In fact, by the time media industries gained formal government recognition in 2002, they had experienced over a hundred years of commercial development in the West.[4] Of course, China did have a film industry and a bevy of film stars, dating from as early as 1913. This industry generated significant commercial presence in Shanghai during the 1930s and as with the field of literature there were vestiges of a revolutionary left-wing consciousness.[5] By the time the Chinese Peoples' Revolution gathered pace in the 1940s, film had been subsumed into the propaganda apparatus of the state. Its scriptwriters were churning out tales of model workers, hard-working peasants and heroic soldiers. It would be another sixty years before film regained its industrial commercial status.

The film industry is just one example. The important point to bear in mind, however, is technology. The technology of cinema was available in China at the same time as the West. The internet is a similar story; its uptake in China closely followed that of the West and lured many skilled entrepreneurs back home, particularly from start-ups in Silicon Valley. Technology forms part of infrastructure. Infrastructure, in a broad sense, refers to any widely shared human constructed resource.[6] Sociotechnical in nature, infrastructures require interoperability to allow smooth functioning.[7] We frequently take it for granted, often as something provided by the government. The term has multiple applications, as will be discussed in the following chapters.

This chapter charts the development of conventional media and cultural industries in China and their transition into digital creative industries. By conventional industries, we refer primarily to the practice of building infrastructure: zones, bases, parks, studios and in many cases centres of low-cost production. It begins with a brief exploration of the cultural market during the time of Deng Xiaoping's economic reforms (1978–93). This topic has been the subject of a number of detailed studies;[8] our purpose here is primarily to show how an industrial mentality emerged in the cultural and media sectors, from where the momentum for reform came, and how it eventually integrated with other industries. The second section focuses on industrialization of the media and cultural industries amid the rhetoric of catch-up. Our discussion shows how China's cultural and creative industries transformed from a preoccupation with material artefacts to an obsession with digital technologies and how the digitalization of production is impacting on China's culture 'going-out' programme. Section three introduces the term 'industry +' to understand the nation's ambition to become a cultural power. This concept builds on the reform era model of society-wide industrialization and the technological gains of the Fourth Industrial Revolution.[9]

Early years

In 2012, the Singaporean media scholar Chua Beng-Huat conceptualized a matrix to explain rankings in the 'transregional media order'. Chua maintained that the more technically developed nations and regions were leading in 'soft power competition' and this was reflected in the quality of products. Because of technical advantages there was 'a greater tendency for production and export to dominate over import and consumption'.[10] A secondary consideration was the size of the domestic market. Chua conceded that size was potentially China's trump card – but he maintained that 'China with its huge market, is still primarily a location of import and consumption due to the weak production quality of its still nascent media industry.'[11] At that time many scholars and commentators viewed China more as a production site for film and TV drama, one that producers from East Asia could exploit for cheap labour and stunning vistas. It was East Asia where the real action was. Once marginal, the region was rising, its soft power capacity clearly evident. Observing these changes, Anthony Fung refers to new forms of structure and operation in the East Asian region, which illustrate 'how Asia is being connected and reconnected to the world'.[12]

A similar process of reconnecting with the world is now occurring in the PRC. China's nascent media industry, the propaganda state model of the past, has transformed. While China is yet to be acknowledged as an export power and yet to shake off the association with censorship, it has changed the landscape of regional production. Chinese producers have elevated the quality of media output, a fact now recognized by the massive investment in China's media and the willingness of regional partners to make content in China.[13] The immense monetary value of culture and its capacity to add value to other sectors could not have been imagined in the past. The great transformation of China's commercial media sector continues to unfold, an unfolding that would make Chairman Mao turn in his grave. A condensed account of the staged evolution of cultural and media industries is therefore required in order to set the context for the following sections (and chapters).

The decentralization of China's cultural sphere began in 1978 following the Third Plenum of the 11th Central Committee of the CCP. During the previous three decades of socialism, Party doctrine was directly distilled into cultural works; media reflected reality, which was often framed as a class struggle. Under a system in which cultural goods were produced according to quotas and distributed according to plan, advertising was redundant. It was associated with the creation of false needs, in contradistinction to the Chinese leadership's definition of people's real needs. Within a few years of the Third Plenum, however, advertising was seen all over Chinese television screens. On 14 January 1979, an editorial appeared in Shanghai's *Wenhuibao* calling for the 'restoration of the good name of advertising'.[14] Two weeks later, China's first television advertisement appeared on Shanghai television promoting a herbal wine.[15] A month later, viewers had the first taste of foreign advertising, a promotion for the Westinghouse Corporation.[16] By November, the CCP Central Committee had formally ratified advertising in the mass media.

The first green shoots of a cultural market emerged in Guangzhou, the capital of Guangdong province, which is geographically proximate to Hong Kong and which uses the same spoken dialect, Cantonese. The former British colony had a bustling media and cultural scene in the 1980s. As Michael Curtin has detailed, its film and television industries in particular were extremely profitable with the influence of the Shaw Brothers allowing Hong Kong content to reach out to South East Asia.[17] A style of broadcasting called 'economic radio' made its way into the PRC from Hong Kong; in contrast to the propagandist format used in the rest of the PRC, economic radio used a mix of talk, pop music and weather reports to establish its popularity in the south. Guangdong province was also prominent because residents used satellite dishes to receive television signals from Hong Kong. In the 1990s *gangtai* culture, a term referring to the pop-oriented commercial culture of Hong Kong (*gang*) and neighbouring Taiwan (*tai*), was highly regarded by many in China's younger generation, as Thomas Gold relates in his essay 'go with your feelings'.[18]

By the time Deng Xiaoping had completed his southern tour of China in 1992, handing over Party leadership to his successor, Jiang Zemin, China's media industries were on notice. The message was to make your own way by generating advertising but be vigilant and observe the boundaries. The expansion of satellite TV stations, which could reach the whole nation in the mid-1990s, provided an economic stimulus, as did China's impending entry into the WTO. The cultural industries were inscribed in the 11th Five-Year Plan.[19] Cultural industries research mushroomed, published in government Blue Books (*lanpishu*). In contradistinction to the practice of saluting the planned economy, scholars now focused on how best to reform the cultural system. The cultural system (*wenhua tizhi*) was a holistic term used by policy makers and academics to denote both representation and production of content. Media institutions such as CCTV and the *People's Daily* were termed *shiye*, while those that had more freedom to become self-reliant were enterprises (*qiye*) or industries (*chanye*).

By 2003, with the passage of a notice referred to as the 'reform of the cultural system', media were officially classified as industries, although the term *shiye* was retained for Party media.[20] The terminology of industries has moved centre stage during the past two decades, although not without controversy. Broadly speaking two approaches have dominated. The first is well documented and has a long legacy in writings on the cultural sphere in China; this is the consensus shared among political elites that culture is an instrument of governance, a means of educating and civilizing 'the people'. Accordingly, cultural workers have a responsibility to produce social goods that have an educative function. While cultural production has become more self-supporting and entrepreneurial over the past three decades in China, the cultural and media spheres are still regarded as sectors that require vigilant supervision, guidance and subsidy. The second approach, as we have discussed in the previous chapter, is that China should build strong cultural industries and extend its influence globally. This ambition has required a more hands-free approach from regulators, which has resulted in openings to creative content, often followed by sudden retractions and edicts.

Industrialization and catch-up

Reading Chinese policy documents, one is constantly reminded of forces of production. Indeed, Jiang Zemin, the Chinese leader who followed Deng Xiaoping, promulgated a theory in 2000 called 'the Three Represents' (*san ge daibiao*): the first representing 'advanced productive forces' (economic production), the second 'the progressive course of China's advanced culture' (cultural development) and the third 'the fundamental interests of the majority' (political legitimacy). The theory was ratified in the 16th Party Congress in 2002. In the same year entrepreneurs were welcomed as members of the CCP, opening the way for private capital to merge with ideology. Today, leading members of China's cultural, media and communications industries rub shoulders with party leaders and government officials.

The industrial nature of Chinese business is never far from the political centre and industry papers are infused with statist dogma. The term 'upgrading' (*shengji*) frequently appears in Chinese industrial economics. The role of state policy in the PRC is to provide the right policy levers and incentives to bring about upgrading while containing excessive outbreaks of unhealthy market activities. In the mid-2000s, the term 'cultural innovation' (*wenhua chuangxin*) began to be used in policy circles. China already had a market economy. How could the cultural market innovate? How could it be more competitive? How should upgrading proceed? It was soon realized that transforming from manufacturing to cultural and creative services entails more than just dispensing loans to enterprises. Real innovation implies a Schumpeterian approach in which entrepreneurial activities produce uncertainty. Arguably, nothing illustrates innovation (and uncertainty) more than the internet, a point that Chinese internet leaders advocated in their support of the 2014 mass entrepreneurship, mass innovation policy.

While convergence had achieved a following among many working across culture and technology fields in the West, the idea took a while to take root in China. It was economic development that proved to be the handmaiden of convergence. To understand this and the emergence of a cultural industry mentality in China, we have identified a stages-of-growth model (Table 2.1).[21]

Table 2.1 Cultural innovation timeline (Keane 2007)

Stage/theme	Strategic form
Standardized production	Subcontracting (fashion, animation, software, toys, furnishings, electronics)
Imitation	Import substitution, local versions and cloning
Collaboration	Co-production and various forms of sharing knowledge
Trade	Beginning of soft power strategy; breaking out of domestic constraints
Clusters	Attempts to harness soft power by industrializing culture
Online creative communities	Borderless social network markets; reaches domestic and international online audiences

Since the 1980s, the 'Made in China' phenomenon has driven China's economic success. The first of six stages of cultural innovation is standardized production. The 'Made in China' brand illustrates how the factory model is transferred into the domain of culture. The freeing up of culture to 'go to the market' in the 1990s required physical labour. Factories were converted into production centres, attracting workers. Technological components, household appliances, medical equipment, tools and machinery were already being produced in factories and sweat shops as well as virtually every household commodity found in supermarkets and hardware outlets globally. Major international consumer product brands established factories to take advantage of low rent and cheap labour. Production line labour in these factories was, and still is, managed by strict routines.

The weakness of the standardized production model, however, is that it perpetuates a bottom-line mentality. The availability of cheap land for factories and clusters, often subsidized by local governments, has implications for innovation. Focusing on an industrial model of production with a high proportion of outsourcing runs the risk of contract work moving to lower cost locations.[22] Another problem with this model is that China is locked into processing with little or no money invested in R&D. Reliance on cheap exports became apparent in the wake of the 2008 global financial crisis, which saw a lessening of overseas demand for China's manufactured products as well as a shift to production in western regions of China and lower cost developing countries. On the other hand, as Richard Baldwin has shown, these processing zones have allowed the transfer of technology and skills, which has over time seen the development of innovative products.[23] Another scenario is that the nation's over-reliance on low-cost manufacturing, characterized by original equipment manufacturing (OEM), forced policy makers to ramp up existing programmes directed at fostering technological innovation as well as providing more latitude for commercial players in order that China could move up the global value chain. As a result, China is arguably leading the world in applications of digital technology and their embeddedness in society, leading to greater efficiencies and social dividends.

Imitation, the second stage, is often negatively associated with Chinese media and cultural products. While generally deemed to be opportunistic, imitation serves a purpose. Copying is intrinsic to all learning activities and engenders novelty, which is in effect differentiation with some intrinsic goal. The practice of important substitution had served China well in the Maoist period when foreign goods were banned. The ban required local industries to become 'self-reliant', to learn how to make local versions. As Yuefan Xiao observes, this reverse engineering often amounted to 'sinifying foreign things'.[24] Local versions accounted for a great deal of audiovisual content, for instance, the propensity to produce cloned versions of 'foreign' reality TV formats such as *The Voice*, *Idol* and *If You Are the One*.[25] The boundary between imitation and creativity can be a fine line. The best example of these practices is the myriad copies of international products collectively described as *shanzhai* (literally home of mountain bandits). *Shanzhai* occurs across a range of consumer items but is extremely prevalent in electronics and fashion, where the logo, brand name or brand image is given a minor change. As Lena Scheen points out, the *shanzhai* product is meant to be similar enough to its prototype to give the customer positive associations with the original brand, but different enough to compete with it and to avoid – with varying success – violating intellectual property rights (IPR).[26] An example of how copying, in the name of urban development, led to a 'celebration of individual creativity' is illustrated in Winnie Wong's account of the extraordinary success of the Dafen Oil Painting Village in the southern city of Shenzhen. Initially the art scene began as a painting contest organized by officials. Now one can order a Van Gogh (copy) online. Influential art world figures and dealers have spent time in Dafen lecturing and advising the local painters how to break into the 'real' art world.[27]

The third stage is collaboration. The search for market success has led many to collaborations with foreign partners; in many cases these partners come from Taiwan, Hong Kong and South Korea.[28] Collaboration accelerates learning and engenders long-term relationships, although the results of collaboration don't always bear market fruit. But there are reasons for this mixed result, mostly to do with the creative compromises that are necessary to work collaboratively. Entrepreneurs from East Asia have moved into media companies in China. Their roles are creative, managerial, consulting and technical, providing professional expertise, alternative approaches to human capital management and new ways of solving problems. These intermediaries bring ideas, investment, technology and know-how into the sector. Collaboration, along with foreign investment, is meant to provide benefits for both parties. The form that collaboration takes varies: in film and animation industries the preferred model is co-production: these can be joint, assisted or commissioned production.[29] In television production, it is generally formatting, a practice that has accelerated in the past two decades globally. When one party is downgraded to a technical or production capacity, however, the result is often akin to exploitation. Certainly, this has occurred in film and TV drama production when the foreign entity, often South Korean, Taiwanese or Hong Kong, has assumed the role of creative executive producer.

Trade, or 'going out', is the fourth stage in development. It was not always so. China's large domestic market has mitigated against the need for the export of cultural and media products. But reputational effects have come into play, especially as more foreign products have entered China from East Asia. Markets for China's cultural goods, especially cinema, TV and animation, are primarily in East and South East Asia despite the national government's desire to challenge US entertainment and news conglomerates. The strategy here is to build soft power, as we discuss elsewhere in the book. Moreover, the lesson to draw from history is that rejuvenation is needed. China's exports to the world – ceramics, silk and philosophy, as well as its inventions, paper, printing and gunpowder – had created the impression of a wondrous world in the eyes of travellers and writers from Europe. In other words, China had a reputation as a creative nation a thousand years ago. As Ding has convincingly argued it had soft power in abundance: 'Throughout history, China's cultural power frequently "conquered" neighbouring regions through osmosis rather than military victory.'[30] But can China regain its lost soft power through trade?

Technology, however, is an area where China is developing a formidable reputation. Chinese phones are achieving large sales in many parts of the world, notably the subcontinent. A Made-in-China brand like Xiaomi, which was once just about the production of cheaper smart phones, now offers consumers enhanced Internet of Things (IoT) products that promote a digital lifestyle. While audiovisual sectors have the greatest opportunity to reach out, efforts by the state to increase soft power, for instance by establishing international television channels, are largely counterproductive. Moreover, because such television channels are heavily regulated, they are viewed as conduits for state ideology. Cinema is another domain of influence; as noted above, co-production and the borrowing of ideas from East Asia have invigorated Chinese cinema, although international recognition such as that achieved by South Korea at the 2020 Academy Awards remains as far away as ever.

The fifth stage of the cultural innovation timeline began two decade ago, when China's leaders decided the nation needed to industrialize culture through clustering and innovation. It provides evidence of the integration of technology and culture, even before the idea made it to Chinese think tanks. And it is similar in some respects to the first stage (standardized production), except that innovation is the desired benefit. From 1988 onwards, Economic and Technology Zones (ETZs) appeared, first in the southern coastal areas of China, later extending to a large number of 'open' cities.[31] Many of the ETZs featured high-technology parks or innovation parks; these were meant to attract foreign investment often through South East Asian ethnic Chinese networks.[32] By the 1990s a consensus was achieved among economic reformers that agglomeration economies were the best way of utilizing material resources and managing low-cost human capital. Following the widespread success of industrial clusters, the cluster model was grafted onto cultural production. Scores of parks, bases, and zones sprang up, often in old industrial sites. These industrial spaces replicated the industrialization of Chinese society over the past decade: in instances such as Beijing's 798 Art Zone and Shanghai's Tianzifang they provide opportunities for consumption. Originating from British neoclassical economist Alfred Marshall's 'industrial districts', clusters gained new significance following Michael Porter's influential account of *The Competitive Advantage of Nations*.[33]

Predating the current focus on clusters, however, was the formation of state media groups in order to stimulate 'managed competition'. Joseph Man Chan has noted how most media conglomerates 'are organized by administrative fiat', resulting in inefficiencies, duplication and new cost burdens.[34] By 2012, China had 30 media groups. The media groups have in the past decade been challenged by new players, including the digital technology giants known as BAT, which have actively entered into the production of media content. In Shenzhen for instance one finds the Shenzhen Media Group, which has to contend with the rising star on the block, Tencent, also based in Shenzhen but which has a much more commercial ethos and heavy investment in social media and gaming.

By the beginning of the second decade the creative cluster model was failing to deliver the promised benefits, aside from raising real estate prices and favouring enterprises with links to powerful players. Shanghai, the leader in designating creative parks, was most culpable in this regard, with creative freedom often shut down because of the political connections of the managers of the spaces.[35] Spaces such as the Songzhuang Art District outside Beijing suffered the same kinds of restrictions after an early period of creative optimism.[36] Aside from a few commercial success stories such as the 798 Arts District at Dashanzi in Beijing, the OCT Loft in Shenzhen and Creative 100 in Qingdao, the idea of putting people together in designated spaces had not translated into meaningful creative breakthroughs. The aforementioned sites were mostly successful as places to go, for instance as tourists, rather than to create. But this was before online technologies provided people with the means to create and collaborate, before 'mass entrepreneurship, mass innovation'.

In 2014, the creative cluster movement morphed into the digital era, following the announcement by Premier Li Keqiang that grassroots innovation was to be the approved development strategy. The mantra of 'mass entrepreneurship, mass innovation' coincided with a recognition of start-up culture and the Internet + initiative. The graduates of China's universities would now use their skills to become entrepreneurs. Money and resources were poured into so-called mass innovation spaces or, as they are more commonly known globally, makerspaces. Incubators, fab labs and co-working spaces blossomed, surrounded by coffee shops with funky names where young entrepreneurs can meet up and dream big about the development and production of internet-related products ranging from fashion accessories to sexualized robots to VR apps.

Aspiring creatives could now receive direct mentorship from digital industry elites. An example of the new digital cluster model is Dream Town in Hangzhou. Work on the project commenced in August 2014. According to reports Dream Town had the stated purpose of developing IT industries and 'special-feature' (*tese*) towns.[37] On 28 March 2015, the governor of Zhejiang province reported that Dream Town was actually 'a new type of mass entrepreneurial space, a giant incubator, a young entrepreneurial community, a new information economy motor, an Internet start-up ecosystem'.[38] The project attracted talent from China's leading educational institutions along with returning overseas talent. Innovation vouchers allow selected participants to utilize the services of companies within the villages.[39] By June 2016, just over a year after its inception, Dream Town had 15 commercial incubators and a total of 640 projects employing 5,900 workers.[40]

The last stage, online creative communities and user-generated content, is the most important in an evolutionary sense and draws the previous stages into the convergent industry model now championed by China's internet companies. The five previous stages in the innovation timeline (OEM, imitation, formatting, market expansion in Asia, and clustering) indicate formal mechanisms to initiate projects, often supported by and reliant on government policy: some of these strategies are simple, for example, find factory space, acquire workers and look for outsourcing work. Others are expedient: imitate, borrow, adapt or even steal ideas. Collaborating and clustering were early attempts to professionalize and to share skill. Exports were a possibility but not easily achieved. With the development of creative online communities, artistic and cultural production became variegated, heterogeneous and informal. Activities are conducted by both professionals and amateurs; and the crossover between amateur and professional has accelerated. In the parlance of the digital industries this kind of disruption is good. And as the opportunities for creative expression spread, grassroots communities have evolved, extending opportunities for productive sharing, reuse and remixing of content and collective authoring.

Looking at the massive transformation of Chinese society, it is possible to see how China has transformed from its strengths in material culture (theme parks, jewellery, artefacts, goods, performances) towards the intangibles of the digital culture and economy, one in which markets are complex and fragmented but where people's consumption is individualized.[41] In China today, convergence has become so visible that the concept seems anarchic. Production (and distribution) of content has moved from designated professionals to amateurs. The stages illustrate China's catch-up strategies and explain to some extent why Chinese policy makers have prescribed industrial (economic) models for culture. The stages also reveal the insecurity of China's soft power, namely a sense of frustration of China being typecast as a derivative uncreative nation by its East Asian neighbours, South Korea, Japan, as well as the Special Autonomous Region of Hong Kong and Taiwan, which individually and collectively have harvested the gains of commercial contemporary media and the kudos of critics.

Industry +

The Chinese economy, like the newly industrializing nations of East Asia, has risen to its present commanding heights thanks largely to export-oriented industrialization, what some characterize as 'Made in China'. The internet revolution has however changed the way that economies function and has allowed industrial latecomers to catch up. The Japanese economist Terutomo Ozawa says that the late twentieth-century American growth model was a virtuous circle sequence of 'IT revolution – investment – stock market gains – wealth effect – consumption and investment – and economic boom'.[42] Japan, Taiwan, South Korea and Singapore quickly emulated this path, albeit with a great deal of state planning and investment. China is now set to take on the mantle of AI superpower according to the venture capitalist Kai-fu Lee.[43] In the 1990s, foreign investment flowed into China, echoing Richard Baldwin's notion of the 'great convergence', whereby developed nations sent their managerial know-how to places where they had assembly and processing plants,[44] for instance, south China, allowing these places to transform and become significant players in global supply chains.

As discussed above, industrialization was a key word in the Chinese developmental lexicon in the 1980s, along with other economic terms such as development (*fazhan*), transformation (*zhuanxing/zhuanbian*) and upgrading (*shengji*). With the opening to foreign investment, mostly in designated areas and industries, information and communication technologies (ICTs) became central to the reform agenda. Communications infrastructure facilitated the so-called 'four modernizations' (industry, science and technology, defence and agriculture). By the mid-2000s, China had set its course to promote 'indigenous innovation' (*zizhu chuangxin*) and in doing so the nation began to move away from reliance on manufacturing component processing. Grassroots entrepreneurship received the warm endorsement of the government and although most headlines were initially directed at emerging technologies such as quantum computing, robotics and smart grids, the new programme directly impacted on the cultural and creative industries, which by now had received directives to go global. Projects began to be rolled out in response to a grassroots model of entrepreneurial industrialization.

The 'upgrading' of traditional industries through emerging technologies such as cloud computing, the IoT, robotics, data analytics and enhanced automation – and the recognition of the value of such disruptive technologies in the creative industries – is what we call 'industry +', sometimes referred to as the 'future industry' (*weilai chanye*). In China 'mass innovation' signals a collective ambition. Whereas the American Dream is about how an individual becomes a success, China's techno-utopian dreamscape is founded on connecting people (the masses) with technology. This began with the ICT revolution of the late 1980s and 1990s.

The ICT sector was the precursor to the internet boom. This state-supported sector had seen the scaling up of Chinese start-ups such as Lenovo, Huawei and ZTE. Zhou maintains that China's IT industries originally operated on slim profit margins, competing on price while eschewing frontier innovation.[45] Elsewhere, Liu and Zhou say that Chinese IT firms started with a low level of technological capability and with the assistance of government 'placed a heavy emphasis on reverse engineering and technology imports in their strategic development'.[46] Kai-fu Lee has called this practice 'gladiatorial entrepreneurship', but believes that such competition has led to real cutting-edge innovation.[47]

While imitation and borrowing are part of the narrative of ICT industrialization, so too is innovation. Despite imitating Western prototypes, and despite adopting Western branding strategies, China's digital media industries are extremely profitable and are reaching out into the Diaspora – as we show later in Chapters 6, 7 and 8. As we also argue in Chapter 5, while statistics from China are hard to verify, the indications are that domestic media sectors have experienced high growth and in doing so are providing more opportunities for employment, as well as attracting creative talent and investment from East Asia to the mainland.[48] The big change in China's cultural landscape in the past decade, however, as we shall see, has been industrial convergence.

Convergence did not happen through international market pressure, although foreign developments and players certainly influenced Chinese decision making. In a study of telecommunications in China, Eric Harwit considers the key role of industrial policy in the 1990s.[49] Administered by top decision makers in the State Council, industrial policy allowed an important, albeit limited role for overseas companies. Because foreign interests were kept at bay, domestic players were able to contend for the spoils of what was rapidly becoming a massive market. In the process of building national champions, Chinese policy makers had carefully scrutinized international models. The Ministry of Posts and Telecommunication's (MPT) monopoly over valuable communications services sectors, including mobile phones and internet, was challenged however not by international competition but by coalitions of institutional partners. China Telecom was instituted in 1995 under the administration of the MPT. Prior to this period the MPT was the sole industry player. By July 1995, China Unicom had managed to draw resources together from three ministries (Ministry of Electronic Industry, Ministry of Electric Power and Ministry of Railways), as well as 13 state-owned corporations. Unicom began to offer mobile services, leading to a series of price wars that drove prices down, signalling a first wave of industry turf wars. Yu Hong shows how the development of 3G networks provided an opportunity for domestic players in both physical devices and value-added network services.[50] The role played by state industrial policy included developing the China-only TDSCDMA standard. To establish this standard the state created an industrial alliance, set up a TDSCDMA R&D and industrialization fund, assigned favourable frequencies and forced the dominant telecom player China Mobile to adopt it. Media infrastructure expanded, from basic services to value-added broadband. By this time policy makers around the world had turned to broadband internet. In 2009, China's big three telecommunication providers, China Mobile, Chine Telecom and China Unicom, acquired 3G mobile communication licenses. Value-added services were now expanded into all aspects of social life, and this led to further 4G and 5G innovations.

In 2016, the existing National Informatization Development Strategy, initiated in 2006, was modified 'on the basis of new circumstances', namely the exponential growth of the internet technology sector which was unimaginable in 2006, and the more recent implementation of the BRI, which will allow the rollout of China's networks and platforms into new territories, establishing what the State Council calls a China-ASEAN 'information port' or even a digital Silk Road. An important addendum to the revised document is China's commitment to cyber-sovereignty, which may complicate the terrain for foreign internet-related businesses in China.

Prior to the development of China's commercial internet industries, local governments had developed an obsession with industrial clustering, particularly in software and IT component production. In the late 1980s, the government initiated the Torch Program to promote Science and Technology Industrial Parks, Software Parks, Science-Tech Business Incubators and Productivity Promotion Centres. The 863 programme was later established to encourage science and technology talent to return home from abroad. Technology parks and bases mushroomed in the 1990s as many regions and districts acquired technological learning from foreign firms. One practice was import substitution, the practice of replacing foreign brands with locally made ones; another strategy was export-focused, capitalizing on the need for cheap labour to attract foreign investment. However, after the global financial crisis of 2008, the Chinese government began to revaluate the export-led development strategy. As Xiao notes, a shift occurred 'from export-oriented growth to innovation-driven development, or transformation and upgrade'.[51] While this industrial model has remained largely intact, the sphere of cultural and media production was eventually overshadowed by the rapid development of the commercial internet. Digital production of content was no longer confined to parks and bases. However, the boom that eventuated can be dated back to the late 1990s when the seeds of China's internet revolution were being fed by venture capital. This is discussed in the next chapter.

Despite the attention currently attributed to the digital content sectors, cultural and media industries are a relatively new designation in the PRC, their origin dating from the early 1990s when the Chinese commodity economy was officially unleashed by Deng Xiaoping. Official recognition of industrial status is now more than two decades old. Today, China maintains a heavily commercialized and heavily protected media sector, one in which leading film actresses and directors are indicted with massive tax evasion and made scapegoats for the excesses of capitalism.

Notwithstanding the vicariousness of its idols and the sometimes blind eye turning of officials, the legacy of socialist ideology persists. Regulatory bureaux in China have carefully monitored the development of commercial media. The regulatory apparatus frequently changes name. In the 1990s, the Ministry of Radio, Film and Television (MRFT) operated in tandem with the Central Propaganda Department and provincial offices. Later other organs were added to the industrial remit, including State Administration of Industry and Commerce (SAIC) (for DVDs), the Ministry of Information Industry (MII) (for information network supervision), while the State Administration of Radio, Film and Television (SARFT) morphed into SAPPRFT, before being absorbed into a super ministry in 2018. Communication is arguably more important to China than it was in the heady days of propaganda cadres inveigling the masses.

Conclusion

This chapter has shown the importance of industrial development to China, a developing nation according to the United Nations, a nation that aspires to be a great global power. China achieved significant heights of both economic and cultural power in the first millennium and for most of the second millennium. The rise of West, from the eighteenth century, its leading role in the first and second industrial revolutions, was assisted by mercantile capitalism and colonial ambition. Western civilization globalized and this allowed ideas about liberalism and democracy to resettle in what were previously autocratic states. From the 1940s onwards, Western culture (film and television) crossed into new territories and was counted as trade data.

The Third Industrial Revolution, the age of computers, and the so-called Fourth Industrial Revolution, the age of automated technologies and smart devices, is allowing China to establish greater cultural presence. China's rise as a digital superpower is no longer contingent on expertise alone. The capacity of China's platforms to harness massive amounts of data allows China to 'leap forward' by machine learning. Similarly, the use of algorithms to aggregate and recommend content, which is then shared by users, accelerates the renewal of China's cultural resources. But does this data-driven model make Chinese culture more amenable to global audiences? Does technology allow 'China to tell its stories better'? In short, the proposition we need to test is: culture + technology = cultural power.

Finally, it is important to note the evolution of industrial policy as it applies to the cultural sphere. The cultural industries remain the default national terminology in China. However, the foreign variant 'creative industries' were incorporated within the 13th Five-Year Plan (2016–20). The 'digital creative industries' is listed as one of the five key development priorities. The attribution 'digital' before creative industries serves to differentiate it from foreign usages: in effect, adding digital mitigates the negative threat associated with disruption, echoing a view that technology is not ideological while accommodating the benefits of grassroots collaboration. The incorporation of digital technology as a driver of creativity was not something that the state had envisioned at the time the cultural industries were legislated in 2001. Technological developments, namely web 2.0 and then 3G, 4G and now 5G technology, have provided the means for an expansion of creative expression beyond the designated work units, television stations, media parks and clusters that served China in the planned economy. A generation born with the affordances of technology has an opportunity to remake Chinese culture.

Online creative communities thus represent the creative potential of China. An example is internet publishing which has generated its own momentum and spread its wings into South East Asia.[52] Moreover, it is the informality of online creativity that renders it so powerful. Many participants operate on the edge of regulation, partly visible to regulators. We see adventures in online networked production, amateur film-making and informal innovative activities. Many outputs are not brought to market. The perennial constraint of state regulation is obviated to some extent by Chinese digital platforms, which promise more creative freedom and operate at a greater distance from the state, albeit not as far as their Western counterparts. Some have internationalized and are global brands. The short video platform TikTok, owned by Bytedance, is not recognizable to most people in the world as being of Chinese origin. This will be discussed in the following chapters.

Chapter 3

INTERNET +

Chapters 1 and 2 charted the 'upgrading' of Chinese media, cultural and creative industries from the late 1980s to the present. The 'two cultures' – the domains of the sciences and the humanities – have come closer together.[1] In this chapter we focus on the most significant addition to the industrial convergence lexicon in China, Internet +.

The history of internet development in China is often depicted as the history of the 'Chinese internet'. Yet, scholars don't speak of an American internet, where the technology originated, or a South Korean, African or Australian internet. Of course, there are good reasons why the description Chinese internet applies, notably the draconian content filtering architecture known as the Great Firewall of China (GFC), the retention of user data on servers within China and the use of surveillance technologies to monitor the movements of Chinese citizens. Recent arguments have even made a compelling case for the emergence of 'splinternets' or alternative internets and sovereign understandings of how the internet is governed.[2]

As discussed in previous chapters, media and cultural industries were regarded as the superstructure – the realm of ideology in China. The superstructure was the absolute embodiment of political culture; it reflected economic development, that is, the material base of objects, commodities and things. The superstructure had adapted the *tiyong* model of the early reformers, purging the *ti* of its feudal traditional elements and replacing it with Marxist theory. This base superstructure model offered a functionalist explanation of the world in the era prior to the 1980s. However, as Scott Lash and Celia Lury point out, 'cultural objects are everywhere; as information, as communications, as branded products, as financial services, as media products, as transport and leisure services'.[3] Culture has seeped out of the superstructure, infiltrating the infrastructure and becoming infrastructure.

To better understand the ramifications of China's global connectivity and how digital infrastructure is viewed in meeting the country's ideological agenda, this chapter sketches an outline of the development of the internet both as it pertains to international content entering China and Chinese content going out. With China's inevitable rise as a technological superpower, together with growing apprehension in the West about Chinese influence, research on Chinese internet control continues to grow. After some initial enthusiasm about the potential of the internet to democratize China, most scholars soon recognized that the internet is not that dissimilar to China's traditional media sphere. Content restriction and monitoring were applied to media producers prior to the advent of online platforms, for instance prepublication censorship, and the abrupt withdrawal of foreign satellite television connections.[4] Practices of restriction and monitoring are now operationalized online by state security apparatuses through an arsenal of human monitors as well as a first defence shield of machine learning algorithms.

The internet is evolving beyond its technical infrastructure and standards. The governance of cyberspace is a contested domain. It relates directly to the management of financial technology (FinTech), which includes decisions about investment in technologies that impact on cultural and media industries, for instance, the digitalization of heritage and VR. This chapter describes how the internet evolved in China, from being a technology of hope to one of social management, from a communications network that needed to be closely monitored to one that would revolutionize peoples' social transactions, together with their aspirations for a better life. While the internet has generated a greater splintering of Chinese society, for instance, numerous disputing communities, it has fermented user-generated creativity on an unprecedented scale. And it has made China the world's largest digital economy and a global leader in next-generation technologies.

This chapter is organized as follows. Section 1 provides a brief review of the history of the internet in China with a focus on significant events, major milestones and key players over the last 25 years. It examines how a Chinese internet ecosystem was formed. It considers how the system is becoming more authoritarian under the control of the Chinese party-state. Section 2 examines Internet + and several policy and industry responses that are aimed at structurally transforming the Chinese economy from manufacturing to digital services. The chapter discusses how Internet + has evolved to become a comprehensive blueprint for next-generation technology and how it is integrated with the composite idea of Social +. Section 3 then considers how Internet + is contributing to the rise of China as a global power; and how it has also motivated Chinese internet companies, such as social media and video-sharing platforms, to be part of the 'culture going out' efforts. Finally, Section 4 discusses the impact of the Chinese discourse of Internet + on global internet governance.

The Chinese internet ecosystem

The World Wide Web transformed the internet from an academic curiosity to a technology that would change the way people live. Some of the key moments that relate to internet history are the first Web browser Mosaic (1992), the Google algorithm (1998), Wikipedia (2001), Facebook (2004) and the iPhone (2007). Indeed, the history of the web is frequently related to Silicon Valley and associated with a kind of utopian spirit. The internet thus evokes the ethos of freedom, at least the kind of freedom espoused in liberal democracies. Even when the corporate world began to irrevocably monetize the internet, the ideal of a World Wide Web retained the collective ethos of sharing.

A Chinese history of the internet followed closely in the wake of Western innovation. The first email ('Across the Great Wall we can reach every corner of the world') was sent from Beijing to Germany in 1986 between academics of two research institutions. China was linked to the World Wide Web in 1994 through a dedicated line with the United States; then in 1996 the internet was opened to the Chinese public. In China the internet was simply understood as the WWW.[5]

The development of internet infrastructure has enabled Chinese people to cross the new Great Wall and communicate with strangers in and outside China. Despite a high barrier to entry for ordinary Chinese people to connect via expensive dial-up telephone lines, modems and the difficulty of learning the Chinese script input system in text-only formats (emails and bulletin board services), the internet was a social technology from the beginning. The internet developed out of a nebulous environment in which the party-state, the fledgling IT industry and computer and information technology enthusiasts, both professional and amateur, explored the new opportunities provided by internet-mediated communications. Because it was self-regulated by IT engineers and enthusiasts, it embodied a spirit of freedom as in many other nations.

The first campaign to 'civilize' Chinese cyberspace did not start until 2000. Referred to as the 'Network Civilization Project', it was jointly launched by eight key ministries and governmental agencies. The aim was to regulate the nature of content on the internet and the behaviour of users. Since then, the internet *within China* has become less free, with the government taking over development of infrastructure, including implementation of the so-called Great Firewall, intended to prevent Chinese people from reaching 'every corner of the world'. Because of the fears of foreign ideas flooding into China, the world's largest intranet was born. Rather than speaking of the internet in China, scholars often speak of a Chinese internet, one that is tamed and 'domesticated'.⁶

In fact, governance infrastructure started to be assembled in 1996 when the internet was opened to the public. Political elites in Beijing sensed the importance of infrastructure from the very beginning.⁷ The government enacted interim provisions for governing computer information in that year, and then in 1998 the Ministry of Public Security launched the Golden Shield project for internet security, a national filter that blocked politically sensitive content from entering the domestic network. Today the Golden Shield project is one of 12 Golden projects, including Golden Bridges (for public economic information), Golden Customs (for foreign trade), Golden Card (for electronic currencies), Golden Finance (for financial management), Golden Agriculture (for agricultural information), Golden Taxation (for taxation), Golden Water (for water conservancy information) and Golden Quality (for quality supervision). The importance given to the Golden Shield project, as the first of the projects, is illustrative of the way the Chinese government manages its internet ecosystem, which evolved from early fragmentation to a highly coordinated and integrated structure by the turn of the twenty-first century.⁸

It is well documented that the Chinese government regards its media and communication sectors as key to the nation's technological catch-up. Technology has always been critical in China's competition with developed Western economies. Technology has allowed China to thrive in the global market economy. By the early 2000s, the term 'neo-technonationalism' described China's communications policy.⁹ As some scholars have noted, the internet has become an integral part of strategies used by the Chinese government and the Chinese Communist Party to extend control over information management, enhance legitimacy and promote national soft power on the international stage.¹⁰ The government has spared no effort and resources in ensuring that China's internet is safeguarded against unwanted information and foreign influence while at the same time serving its national and commercial goals. Such an internet governance framework balances political imperatives and market logic, public security with economic development and encourages a mutual incorporation and convergence of public and private interests at both national and transnational levels. These balances will be further discussed in this chapter.

Infrastructural development is key to growing user adoption. As shown in the previous chapter, the digital transformation of Chinese society was a direct consequence of competition between telecommunications giants like China Mobile, China Netcom and China Unicom, which led to more broadband infrastructure and cheaper devices. Even though it would take years for people in remote areas to go online, Chinese society was now connected, completing a nation-building project that had begun decades earlier with the extension of radio and television networks. In fact, the initial development of the commercial internet in China followed from the state's policy elevation of the role of the ICT industry as a pillar of the Chinese economy. Reflecting the argument about 'the great convergence'[11] noted in the previous chapter, this model was founded on a foreign direct investment (FDI)-driven and export-oriented model.[12]

China's aspiration to develop indigenous and proprietary technologies has a history dating back to the 1990s. After China's entry into the World Trade Organization (WTO) in December 2001, it became imperative for the national economy to become self-reliant and elevate its position within global industry chains. The term 'indigenous innovation' (*zizhu chuangxin*) carried the hope of transforming China's status from the world's factory into a technological leader.[13] Several attempts were made in this regard, in 3G and 4G technological standards, as well as Wi-Fi security standards. The race to 5G is the latest contested field on the global stage and is perceived as a strategic high ground for unlocking the future benefits of the digital economy.

Technological evolution has propelled the development of various forms of the internet. In the late 1990s, leading web portals including Sina, NetEase and Sohu began to play an important role in providing content for the consumption of Chinese users.[14] All three portals profited from the rapid growth of the Chinese market and were listed on NASDAQ in 2000. The availability of bulletin boards allowed users to be content creators, connecting with each other and engaging in public discussions online. The first wave of internet celebrities in China soon followed.[15]

The late 1990s marked a significant watershed moment for China's new digital giants, the 'three kingdoms', which were collectively known as BAT. Tencent, established in 1998, launched its messaging tool QICQ, renamed QQ in 2000. Alibaba planted seeds in e-commerce in 1999, resulting in the launch of Taobao site in 2003, and Baidu established a stronghold with its search engine launched in 2000. Since then, with their competitive edge established in social networking, e-commerce and search, Tencent, Alibaba and Baidu built up broader ecosystems and became the leading players in China's digital economy. These players also became the instigators of China's sharing economy, which has now become mainstream and whose definition is flexible, ranging from informal video sharing to new business ventures. The sudden manifestation of the sharing economy in China generated a proliferation of apps, such as Didi (known as Chinese Uber) in ride sharing and Dianping (known as Chinese Yelp) in consumer review/rating and sharing. According to a 2017 government think tank report, in 2016, 600 million Chinese people participated in China's new sharing economy. The report did not specify if these numbers applied to overseas Chinese, but one senses that the influx of overseas technology capital is crucial. The report projected that the sharing economy would contribute 10 per cent of gross domestic product (GDP) by 2020.[16]

From the early 2000s, the internet has become a popular space for video content sharing. Bit torrent and other peer-to-peer sharing technologies led to the growth of domestic sites including BTChina, Xunlei and Very CD. These technologies provided a way for audiences to access and redistribute restricted overseas content from Hollywood films to Japanese and Korean TV serials. A wave of video-sharing platforms followed, most notably Tudou and Youku, and this began to draw even more users online. Others took a different path. LeTV and PPTV, for example, rebroadcast professionally produced content from television networks and movie studios. As well as the outbreak of video service providers, subtitling communities made consumption of overseas content easier for viewers with less foreign linguistic literacy. For many the plethora of free sites seemed like a gift from the heavens; China's net generation now had almost unlimited access to content.

However, attempts to reduce piracy were gaining momentum, with several campaigns carried out by the government.[17] Externally, pressure was coming from copyright owners such as Motion Picture Association of America (MPAA). In December 2007, the State Administration of Radio, Film and Television (SARFT) and the Ministry of Industry and Information Technology (MIIT) introduced the Administrative Provisions on Internet Audio-Visual Program Service.[18] These Provisions introduced new licensing regulations. The carnival was over. The state's intervention in Internet Protocol (IP) regulation was an attempt to appease the international community as much as it was designed to extend domestic ideological control online. As a result, many service providers started to seek a transition path to the formalized sector. Many more disappeared. The licensing requirement accelerated the industry shakeout. New market entrants such as iQiyi (later acquired by Baidu) and Tencent Video quickly dominated the market, while Youku and Tudou merged into one corporation which was later bought by Alibaba.

The advent of the mobile internet further extended the mediatization of Chinese society, especially with the adoption of smart phones. Mobile internet users exceeded PC users for the first time by mid-2012, reaching 380 million.[19] The debut of the iPhone in 2008 saw enthusiastic fans going to great lengths to obtain the device, often via parallel dealers before it was formally introduced to China in 2009. Following the launch of App Store and Google Play in the United States, the rise of local third-party app distributors was a precursor to what would quickly become a booming app economy. Local smart phone brands capitalized on the open-source Android. Huawei, a major market player in telecom network equipment, launched its first Android smart phone in 2009 and has since risen to become the world's third largest smart phone provider. Xiaomi, established in 2010, has broken into several international markets including India, Indonesia and Europe, and became the youngest company on the Fortune Global 500 list.[20] Taking a different path than incumbent brands, Xiaomi engaged informal creative energy in product development and cultivated a distinctive patriotic brand identity by aligning with the state project of rebranding 'Made in China'.[21]

The mobile app economy significantly changed user behaviour in China. While search engines and browsers provided the gateway to the internet, mobile apps have allowed multiple entry points to a diversified range of content and services. Baidu, which had relied on its search engine to drive its advertising business, soon encountered industrial disruption. The search engine giant spent extravagantly on a deal to acquire the leading mobile app distributor 91Wireless in order to secure its market position. The latter became a new gateway to the Chinese internet by navigating the boundaries between the formal and informal media economy, and across geographical borders, to create value networks.[22]

The year 2010 witnessed a growing number of e-commerce apps on the market. The Double 11 Shopping Festival, then in its second year, had already started to attract a large number of users; 11 November has since become the biggest occasion for online shoppers in China who flock to sites such as Taobao.com and JD.com. Mobile payment assumed a crucial role in propelling m-commerce. While Alipay has dominated the Chinese e-payment market since its debut in 2004, the launch of WeChat in 2011 soon saw the Shenzhen-based digital giant adding the feature of mobile payments. WeChat Pay arrived in 2013 and was followed by QQ Wallet in 2014. Alipay and WeChat Pay are leading China's road to a cashless economy. According to one survey, 92 per cent of people in China's largest cities use WeChat Pay or Alipay as their main means of payment; in rural China, 47 per cent of the population is reported to use mobile payments regularly. In 2018, around 83 per cent of all payments were made via mobile payment modes.[23] Both companies have attempted to tap further into overseas markets, starting with diasporic populations.

A timeline of internet development shows just how critical the new technology has been for China's innovative nation project. By the end of the second millennium, the internet had achieved critical mass in China. In 2008, China became the largest internet population in the world by registered users; in 2011, it replaced the United States as the world leader in terms of installed telecommunication bandwidth; in 2014 it became the world's largest e-commerce market; in 2018, China became the second largest digital economy in the world, behind the United States but surpassing Japan and the UK. As of March 2020, China had 897 million mobile internet users, accounting for 99.3% of its all netizens.[24]

Clearly, technological advancement has introduced significant changes in how people access information, communicate, consume entertainment content and conduct transactions. A myriad of tech start-ups, large, medium and small, many of which were funded by international capital, have been driving such transformations.[25] By the early 2010s, BAT had established themselves as Chinese frontrunners in the digital economy, while the new-generation unicorns and start-ups like BMD (ByteDance, Meituan-Dianping, Didi Chuxing) started to emerge and would strengthen their proprietary platform system and soon pose as serious challengers to BAT. These internet enterprises have more in common with Silicon Valley entrepreneurialism than Chinese SOE-style management. They have sought to expand into international markets, with some initial successes. The overseas ambitions of these platforms will be illustrated in Chapter 4.

From the Chinese internet to Internet +

The Chinese state's push to develop the internet as a new engine of growth requires maintaining a tight grip over content while encouraging the entrepreneurial energy and creativity for economic restructuring. In 2014, Xi Jinping stressed the need to build China into a strong cyberpower (*wangluo qiangguo*). The intent of this directive was to strengthen innovation capacity, develop the digital economy and enhance cybersecurity.[26] Then in 2015, a key policy framework on the development of the internet and digital economy in China was announced.

Internet +, the name given to this initiative, aims to redefine how the internet is understood in everyday life and extend its remit to economic development and social governance. Along with its doppelganger concept 'Made in China 2025' (hereafter MIC25) (see below), its objectives are to upgrade China's manufacturing industry through mobile Internet, cloud computing big data, and the Internet of Things (IoT) and to encourage Chinese digital companies to grow stronger and more competitive in the international market. Internet + extends beyond manufacturing and smart factories to a broader range of industrial digitalization projects such as connected health care, digital hospitality and tourism, and digital education. In the context of building soft power capability, the final objective 'to get Internet-based companies to increase their presence in the international market' is critical. Can digital platforms have a presence in the international market and, in doing so, disseminate Chinese culture, overcoming the limitations of previous more official channels of cultural diplomacy such as Confucius Institutes, film festivals and cultural troupes? This will be addressed in the following chapters.

Certainly Internet + is a bold policy blueprint for a whole range of modern industries and social and economic governance, evolving around the integration of cloud computer, big data, IoT and artificial intelligence (AI). It is one of a series of initiatives to boost economic development, transform economic structure and improve government capabilities. It demonstrates a robust commitment to the digital economy and a willingness to engage with transnational capital and build corporate dynamism. Whether through encouraging, taming or mainstreaming, the pivot to Internet + is the Chinese state's ambition to use digital technologies to remould the national economic structure and the nation's future.[27] As Table 3.1 shows, the Chinese government and its agencies have taken a top-down approach to the grand strategy of transforming China's internet industries, building innovative capacities and taking on the world's leading high-tech powers by 2030. Tech entrepreneurs meanwhile have gained remarkable political influence and been hailed as entrepreneurial model leaders; disruptive innovation is promoted among society as part of the strategy to stimulate mass entrepreneurship and mass innovation.

In effect, Internet + was implemented through a portfolio of plans, including the 13th Five-Year Plan (13th FYP) (2016–20) and MIC25. The 13th FYP charts a development vision, one in which the internet becomes a strong force in delivering economic transformation and restructuring. It aims to invigorate the digital economy and elevate China's status as a digital superpower. Specific initiatives include improving information infrastructure, promoting the penetration of broadband usage and increasing government funding for research and development (R&D). As Hong argues, the industrial policy expressed in the 13th FYP, which is tied to the state's new services-led development agenda, is part and parcel of a global trend since the 2008 global economic crisis.[28] Many countries have scrambled for new industrial policies and resorted to next-generation technologies to achieve competitive advantages. As a contender state, China is keen to be in the forefront of the coming technoeconomic revolution and become 'a new epicentre of digital capitalist development' and to 'contend in the existing world order and better China's position therein'.[29]

While Internet + was put forward by Li Keqiang as an initiative, 'MIC25' has become more well known as China's industrial policy in its quest for global tech leadership – to reduce reliance on foreign technology, catch up with Western industrialized countries and gain a competitive, if not leadership, edge in high-tech and emerging technologies. MIC25 is characteristic of the East Asian development model with a strong government and political target that aligns with business interests, as long as the businesses toe the government

Table 3.1 From Internet + to Intelligent + (complied by authors)

2015	**Internet +** (endorsed by Chinese Premier Li Keqiang in his government work report at the third session of China's 12th National People's Congress) **Made in China 2025** (a strategic plan issued in May, a blueprint to upgrade manufacturing capabilities to high technology-driven fields including IT and robotics, automotive, pharmaceutical, aerospace and semiconductor industries) Internet Plus Action Plan (to integrate mobile internet, cloud computer, big data and the IoT with traditional industries) Mass entrepreneurship, mass innovation
2016	Three-Year Guidance for Internet Plus Artificial Intelligence Plan (2016–18) The robot industry development plan (2016–20) 13th Five-Year Plan for Developing National Strategic and Emerging Industries (2016–20)
2017	New Generation AI Development Plan (to establish China as the premier global AI innovation centre by 2030) Artificial Intelligence 2.0 (by Chinese Academy of Engineering, adding AI to its list of 15 Sci-Tech Innovation 2030-Megaprojects)
2018	**Three-Year Action Plan for Promoting Development of a New Generation Artificial Intelligence Industry (2018–20)** (MIIT action plan in response to State Council's AI Plan and 'Made in China 2025') White paper on AI Standardization Three-Year Action Plan for Developing Industrial IoT (2018–20), by MIIT Tencent Research: 2018 Report on China's Internet + Index
2019	**Intelligence +** proposed by the State Council to develop and apply big data and AI in the Industrial IoT AliResearch: From connection to empowerment: Intelligence + to power China's high-quality economic growth

---

line.[30] Similar in many respects to Germany's Industrie 4.0 and the United States' Industrial Internet, MIC25 was proposed in 2015 by Xi Jinping as a signature project to achieve his Chinese Dream and assure China's future development in six strategic emerging industries.[31] In short, MIC25 expands next-generation ICT industries and the digital economy into the new pillars of China's economic transformation.

MIC25 has triggered foreign criticism and raised concerns about China's intention to push other countries out of both the Chinese and emerging markets, and has drawn attention to China's unfair business and technology theft practices. As it did with its other signature theme 'the peaceful rise of China' a decade earlier, the Chinese leadership has toned down the rhetoric while quietly moving from blueprint to implementation. Like all other state-led projects, MIC25 has been piloted in more than 30 cities, each with the task to develop specific high-tech industries included in the MIC25 remit. The emphasis is on next-generation ICT technologies (like 5G), new energy and intelligent vehicles, AI, big data, facial recognition and smart communication systems. The private sector is tasked with development, along with selected state-owned enterprises, in the strategic industries that are associated with MIC25. Huawei and Alibaba, two of China's digital hegemons, are among the top R&D spenders in the nation. The R&D expenditures by both the state and commercial enterprises have been on the rise since 2015. By 2019, China's R&D expenditure, in terms of percentage of GDP, had already surpassed that of the EU and is only second to the United States.[32]

With a trade war ongoing between China and the United States at the time of writing, and particularly in the wake of the arrest of Huawei CFO (chief financial officer) Meng Wanzhou and the sanctions on Huawei and ZTE, it is likely that China will witness a significant rise in future R&D spending in the future, not only in utility research and patents but also in primary research and invention patents. Technonationalism, which has characterized China's pursuit of leadership in emerging technologies, has seen a renewed enthusiasm in the Chinese public discourse in strengthening foundational technologies (e.g. chips, new materials and semiconductors) in order to reduce reliance on foreign supplies and better protect national industrial security. It is recognized that while China is stronger in adaptation and implementation of new technologies and best practices than developing new ones – common to latecomers' catch-up process, China is now trying to balance quantity with quality, particularly in enabling digital technologies, such as AI and analytics.

Indeed, significant parts of the Chinese economy – from commerce, finance, transportation, to health care, media and entertainment – have been digitalized and upgraded. The internet is collapsing industry boundaries, creating new markets, introducing new business models and transforming people's everyday lives. As the integration process unfolds, it produces and connects unprecedented amounts of data, which further underpins the development of the digital economy. With its large population and high penetration of mobile internet, China therefore occupies an advantageous position in generating and exploiting big data. Leading internet companies have commanded a wealth of data from online search histories, social graphs, transactions and physical locations.

The IoT further powers the process of capturing data, as QR codes, RFID tags, surveillance cameras, microphones and various kinds of sensors, that speak to each other via networks. Data are produced at an accelerated pace and this is crucial to sharpen machine learning capacity and advance AI. Following the Internet + strategy, the state launched several policy documents, which elevated AI to the level of national strategy. The State Council first put AI on the development agenda with the 'Three-Year Guidance for Internet

Plus Artificial Intelligence Plan (2016–2018)',[33] as a follow-up to the Internet + strategy to promote emerging industries. In 2017, AI officially became a national strategy with the release of the New Generation AI Development Plan, in which the state has set an objective to establish China as the 'premier global AI innovation centre' by 2030.[34] The MIIT quickly followed up with the 'Three-Year Action Plan for Promoting Development of a New Generation Artificial Intelligence Industry (2018–2020)'.

China's digital champions have responded enthusiastically to Internet +. In fact, Tencent CEO Ma Huateng had proposed an earlier term 'Internet Thinking' in 2013, two years before Internet + entered into the policy domain. At a time when mobile internet users showed leapfrogging growth, the opportunity to capitalize further was high on the agenda. A delegate to the National People's Congress, Ma had supported adopting the Internet + strategy in the 2015 session to power economic restructuring and development in China. Since then, big data, cloud computing and AI featured prominently in the discussion of Internet +. Soon after, Tencent released its own Internet + solution, which is aimed at enabling transformation in a variety of industries.

In April 2015, a month after the Chinese government released the Internet + blueprint, Alibaba Research Centre promoted a vision called 'from IT to DT (data technology)'.[35] According to this report, simply entitled Internet +, 16 industrial domains and sectors would be transformed by the internet, including Internet + agriculture, finance, credit, logistics, health, education, tourism, governance and public welfare. Chapter 20 of this report, entitled Internet + Culture, describes how the technology of the internet would facilitate cultural consumption by revolutionizing 'screen to online' models, by facilitating interaction between audiences and creators. With Alibaba owning significant media content assets, the digital transformation of user consumption was a clear sign of their intent. Baidu likewise announced AI and IoT initiatives. Other tech companies have entered into the euphoria about China's rise and the renovation of its national image.

From Internet + to Intelligent +

As discussed above, there is a sense of urgency in China's aspiration to be the world's leader in next-generation technologies and economy. A nationalistic discourse has characterized the desire to lead: it is sometimes reported in the mainstream media discourse that China missed the best opportunities in the First, Second and Third Industrial Revolutions; it must therefore seize the current opportunity and lead the so-called Fourth Industrial Revolution[36] to realize the Chinese Dream of national rejuvenation.[37] Such a grand strategy cannot be implemented without the help of China's own digital champions, who have developed increasingly similar portfolios as their Western counterparts together with a deep entanglement with transnational capital and the support of the Chinese government for continual growth and expansion. Such a symbiotic relationship between digital platforms and the national government agenda is central to the burgeoning Chinese digital economy. This symbiosis has been a central tenant in numerous publications and reports on China's digital capitalism.

The internet, with the 5G revolution now reshaping the Chinese economy, is exerting an enormous impact on services. Because of this, non-manufacturing transaction-intensive sectors such as finance, telecommunications, distribution and government services are being dramatically impacted. Chinese tech giants and digital platforms have pioneered a nationwide digital lifestyle and a new type of business model, known as Social +.[38] It embeds the internet as a crosscutting agent in aspects of such digital lifestyle and combines social networking and entertainment in the context of e-commerce transactions, philanthropy, poverty alleviation, social governance and many other areas of contemporary socioeconomic lives. China's tech giants have all extended their Social + plans to drive user engagement and growth.

While digital payments are prevalent throughout China, digital health is another area transformed by new technologies. Encouraged by Internet + and the 'mass entrepreneurship, mass innovation' mantra of the central government, the Chinese digital ecosystem has expanded with a robust start-up culture. Digital health care is a key sector. It has been designated by the government to integrate technology with the 'healthy China' plan, formulated in the 13th FYP. Again, private enterprises are leading the way in using AI-assisted screening, consultation and diagnosis. Doctor–patient service platforms have increased, alleviating the pressure on public hospitals. The most notable health care portals or platforms are: Ping An Good Doctor, Tencent's Doctorwork and Alibaba's DoctorYou. The internet and AI analytics play a leading role in such systems and form the backbone of the necessary digital infrastructure for the healthy China project, including real-time sharing of digital health records, medical resources and care management systems. The outbreak of COVID-19 in China and the rest of the world has seen increasing investment and resources from Beijing and its industry collaborators in the areas of digital health, involving interoperability of both online (powered by AI) and offline (aided by robotics and automated decision-making facilities) health datasets and services. This is an important area that deserves more research and critical analysis.

What we have witnessed since the Internet + was proposed in 2015 is the increasing integration of the internet and next-generation technologies in all aspects of social lives. Chinese tech enterprises have played a very active role in responding to the Chinese government's initiatives and pioneering innovative applications of digital technologies in transforming not only the economic structure but also the infrastructure and the ideological superstructure of digital China. China is using AI on a massive scale; it is also racing ahead with 5G; all of these endeavours are spearheaded by private enterprises working closely with the state. The AliResearch (2019) report on Intelligent + is an example of how the public–private dynamic operates in China.

'Intelligent +' was first presented in the 2019 Chinese Government Work Report on 6 March of that year, with the aim 'to promote the development and application of leading-edge technologies such as big data and artificial intelligence [...] by establishing industrial internet platforms and expanding on Intelligent Plus initiatives to facilitate transformations and upgrading of manufacturing sector'.[39] It is key to China's vision for high-quality development amid mounting uncertainties and continued economic slowdown. Similarly, to their rapid response to Internet +, Alibaba issued their 'intelligent +' report in March 2019. The report highlights the power of intelligent technology clusters (not individual technologies) as a primary driving force of change in four key areas: economy, innovation, work and lifestyles, and governance. Intelligent + encompasses 'data + computing capacity + algorithms', which will empower 'data-empowered consumers and businesses' to 'push for a revolution in decision-making and tool-harnessing' and 'help optimize resource allocation in the society'.[40]

In such industry reports, China's leapfrog into the digital economy is both celebrated and anticipated. Implied in the confidence in China's intelligent future is the ambition to reposition the country in the 'global value chain revolution', to use the words of Richard Baldwin. Baldwin, writing about the history of technological catch-up in developing nations and regions, argues that the offshoring of production to low-wage nations in the 1980s changed the face of globalization.[41] With production stages moving offshore to capture cheaper labour, Western 'rich-nation' companies needed to send marketing, managerial and technical know-how. Baldwin says that this global value chain revolution redrew the international boundaries of knowledge. The most pertinent example is perhaps Apple. Most of the company's products are designed in California. US operations handle marketing, distribution, after-sales service and many add-on services while the fabrication stages are mostly done in China and organized by companies like Foxconn, an entity formed in Taiwan. Baldwin calls this change in the global economy 'the great convergence'.

Through the blueprint of Internet + and now Intelligent +, China is determined to lead in the new great convergence and lays its bet on intelligent technologies to move up the global value chain. A similar convergence argument was made earlier by the Japanese economist Terutomu Ozawa.[42] In a co-authored paper, he argued that just as the telegraph and later the telephone had upgraded economies in the previous communications revolutions, the internet revolution is generating more abstract or conceptual goods. Chinese political and technological elites clearly see the tremendous opportunities and impact of the internet and next-generation technologies on abstract or conceptual goods. Culture is one such good.

In the sphere of culture, which is essentially a service according to the WTO's General Agreement on Trade in Services (GATS), a similar argument about cultural technology transfer is applicable. The architecture of today's multisided digital platforms is largely derived from Western innovation, which has been modified to fit Asian contexts. Knowledge has been copied. Technology has been reverse-engineered, often wilfully, ignoring intellectual property rights. In regard to the more symbolic realm of creative content, Western formats have made their way eastwards, from television programmes to blockbuster genres. More recently, however, the tide has shifted with Made-in-China innovations and Made-in-China apps reaching out to the West; China's tech and content industry is said to be copied elsewhere.[43]

Connecting with the world?

This chapter has discussed how the 'Chinese internet' has transformed into IoT and Internet of Everything (IoE), with the internet functioning as the crosscutting ledger to integrate ICTs and next-generation technologies. This final section discusses how Internet + can be interpreted as part of China's remapping of the global internet governance. Instead of speaking of the Chinese internet or the internet in China, it is more pertinent to talk about Chinese approach to the internet industry and governance. Such an analytical framework allows us to examine the Chinese discourse of internet governance as a dual-tracked framework: domestically and internationally. The two tracks mutually sustain each other.

As mentioned earlier, the development of the Chinese internet is characterized by the central role of the state in governance and regulation; moreover, the Chinese internet ecosystem is built collectively by public and private players that respond to the discourses of technonationalism, national security and global financial markets. While the Chinese state hails the internet as a new growth engine, it exerts tight control over it. China's Great Firewall is a classic example of information control infrastructure.[44] With this ring-fence approach effectively keeping major global internet players at bay outside China, the Chinese government has nurtured an enclosed universe where its domestic enterprises dominate. For more sophisticated users, and those that are seeking to jump the wall, VPNs come to their assistance and enable them to access banned content and services. Periodic government crackdowns on VPNs, however, can make it difficult to scale the wall.

Undeniably, the internet is expected to propel the development of media industries, and cultural and creative industries more broadly in China. The call for the convergence of technological innovation and cultural creativity (*keji chuangxin yu wenhua chuangyi ronghe*) is a prominent policy theme in the media system reform. Media industries have co-evolved with the internet, unleashing waves of content production and new models of distribution and consumption. Media entertainment, in particular, has witnessed vigorous growth. OTT video markets, for example, recorded 115 per cent growth in revenue[45] between 2014 and 2018 in China, more than doubling the growth rate in the Asia-Pacific.

The potential of facilitating creativity and innovation is however accompanied by potentially disruptive behaviour, of which Chinese authorities are acutely aware. The state has consolidated and escalated internet content regulation in recent years. While internet content regulation was previously overseen by multiple state agencies, China established the State Internet Information Office (SIIO) under the State Council Information Office in 2011 to consolidate regulatory power. In 2014, SIIO transformed into the Cyberspace Administration of China (CAC), also known as the Central Cyberspace Affairs Commission. Under the direct leadership of Xi Jinping, CAC is a top-level internet governance apparatus aiming to 'make the positions of the Party the strongest voices in the online space' and 'distribute positive energy online'.[46]

Rebecca McKinnon has proposed an apt description 'networked authoritarianism' to characterize the Chinese internet ecosystem.[47] As Tim Oakes points out, however, the boundary between official and informal media can be fuzzy in China.[48] Certainly, the party-state has been adept in exploiting fuzziness. It has continued to block Silicon Valley heavyweights such as Google, Twitter, YouTube and Facebook. This obstruction provides a shield for home-grown digital platforms from head-on competition with global internet giants in China while fending off so-called unhealthy and content critical of the regime. In short, home-grown platforms share similarities with their global counterparts, but they operate in a different social and political environment.

Domestically, the internet is viewed not only as a single technical infrastructure but an aggregator of ICTs, a facilitator of government intervention, control and surveillance and a space for communication and organization by the masses. It is subject to myriad overlapping industries, jurisdictions and interests. The Internet + blueprint, although announced in 2015, had been a grand strategy in the making for more than a decade, particularly epitomized in the informatization (*xinxihua*) discourse of the Hu Jintao–Wen Jiabao government.

China's leadership has given high priority to the internet and viewed tech giants of the private sector (such as Huawei and Alibaba) as strategic partners in occupying the commanding heights (*zhigaodian*) in domestic economic and social governance on the one hand and participating in the global regime of internet governance dominated by the United States on the other hand.

In China, occupying the commanding height has seen the increasing active role of the state in the management of internet content and sinification of ICT resources (both hardware and software) by increasing regulatory barriers for foreign technologies and encouraging indigenous innovation and patents. All these are done in the name of internet security and sovereignty. As discussed earlier, through the Golden Shield Project and later the GFC the Chinese government blocks foreign content, censors network traffic and suppresses popular dissidence online. At the same time, it encourages self-censorship and behavioural change in Chinese internet users via flooding, nudging and mass surveillance.[49] A large army of internet police and opinion-setters are employed to guide and direct online public opinion during contentious events and times. Closed and semi-public social media platforms such as WeChat are encouraged, instead of the more open and public platforms like Weibo.[50] Another example is the Social Credit System, announced in June 2014 and nationally implemented since January 2020. Although a much more complicated project than simply a digital surveillance project, it is understood as a key mechanism to strengthen the state's social governance capacity and channel 'good/trustworthy' behaviours into a new norm by giving credit scores to and ranking individuals and organizations.[51]

Internet + was proposed and has evolved under Xi Jinping's leadership. It has been noted that since his taking office in November 2012 we have witnessed a revival and reappropriation of Maoist ideology and practices in Chinese internet and social governance. As Guobin Yang observed in 2014, Chinese internet governance is likely to 'combine Mao-style mass campaigns with the mobilization of law and civil society to proactively mould online expression and behaviour' and more emphasis will be put on 'winning the hearts and minds of the people and generating bankable stories in the global marketplace of internet narratives'.[52] Internet + is one of the big bankable stories; and internet sovereignty is a key narrative when confronting the global internet.

Hong Shen has observed that the Chinese discourse on internet sovereignty has evolved through three stages over three decades: the first stage being the initial connection and engagement with the global internet in the 1990s; the second stage being rebalancing the system through resisting its established standards while quietly encouraging certain compliance with global norms in the first decade of the twenty-first century; and the third stage being integrating into global internet governance through re-engaging with the US-led global internet governance regime in order to reset it by asserting a stronger Chinese voice.[53] Such strategies of selected engagement, resistance and compliance have seen China's increasing influence and control over three areas: technical standardization, critical internet resources and public policy for the internet. China now has control over the Chinese domain name (.cn) market, IPv6 (a Chinese IP to replace the IPv4) and the Chinese ccTLDs (country code top-level domain names) – all key internet resources, managed by the China Internet Network Information Centre (CNNIC).

China's claim to internet sovereignty is designed to serve two purposes: to rebalance the power structure of global internet governance internationally and to legitimize its own internet control and censorship domestically. The Internet White Paper, issued by the State Council Information Office in 2010, states: 'Within Chinese territory the Internet is under the jurisdiction of Chinese sovereignty. The Internet sovereignty of China should be respected and protected.'[54] Then in 2014, the Central Cyber Security and Informatization Leading Group was formed, led by Xi Jinping himself, to accord internet governance the highest point of command. The Leading Group and its administrative office (CAC) are the top bodies in charge of the internet technological and infrastructure development, security, governance and international relations.

The promotion of internet sovereignty was given a boost by Xi during the World Internet Conference in Wuzhen in 2015, the same year Internet + was unveiled. Xi asserted China's position on regulating cyberspace and emerging technologies in his address to the conference, insisting that 'We should respect the right of individual countries to independently choose their own path of cyber development and model of cyber regulation and participate in international cyberspace governance on an equal footing'.[55] Internet +, when viewed in the context of China's assertion on sovereignty and its implied contestation of the US-led open internet, should be viewed as the tip of the iceberg of the complex and still evolving policy and regulatory framework spanning from ICT, digital economy, internet industry, online content, to cybersecurity, regime security and global power struggle.

The Chinese government has viewed the internet as a crucial battlefield and is cautious about the subversive potential of information technology, particularly since it views the US government and transnational corporations as China's biggest threat in its effort to maintain domestic stability and its aspiration to play a leadership role on the global stage.[56] The Snowden revelations in 2013 of massive US cyber-espionage and surveillance alerted China to its own vulnerability in technological infrastructure and thus accelerated 'a drive towards indigenization of software and hardware, as well as greater assertiveness concerning the thorny question of cross-border hacking, surveillance and intelligence'.[57]

As the geopolitics of the internet continues to unfold, China is increasingly engaging in the global forum of internet governance. While the cyber sovereignty model advocated by China is often contrasted with multi-stakeholderism championed by the United States, China's approach has its complexities and contingencies.[58] Its pursuit of internet sovereignty is 'both a justification of its domestic policies and an attempt to ward off foreign interference both "hard" and "soft"'.[59] The result of these tensions is increasingly visible: China has enhanced its effective control over key internet resources, technological infrastructure, online content and cross-border data flow; and its model of internet sovereignty and data localization has been supported, or partly accepted, by an increasing number of countries.

In 2017, the Chinese government issued two further laws, 'The General Principles of Civil Law' and the 'Cybersecurity Law', to establish the parameters for data protection and data localization in China. They state core principles on the collection, use and transfer of personal data as 'key information infrastructure', and hence the export of 'personal and important data' is banned and corporations must set up data centres in China. China is not alone in imposing restriction on cross-border data flow, requiring data localization with storage and processing requirements. Governments across the world are eager to increase control over the internet and national data, driven by concerns over privacy, security and surveillance. From Vietnam to Russia, from BRICS to the EU, national governments are putting up barriers to restrict the free flow of information and data across borders while strengthening data protection within borders.[60]

China's approach to internet governance certainly has had its impact on how global internet players engage with the changing internet. The state sovereignty approach has assumed growing importance in internet governance beyond China. It is likely that China will continue to promote its position and leadership through the Shanghai Cooperation Organization and the One Belt One Road initiative; it will continue to consolidate its leadership in the new industrial revolution by developing more Made-in-China innovative hardware and software, as well as by setting standards and regulatory frameworks of new and emerging technologies and systems that reflect China's interests. Internet + is thus pivotal to China's insertion in the global internet governance framework, currently dominated by the US-led multi-stakeholder approach, through its discourse of internet sovereignty.

Conclusion

This chapter has examined how the Internet + blueprint arose, how it has provided China's digital enterprises with an ideological prop for their capitalist ambitions and how it is pivotal to China's solution to sustained development, regime stability and global cybergovernance. Understanding how Chinese internet policy and governance has evolved and how the internet functions assists our interpretation of China's role in global internet and technological governance. Comprehending the geopolitics of Internet + may also help us to reorient scholarship on the Chinese internet from within to without.

One of the aims of Internet + and Chinese internet governance is 'to allow Chinese culture to go to the word' and have 'its voice heard'.[61] In the next chapter we will investigate China's culture going out through the framework of platform + – what we will refer to as the amalgamation of the internet, networks, technologies and platforms. Aside from intellectual property rights and restrictions on terror or national security-related postings, there are no barriers to restrict China's media going to the Asia-Pacific or even going global, as there are with foreign content entering China. The global (or free world) internet thus provides a mechanism for globally dispersed audiences and users to access Made-in-China content, shares ideas and memes in real time or at their leisure via platforms made in China or with Chinese investment. The main challenges, however, as we will see, are cultural literacy and ideology.

Chapter 4

PLATFORM +

Sichuan opera, one of the most treasured of all Chinese arts forms, is well-known for a virtuoso performance called 'face changing' (*bian lian*), in which a performer uses colourful masks to rapidly change face. From a cultural perspective the meaning of *bian lian* in Chinese signifies agility and mastery, as well as having connotations of secrecy. With the Chinese state hoping to capitalize on the potential of digital technologies, the role played by indigenous online platforms is critical for driving economic growth, ensuring cultural revitalization and projecting national soft power.

The runaway success of the digital economy *within* the *PRC* over the past decade came as no great surprise to astute observers of China's technology sector. A burgeoning commercial internet, driven to new heights by mobile-only internet phone usage, precipitated a bull run in venture capital markets between 2015 and 2019. Many Chinese internet companies listed publicly. By 2016, Baidu, QQ and Taobao were among the top 12 globally in terms of traffic[1] owned by Baidu, Alibaba and Tencent; by 2015, these platforms had bought out 75 per cent of successful start-ups in China.[2] Their founders and CEOs are the new faces of digital China, the digital version of the Chinese dream.

This chapter examines industry and policy debates concerning the platform economy. We show how China's digital platforms are advancing commercial empires in the Asia-Pacific. We consider how these platforms represent a new image for China's communications industries. Once fully state-owned and weighed down by political baggage, the leading players are young, smart and innovative. China's digital champions are now wearing international masks. We look at how these anointed digital champions are promoting public–private diplomacy within the 'going out' initiative.

In the first section we examine the concept of platforms and the cross-disciplinary field of platform studies. Following this, our analysis of the hyper-competitive market behaviour of Chinese online platforms reveals a paradoxical alignment with government national development agendas on the one hand and a desire to build a series of capitalist empires beyond the

PRC on the other. It is no wonder that the leading players, BAT, have been referred to as the 'three kingdoms'. But kingdoms need to defend their territories. Contenders include BMD (ByteDance, Meituan-Dianping and Didi Chuxing). The third section of the chapter looks at how and where Chinese platforms are strategically entering overseas markets; their relationships with transnational and regional market players; their infrastructural capacity; and their allegiance to the national 'going out' agenda.

From platforms to infrastructures

Whereas Internet + offers a strategic blueprint to revitalize industries, the description 'Platform +' opens up the discursive field of the 'platform economy',[3] a value-neutral term frequently used by economists and communications scholars within the PRC to describe an expanding universe of technological possibilities. In this techno-utopian landscape industry leaders speak of disruption, paying lip service to a benign model of social capitalism that will deliver China and its people into a prosperous future. Outside the PRC, meanwhile, critical scholarship is more inclined to consider the less benign impacts of 'platform capitalism'[4] or 'digital capitalism'.[5] In using the term 'Platform +' therefore, we bring together emerging critical literature that informs Chinese political and social development.[6] We frame an expanding field of economic, political and social enquiry in which various internets (mobile internet, cloud computing, and Internet of Things) shape and are shaped by infrastructures (transport, logistics, banking, regulation, education and training) and in which emerging technologies (artificial intelligence, big data and robotics) are changing the nature of social transactions. Platform + therefore not only incorporates notions of networks, big data and algorithms, it also implies new modes of economic and cultural production, distribution and consumption – that is, the infrastructure of digital empire.

In a seminal paper on the politics of platforms Tarleton Gillespie writes about 'four semantic territories' found in the Oxford English Dictionary's etymology of the term – these are computational, architectural, figurative and political.[7] Gillespie first considers the broad meaning of platform in current digital communications scholarship. The platform concept emerged from computational studies, where it refers to, among other things, a mainframe, a programming language or a video game console.[8] The architectural usage alludes to the sense that a platform is by definition a raised surface; in the cultural sense a platform provides a means to raise or project ideas or ideologies, reflecting the semantic territory of the political. In a figurative sense, moreover, the platform indicates deliberate climbing to greater heights, evident in the discussion of platform capitalism, or indeed ideology, which alludes to the fourth semantic territory, the 'political', implying a stage to address an audience, a metaphor that will become critical when we consider how Chinese platforms operate and how far they extend their influence beyond the PRC.

The rapid surge of online platforms is viewed by some communication scholars as a manifestation of 'digital capitalism'.[9] The suggestion here is that platforms, largely owned and operated by capitalists, are an extension of capitalist ideology. This is in line with Gillespie's analysis while also recalling Marshall McLuhan's famous adage[10] that the medium is the message. A platform is the medium that enables interactions between two or more distinct parties.[11] Even though platform owners claim neutrality with regard to the nature, function and activity, they, their intermediaries and users are never free from ideology and politics, be it content-hosting or service-provision.

Plantin et al. argue that platforms such as Google and Facebook have undergone infrastructural evolution and increasingly taken on features like scale and ubiquity, or embeddedness in everyday life, while public infrastructure like the internet (including the World Wide Web and cloud computing) has been splintered and privatized.[12] This has allowed platforms, which are usually large enterprises, to build walled, closed and monopolized ecosystems. Interoperability is replaced by programmability; open access is replaced by platform-controlled ecology. 'System builders' – the infrastructures of the past – are replaced by 'ecosystem-builders' (large networks of platforms), which 'leverage programmability and interconnection to achieve control, rather than relying on direct provision and expansion'.[13]

Another useful metaphor is 'assemblage', that is, technical platforms incorporate well-defined interfaces: 'communication circuits between sensors, actuators, processors, storage media and distribution networks'.[14] Both Facebook and Google are networks of proprietary platforms. Moreover, their systems and services are embedded in our daily existence like the roads and electric utilities that we use every day.

Platform studies connect technical details and computational capacities to governance and culture. It not only 'investigates the relationships between the hardware and software design of computing systems (platforms)' or 'the creative works produced on these systems'[15] but also emphasizes 'the socio-technical assemblages', 'complex institutions' and the meaning-making mechanisms that are governed by and of platforms.[16] Platform studies also bridge the boundaries of a number of disciplines, including but not limited to digital media studies, social studies of science and technology, business, software/computer science and political science. In the area of digital humanities, the most widely used and discussed platforms include search engines, online marketplaces, news aggregators, media platforms, video-sharing platforms and social network platforms. Because of the emphasis of online platforms and their ubiquity in transactions, as well as the impact on social relations, platform studies often focus on social media platforms and cross-format platforms, such as Facebook, Twitter, YouTube, Google and Airbnb or Uber; or in the Chinese case, the platforms owned by BAT or even BMD (to be discussed later in the chapter).

Scholars in the field of communications argue that platforms have taken on the role of infrastructure and we have entered the era of the platformization of infrastructure and everyday life. Plantin et al. point out that infrastructure and platform both refer to sociotechnical systems and structures that underline or support other things (platforms or systems) and which enable programmability, interoperability and heterogeneity within networks, particularly in the digital media environment.[17] Neither infrastructure nor platform is neutral in their political and commercial agendas. The rise of digital technologies, they say, has 'made possible a "platformization" of infrastructure and an "infrastructuralization" of platforms'.[18] Platforms can scale up such that they can 'co-exist' and 'compete with or even supplant' infrastructures.[19] As the boundaries between platforms and public infrastructures have become increasingly porous, platforms are more and more a part of 'our everyday lives (infrastructures)', which are 'dominated by corporate entities (platforms)'.[20] This development is not only demonstrated through a close examination of Facebook, Google or eBay[21] but is seen in the Chinese burgeoning tech field, represented by the infrastructural platforms BAT and BMD.

BAT and B/JAT

China offers a unique case to examine the relationship between platforms, platform economy and the platform society. In the Chinese academy these terms offer more neutral descriptions, which are amenable to political support in the context of assuring the commercial expansion of Chinese platforms. Chinese sources generally offer a positive spin: for instance, the platform economy allows the logic of the former planned economy to transfer into a consumer-driven society. This is the so-called 'new normal', whereby the potential market demand hidden in the long tail can be exploited. For instance, Wang and Li contend: 'Under the new normal of the Chinese economy, imitative large-scale consumption has ended, and personalized and diversified consumption has come.'[22] In China, the 'platform economy' and more broadly the 'platform society'[23] are said to reconfigure the way that people connect, share information, consume services and conduct commerce.

A recent paper by Jeroen De Kloet, Thomas Poell, Guohua Zeng and Yiu Fai Chow draws on three frameworks to analyse institutional and cultural processes within the Chinese platform society: infrastructure, governance and practices.[24] They argue that the 'platformization of Chinese society' includes the entanglement not only between platform and infrastructure but also between the state and corporations. Hence it is critically important to consider the infiltration of the Party-state in platform infrastructures. Combined with the penetration of platform infrastructures in the everyday sphere of life, this has profound implications for platform governance and user practices.

As current scholarship has demonstrated, Chinese internet and social media companies are on the frontiers of Chinese state-capitalist expansion and national economic restructuring.[25] The logic of mercantile capitalism, expansionism and data accumulation has characterized these companies' marketing, financing, operational and investment strategies. Chinese and Western/US digital platforms therefore have much in common. A comparative political economy analysis of Baidu (search engine), Weibo (microblog) and Renren (social networking site) with the US platforms Google (search engine), Twitter (microblog) and Facebook (social networking site) by Fuchs has shown that commercial and profit logics dominate; and that both realms are shaped by surveillance-industrial complexes that combine capitalist and state control.[26] Jia and Winseck have compared BAT with their US counterparts Google, Facebook and Amazon, focusing on the triangular relationship between the State, internet companies and international finance capital.[27] They argue that these internet companies are thoroughly integrated in the world economy in terms of the structure of capital, ownership and control. Indeed, the Chinese government's protective policies in information industry development and push to develop the country's digital economy, exemplified by Internet +, has propelled these enterprises to embrace innovation, international finance capital and the global market.

The logic of commerce, capitalism and advertising dominates the internet and social media both in China and the United States. China's big three BAT, like their US counterparts, are publicly listed and connected to flows of transnational finance capital. They are infrastructural platforms that incorporate many different networks, sets of big data and algorithms; they are multisided platforms that criss-cross diversified modes of cultural production, distribution and consumption. While the most well-known Chinese platforms are probably WeChat (social networking and commerce, owned by Tencent), Taobao (e-commerce, owned by Alibaba), Baidu (search engine), Jingdong (e-commerce), a number of innovative platforms have captured global attention and have been acquired by corporate stakeholders. The most notable ones are China's famous unicorns and next-generation tech giants ByteDance (owner of news media platform Toutiao and video-sharing platform Douyin/TikTok),

Meituan-Dianping (combining features of Groupon, Deliveroo, Tripadvisor and Yelp!), Didi Chuxing (ride sharing) and Pinduoduo (group purchasing). This latter grouping is known by the acronym BMD (see below).

The Chinese internet space is brutal for both established and new start-up players. To survive Chinese digital entrepreneurs have learned to be not only resilient and creative but also ambitious and protective. One strategy is to build a digital empire that rests on a number of value-adding platforms – hence Platform + – like an octopus with tentacles reaching from a core business or platform to many other related or even unrelated areas and extending its reach upstream and downstream, often in competition as well as collaboration with competitors and companies like themselves. The empires built by Tencent and Alibaba are therefore good examples of the Platform + market strategy: they are not only cross-platform but also cross-sector. Furthermore, as discussed in the next section they cross national boundaries. They are empire builders in that they attract investors, banks, programmers, developers, advertisers, users and corporations to explore opportunities and push boundaries continually without leaving their own ecosystems. In addition, the core strategy embodies building an ecosystem, one that caters to the social and cultural needs of a born-digital generation and which connects with Chinese-speaking communities overseas; using the Chinese lexicon, we can say this is the development of Social + and Culture +. Together these entities make up the 'monopoly board' of the Chinese internet.[28]

The most successful Chinese company in terms of capitalizing its advantages in social networking and gaming services, Tencent is also the most globalized of the major Chinese platforms. Its network of platforms covers instant messaging/social media, games, entertainment (music, video and live streaming), e-commerce and e-payment and ride sharing. Alibaba on the other hand is a conglomerate that ranges from e-commerce (spanning continents), Fintech business with a powerful credit system called Alipay, cloud computing and big data services, digital lifestyles (travels, maps and food delivery), a film-media-entertainment complex with a key role being played by the popular video platform Youku Tudou and social networking services (with part shares in Sina.com).

In order to be protective Chinese platforms have created ecosystems that control all data and raise barriers to entry. Consumers are often caught in the crossfire. In 2010, a dispute broke out between QQ (instant messenger, owned by Tencent) and Qihoo 360 (internet security), forcing users to choose between the two in the name of privacy and security.[29] Again in 2020, sellers were asked by Alibaba to choose between its Tmall and Pinduoduo.[30]

Using the logic of the ecosystem, WeChat has moved to protect its core business and data while remaining open to competition. WeChat combines many of the functions of Facebook, Twitter, WhatsApp, Instagram and PayPal with additional features of e-payment, e-commerce and e-lifestyle; it is the 'digital Swiss Army knife for modern life'[31] and a 'super-sticky all-in-one app' and mega platform.[32] It is extremely agile, versatile and efficient. Within eight years of operation WeChat had garnered over a billion active monthly users[33] and more than 100 million outside China.[34] WeChat is more than a 'platform': it is a 'portal', 'mobile operating system'[35] and even an 'infrastructural platform'.[36] Yet WeChat is only one of many infrastructural platforms within the burgeoning Tencent empire.

One of many means to be protective of the ecosystem is to ensure control of data and set conditions of entry. WeChat's mini programme feature is a perfect example. Mini programmes are mobile applets of less than 10 megabytes nested within the WeChat platform. They rely on WeChat's application programming interface (API) and the platform's ecosystem and abide by the platform's exclusive proprietary rights over their coding languages. App developers do not need to develop separate programmes or terminal adaptation; and users do not have to download these mini apps separately. Mini programmes have made app developers and users willing collaborators in WeChat's e-commerce empire. Since its launch in January 2017, the mini-platform strategy has seen more than one million programmes with more than 200 million daily users, covering 200 categories, ranging from getting news, ordering food, playing mini-games, buying and selling, to finding love and organizing events. Mini programmes have become the way to do all manner of things in China. Large companies with a mobile or native app tend to have a WeChat mini programme and will therefore form strategic partnerships with Tencent.

Outside the BAT triad of power, it is worth mentioning JD.com, which has quickly risen to be China's second largest e-commerce heavyweight and a rival of Alibaba in its B2C business and Baidu in revenue and tech innovation (e.g. investing in drones and AI systems in its logistics network). JD.com was listed in NASDAQ in May 2014. Baidu's recent loss of market position has led many to shout out the acronym JAT instead of BAT, although some might opt for B/JAT. Baidu, with government support, may yet recover its territory. But JD.com has become a strategic partner of the Tencent empire. Of course, Tencent is not alone in building and walling its digital empire through the super-platform strategies. Other Chinese internet heavyweights have also developed their own super apps and super platforms, such as Alibaba's Alipay that combines financial services and life services with social networking and third-party merchant resources. The super app model is leading the way in the infrastructurization of Chinese platforms.

BMD, fast rising and globalizing

BMD – referring to ByteDance, the tech unicorn that owns news app Toutiao and short-video-sharing app Douyin/TikTok; group-buying service Meituan-Dianping; and ride-hailing firm Didi Chuxing – are said to be China's next-generation tech giants. BMD were established in the second decade of the twenty-first century and all are based in Beijing. ByteDance and Didi are ranked top two in the world's most valuable start-ups. BMD or T (Toutiao) MD are among the 2019 Forbes Midas list of top ten in high-tech and life science venture capital.[37]

Meituan was established in 2010 as a group-buying website and became Meituan-Dianping in 2015 through a merger of the two multibillion-dollar companies. It has pioneered China's O2O (offline to online) market by connecting traditional service industries (hotels, restaurants and entertainment venues) with consumers through mobile devices. It is now China's largest food delivery and ticketing platform, equipped with cloud computing and robotic technologies to cater to both enterprise-facing businesses and consumer-facing services. Unlike ByteDance and Didi Chuxing, Meituan-Dianping does not have a 'going out' ambition; instead it has focused on the Chinese domestic market, particularly in the face of competition of Alibaba-backed ele.me.

BMD have adopted the Social + model in growing their business. As discussed in Chapter 3, the Social + model is unique to Chinese digital economy. All Chinese internet platforms are anchored by the social pillar to drive user growth, engagement and loyalty. They also make good use of users' data to provide tailored content and advertising for the best possible outcome. As China's largest AI-powered content platform, ByteDance's Toutiao, for example, gets its traffic from BuzzFeed style content and relies heavily on the Social + model of customized content recommendation and advertising. Its ecosystem contains short videos, social apps, and content creation and curation platforms. It is one of the few Chinese companies that have successfully landed in overseas markets (see the next section).

Didi was established in 2012 and became Didi Chuxing a year later through a merger of Tencent-backed Didi and Alibaba-backed Kuaidi. It offers on-demand and customized services beyond transport (cars, taxis, bike and bus services) into food delivery and AI (driverless cars and robotics). Didi has increased its global reach and invested in overseas ride-sharing platforms such as Grab in South East Asia. Most B/JAT and BMT are listed in the stock market and respond to both the advertising economy and global finance economy (Table 4.1). ByteDance and Didi Chuxing are not yet listed in the

Table 4.1 China's digital companies IPO valuations (Data adopted from https://www.shobserver.com/news/detail?id=190873)

Company	Established	IPO date	Venue	Value (as of 26 November 2019)
JD	6/1998	5/2014	New York	4.77b
Alibaba	4/1999	9/2014	New York	49.72b
Tencent	11/1999	6/2004	Hong Kong	41.39b
Baidu	1/2000	8/2005	New York	4.17b
Meiduan-Dianping	3/2010	9/2018	Hong Kong	7.29b
ByteDance	3/2012	To be listed		
Didi Chuxing	6/2012	To be listed		

stock market but have had initial evaluations and are on their way to IPOs (initial public offerings).

China has emerged as a world leader in building super apps and super platforms. As the next section will show, the country's Platform + companies have gone overseas with their super apps and business know-how in building and localizing super apps for overseas markets. In the many territories where Chinese people reside, which is almost every nation in the world, we can see the take-up of digital affordances provided by B/JAT and BMD. Chinese internet giants and super stars are entering an era of global expansion, another phase of their exponential growth, *chuhai* (going overseas). This expansion is a business decision, driven by platform capitalism; at the same time, it is underpinned by a political imperative, particularly in the context of what appears to be a cosy state–business relationship.

Most research has focused on the entanglement between the Chinese state and internet corporations; for example, the penetration of platform infrastructures in every sphere of life within the state's purview. Florian Schneider points to the importance of the Chinese Communist Party and state agents in 'setting the parameters of discourse but allowing diverse actors to negotiate the exact meanings'.[38] Researchers also illustrate that Chinese digital platforms and platform capitalists are not only data-dominant oligopolies,[39] they are also empire builders working with and alongside the Chinese state in its 'going out' strategy. The term 'Chinese digital empire' has been recently coined to characterize Chinese ambitions of becoming a global digital power, helped by the infrastructural platforms or Platform + corporations mentioned above.[40]

As discussed earlier, a political economy analysis of Chinese internet platforms has shown that the logic of international financial capitalism mandates these companies to continuously grow revenues and increase profits. While massive in scale, the Chinese domestic urban market is arguably reaching saturation. Digital platforms are moving from first- and second-tier cities to the third-, fourth- and fifth-tier cities and the countryside in the name of 'xiachen/sinking market' (meaning moving down into lower tier markets). Alibaba has shifted its growth strategies from the saturated market of first- and second-tier cities to the countryside and elsewhere, including overseas (particularly South East Asia).[41] Many others have had a global vision and strategy as a core part of their business model. BMD, the young Chinese Platform + companies and challengers of BAT, are also expanding their digital empires in and outside China.

Chuhai: Going overseas

In China the rapid development of platforms is a response to social, economic and cultural issues, while at the same time anticipating and reacting to political imperatives. As noted in the first chapter, one of the political imperatives is taking Chinese culture and ideas to the world. Digital platform owners are endeavouring with the support of the Chinese government to promote Chinese brands. However, although Chinese brands may be attractive to consumers, there is the spectre of the authoritarian state. Scholarship in security studies has focused on the penetration of the Chinese Communist Party's influence in private companies, for instance, the establishment of Party Committees in leading Chinese private companies and foreign enterprises and the incorporation of top executives of these enterprises in the Party's key advisory bodies like the Chinese People's Political Consultative Conference (CPPCC).[42] Hawkish commentators meanwhile warn of dire consequences of the increasing global presence and influence of Chinese digital and technology companies like BAT and Huawei which they regard as Trojan horses that enable and export China's digital authoritarianism and surveillance capitalism.[43]

Chinese digital platforms meanwhile have tried to brand themselves as transnational and private businesses and claim their global expansion is not motivated by political imperatives. They assert a mercantilist imperative to capture new markets and generate more efficiency and resources as well as the desire to 'obtain greater integration and control over their supply and value chain'.[44] As pointed out by scholarship in business studies, digital companies often take two distinct approaches to platform expansion – platform bundling and platform constellations.[45] Platform bundling refers to adding features and additional services to one's initial main function and value proposition, as illustrated by WeChat's development of a super app with multifunctions.

Platform constellation is akin to 'platform incorporated', whereby a family or a variety of services are organized in separate apps/platforms that are owned or controlled by the same company. Chinese Platform + companies tend to adopt both approaches in their global expansionist strategies.

The ambition to go overseas is now wired in the design of many Chinese digital platforms; and these Platform + owners are transnational capitalists with global ambitions. Unlike the state capitalists (who are the bosses of large state-owned enterprises), the new capitalist elites are born-again capitalists; the new bosses of digital conglomerates are drivers of the global digital economy. The co-founder of Alibaba, Jack Ma, perhaps best represents China's new capitalist elite, business leaders who are both fluent in English and can talk with global political, business and technology leaders. They see themselves as the new visionary leaders in the new world's order. Ma has repeatedly told his people at Alibaba since 2000 that they are a global company (immediately after its establishment in 1999). In the words of Joseph Tsai, executive vice chairman of Alibaba Group, 'Alibaba is founded by Chinese, but it is founded for the world.'[46]

Chinese outbound activities in Asia-Pacific have been discussed previously. Keane and Yu, for instance, have pointed out that Alibaba adopted a series of strategies in the Asia-Pacific region, mainly in four areas: e-commerce, digital payment, logistics and R&D.[47] For example, in Hong Kong the technology giant (through its financial affiliate, Ant Financial) goes head to head with WeChat Pay and other competitors in the digital payment market; in Korea it invested in Kakao Pay; in India and South East Asia (Malaysia, Thailand, Singapore and the Philippines) it has invested billions of dollars to acquire and form partnerships with local tech companies and start-ups in e-commerce and digital payment and is the controlling shareholder of Lazada, the biggest e-commerce platform in the region.

Alibaba has made many other investments abroad, including Russia, Canada, the United States and Europe. However, Jack Ma's vision for the eWTP (electronic World Trade Platform) and the attempt to knit together a global payment system centred around Alipay have had limited success in mature markets like those of the United States. The company's success in the overseas markets comes primarily from joint ventures with local tech firms and following the Chinese diaspora and tourists abroad.

Aside from the uptake of its video-sharing site iQiyi (see Chapter 6), Baidu has not made significant progress in its going global operations. Its early attempt to globalize its platforms began in 2006 with the launch of its Japanese-language search engine. After its failure and discontinuation, Baidu introduced a Portuguese-language search engine in Brazil in 2014, with the vision of using it to pay the way for key markets in Latin America. It has not taken off either. The company also tried to break into Thailand in 2011, with two products: a Chinese-style web portal Hao123.com and Windows-based desktop optimization software Baidu PC Faster; and Egypt with the launch of an Arabic-language version of Zhidao, Baidu's question-and-answer service, with the aim to use it as launch pad of its Middle East springboard. But none of these business initiatives have met the expected targets and were forced to close or scale down. The company has indeed made a number of acquisitions and investments in overseas tech companies in the hope of accessing local knowledge and talent and expanding its coverage, reach and advertising market, particularly in the area of AI technology.[48] But its main business, the search engine, is pretty much domestic and has had mediocre influence in the overseas market so far.

India has become the next battlefield for Chinese tech giants, after South East Asia. Alibaba and its affiliate Ant Financial have invested in a few Indian unicorns, including India's largest mobile payment platform Paytm and e-commerce platform Snapdeal in 2015, online grocery platform BigBasket in 2017, food delivery platform Zomato and logistics firm Xpressbees in 2018. Tencent has also bet big in Indian start-ups, such as e-commerce platform Flipkart and ride-sharing Ola in 2017, food delivery Swiggy and fantasy football platform Dream 11 in 2018. The two Chinese tech giants had invested in almost half of the 31 unicorns India has as of December 2019.[49]

Tencent's success has come in three of its key business areas: games, instant messaging/social media and payment systems. Its strategies take three directions: follow the Chinese diaspora and tourists (social media and payment systems), shape a global games empire through equity investment in or acquisition of foreign firms (games and entertainment/music) and establish offshore data centres (to serve overseas markets and other Chinese firms with offshore operations).[50] At the time of writing, Tencent had built 11 data centres outside mainland China, in Asia, North America and Europe, as has Alibaba. Such data centres are an important indicator of their global business.

As the largest ride-sharing and mobile transportation platform in China, Didi Chuxing has aggressively pushed its 'going global' mission since 2015, the same year when Didi and Kuaidi were merged, when it made an undisclosed investment in Ola, India's largest taxi aggregator, and an initial investment in Grad, the share-ride leader in South East Asia. Backed by some of the biggest global tech companies including Apple, Alibaba and Tencent, Didi Chuxing defeated Uber China in 2016 and since then has gone on to take on the world. It has invested in ride-sharing platforms in Brazil, Middle East, Europe, Africa, the United States and South East Asia; it has entered Australia and Latin America in 2018 in direct competition as well as collaboration with Uber and other local platforms.

It is important to remember that Chinese digital giants do not always compete directly with each other; they also invest in each other and other digital platform such as Didi Chuxing; and global financial capitals often back up both giants and start-ups. Hence, we have witnessed a complex web of overlapping connections in the footprints of Chinese digital platforms as they go global. Both Alibaba and Tencent own a stake in Didi Chuxing; Didi is an investor in Grab and Ola while Didi Chuxing, Grab and Ola are all backed by SoftBank and form a global alliance together with Alibaba-invested Lyft (US) to share customers and compete with Uber.[51]

When talking about Chinese digital platforms going global, it is impossible to avoid discussion of ByteDance, the owner and operator of the news aggregation app Toutiao and the hugely popular Douyin/TikTok short video platform. ByteDance represents a growing number of Chinese unicorns and start-ups that set their sights on the global market from the very start and have actually made headways into the minds and lives of global consumers beyond the Chinese diaspora. This is in contrast with BAT who have largely followed Chinese immigrants and visitors in their overseas expansion moves. ByteDance is also an example of how China's digital platforms have successfully 'changed face'. Luzhou Li[52] describes the strategy of 'cultural zoning', whereby Chinese platforms operate in different markets using non-Chinese business practices, often flirting with regulations.

ByteDance is a consumer AI-driven success story.[53] Its reliance on AI for user profiling and targeted advertising is typical of 'surveillance capitalism'. As Shoshana Zuboff points out in her book of the same name, the discovery of behavioural surplus, the extraction of such surplus value at a mass scale by means of machine intelligence and the ability to turn such surplus value into corporate products and services constitute the secrets of the 'Big Other' actors, such as Google and Facebook.[54] All Chinese digital giants have learned such secrets from their Western counterparts. But it is ByteDance that has managed to use its AI platforms to take over the world by storm. And it is now eroding the ad revenue share of BAT.[55]

From very early on, ByteDance has attempted to grow its market outside China. The company was founded in 2012, launched Douyin in 2016 and its international version TikTok in 2017. Like other Chinese tech companies, it expanded in the United States by acquiring local companies (Musical.ly, Live.me, Flipgram). However, its biggest market is in Asia, particularly India, with the largest number of users (119.3 million, Feb 2019) and downloads (467 million times; or 277.6 million as of Nov 2019 alone; double the figure from China).[56] TikTok, its international facing app, has struck a chord with younger audiences, just like its Western counterpart Snapchat before it. It is the new hype among teenagers and millennials who care less about the

Made-in-China nature of the company than what the platform enables them to do. It has become the virtual playground for people aged between 16 and 24; for instance 41 per cent of TikTok users spend an average 52 minutes per day on the app compared with 49.5 minutes on Snapchat, 53 minutes on Instagram and 58.5 minutes on Facebook.[57] TikTok is just one of ByteDance's international products and part of its platform constellation. ByteDance is now one of the most valuable private technology firms in the world, reportedly worth $75 billion, and owns a variety of apps from news aggregators to social media services, such as BaBe, a news aggregation app in Indonesia; Dailyhunt, a content aggregation platform in India; and TopBuzz, a platform that recommends trending videos and articles to users. As of 2019, TikTok was available in 75 languages in 155 countries.

Chinese super tech companies like ByteDance are backed by some of the biggest funders in venture capital, including SoftBank and Sequoia Capital. Their expansion into overseas markets is often driven by the capital imperative as discussed earlier. Despite the growing suspicion towards these companies in the West (particularly the United States and its allies), the potential for them to grow in influence and market overseas remains strong. A slowing Chinese economy, an increasing saturation of domestic market, the cut-throat competition with competitors and their copycat competitors in China and the large internet population in emerging economies are all factors that contribute to the motivation of these companies to go overseas for growth.

As Chinese Platform + companies venture into new markets and territories, they are taking many innovative business models into the global market such as the super app concept. Grab, for example, is among digital start-ups in South East Asia that have learned from their Chinese counterparts and are now aiming to replicate their successful concepts.[58] Market observers have championed the leading role that Chinese digital companies play in technology and business innovation with the prediction: 'In the next ten years, China will become an innovation powerhouse and the world will move from "Made in China" to "Copy from China".'[59] The road to be an innovation powerhouse and truly global player, however, is laden with challenges, as we will discuss in Chapter 9.

Conclusion

China is among many Asian countries (particularly Singapore, Indonesia, India and South Korea) that have experienced exponential growth and broad application of digitized information. This involves harnessing knowledge capital, the production of innovative services, investment in start-ups and new modes of consumption. China's deployment of digital information networks and communication technologies – such as the internet, cloud computing, big data, IoT and FinTech – to transform social interactions, drive productivity and stimulate innovation is seen as trailblazing.[60] From hardware (e.g. Lenovo, Huawei and ZTE) to software (AI, robotics and various digital payment systems), China's digital revolution is enabling its native digital giants not only to build a massive ecosystem of platforms in China but also to challenge the West's supremacy in a digital landscape dominated by US-based digital platforms (such as Amazon and Facebook). The competition is global in scope, with the Asia-Pacific and the Sinophone world as the first battlefield. Until now the BAT trio have led in the going global moves. However, second-generation Chinese tech companies like BMD have been able to rival their success and defy conventional territories by breaking into the heartlands of mainstream population in foreign countries. This is achieved despite the political and ideology burden that they carry as Made-in-China platforms.

As discussed earlier, platforms can be understood as technological architectures with modular systems and layers that can be reprogrammed and coordinated among multiple constituencies; they are studied as organizational structures or meta-organization that coordinate multiple agents and economies (e.g. advertising economy and global finance economy); they can also be viewed as infrastructures especially when they take on features like ordering everyday life and society. The economic imperative is only one part of the story about Chinese Platform +. It is an ongoing narrative with interesting twists and turns.

China's digital platforms have built their empires in the Chinese mainland, leveraging Internet + and government protectionism and benefitting from the massive numbers of people online. They have also made inroads into a number of overseas markets, as discussed in this chapter. In addition to expanding markets and increasing revenues, these platforms are themselves transmitters of Chinese models, ideas and styles, both within the Chinese mainland and to territories outside China, servicing the cultural needs of the Chinese diaspora and reaching out to new converts. A detailed content and consumer market analysis is therefore required to explain the extent of the platform-driven countercultural flow by non-Western digital platforms.[61]

In this chapter we have emphasized the cultural and political dimension of Chinese digital platforms in the global geo-technical landscape. We have discussed the complex web of interests in which these platforms are entangled. They can work together with the Chinese government as well as with international finance capital and partners of multiple nationalities depending on strategic advantages; in fact, they are playing a long game in and outside the People's Republic of China. This is a calculated choice, at both the corporate and national levels.

PART 2

THE ASIA-PACIFIC AS A CHINESE CULTURAL LANDING PAD

Chapter 5

ASSESSING THE EVIDENCE

When trying to assess the evidence of a nation's cultural outputs it is tempting to use proxies of international success, for instance, Academy Awards Oscars or Nobel Prizes. Such global awards seldom countenance creative offerings from Asia and when this happens it is exceptional, for example, the spectacular success of the South Korean film *The Parasite* at the 2020 Academy Awards. Chinese films have received no Oscars to date, despite submitting 20 films for nomination. Chinese writers have been awarded only two Nobel Prizes for literature. One Nobel Prize-winning author lives in France, another in Shandong, China. In contrast, France has received 15 Nobel Prizes in literature since 1901, the United States and Great Britain, 12 each.[1]

For most people living in the West the most representative Chinese actor-celebrity is probably Jackie Chan and the most recognizable Chinese film genre is kung fu. Celebrity status brings visibility on the world stage. In order to achieve global recognition, it is important to feature in films 'made in Hollywood', the centre of the global film industry. Chan has done this since his early years in Hong Kong, like Bruce Lee before him, and he has been welcomed into the golden temple of the academy awards, receiving an honorary Oscar in 2016.[2] Global stars like Chan are a cultural bridge and the publicity machines of Western film and TV industries, their eyes fixed on new markets, endeavour to supercharge their celebrity investments. Expensive promotional sound bites add to entertainment industry news which is widely consumed in China. Aside from recent attempts to coproduce and to use other cross-over stars, for instance, the US actor Matt Damon in *The Great Wall* (2017) and the Chinese actress Li Bingbing in *The Meg* (2018), China's success is culturally and geographically specific. When it comes to narrative forms, some genres work better in China, for instance, historical epics and melodramas. In the global context, however, misunderstandings and 'cultural discounts' apply;[3] the question remains: how is success measured? Can big data or social media tell us anything we don't know?

This chapter delves into the inherent messiness of cultural data. It provides examples of cultural data that are widely used and have acquired strong reputational effects, for instance, the Portland Soft Power 30 index, but which are not without methodological problems. We look briefly at industry metrics such as box office takings, film industry review sites like IMDB and Rotten Tomatoes, which aggregate critical reviews and fans comments, as well as considering the buzz generated by social media. The chapter also considers the validity of academic research reports that are used to measure specific sub-sectors, for instance, film, TV and animation, as well as looking at a survey of the consumption of Chinese film in North America. We conclude that there is considerable variance depending on the kinds of metrics used and the kinds of questions asked, before outlining how we sought to circumvent some of these problems. In order to do this, we developed an online survey on 'China's Media Consumption in the Asia-Pacific' and devised focus groups to capture qualitative aspects of media consumption. As we will show in the four chapters in Part 2, the findings fill in some of the gaps in our knowledge of the effectiveness of Chinese media and culture in overseas markets.

Data and the problem of rankings

In an account of research in the online world, *Big Data, Little Data, No Data*, Christine Borgman writes, 'As more of daily life is instrumented with information technologies, traces of human behaviour are easily captured.'[4] A key point to note is that digital communications can rapidly aggregate information that was once left to professional survey teams. People leave traces of their uses of media and these traces can allow companies to target consumers with customized offerings. The US historian Jerry Muller says metrics are frequently used in ways that are dysfunctional; instead of rushing to believe the data we should be careful to balance measurement with judgement.[5] The 'attention economy' is partly to blame for such dysfunctionality.[6] Thanks to the ease of accumulating data, there are indices for soft power, social progress, innovation, happiness, food security, standards of living, press freedoms and internet connection speeds.

Counting tangibles such as the number of people in employment or the number of patents registered, however, is easier than designing methods to measure the value of cultural products and services, which is often intangible and always subjective. Debates have ensued about the usefulness of statistics beyond mere economic indicators, particularly when results are used to inform cultural policy; that is, statistics can be used to direct resources. The Chinese authorities poured millions of dollars into extending overseas media resources during the Hu Jintao era (2002–12) when confronted with the reality of China's lack of global media influence and its 'cultural trade deficit', which as discussed in Chapter 1 referred specifically to the excess of audiovisual content 'coming in' to China.

The online world has changed the way that we count culture; and this has ramifications for assessing how China's culture travels beyond the PRC. Until the late twentieth century trade in culture was predicated on the movement of physical products; even cross-border trade in movies and television programmes was in the 'can', referring to the physical container that was delivered by air freight across national boundaries. Customs declarations provided the principal means of counting: mostly sales of artworks, artefacts and printed goods. Now most forms of culture are disseminated online and some are *only* accessible online. Advances in digital compression technologies allow artists, musicians and film-makers to express new combinations of image and sound. In addition to reducing the cost of making and transmitting culture and extending its geographical reach, it transforms the manner and time frame in which culture is consumed and the relationships between producers and consumers. Digital platforms have extended the reception of culture and disrupted the linearity of consumption; for instance, digital content platforms like Netflix or iQiyi allow viewers to binge watch. Advances in technology have in turn impacted on the forms, genres and styles of culture that are produced, disseminated and consumed, both online and offline.

What people think and what they say about cultural products has an extended social life because of social media.[7] This applies to opinions about one's own culture or a foreign movie. People tweet, share and comment, usually in their home language. And this social media commentary mostly reaches people with similar world views, for instance, those in one's social media groups. Chinese online commentaries do not reach English readers unless there are cultural intermediaries that can translate. In some cases, bilingual intermediaries report what is said across social media platforms, for instance, commentaries about China in the Western media might be shared in Chinese social media. In addition, banal content such as memes and short videos from China can and do 'go global', usually when they are visual, that is, without the need for translation. The 'net effect', real or imagined, is therefore something we need to take seriously, including its 'illusions'; for instance, 'confirmation bias'. The internet is designed with confirmation bias as a key part of its algorithmic logic. People bookmark, save, select, review and share what they like or agree to. And people filter out what they don't like. Algorithms recognize such likes and feed us more of the same, reinforcing our perceptions. As a result, we may suffer from the information overload disease, 'hardening of the categories'. Most people, for instance, have favourable views of their own culture and will therefore be drawn to opinion and commentary that reinforces their beliefs (or biases), while ignoring critical views which may be perfectly logical.

It is therefore important to be aware of 'confirmation bias' in reviews, especially when they are posted on free online platforms.[8]

Online consumption remains somewhat of a black box. Word clouds allow us to see trending topics while big data methods and sentiment analysis can isolate events where there are peaks of activity. But how valid are hits and shares on social media when evaluating the influence of culture? Does big data offer a better lens to understand cultural influence than qualitative data such as focus groups? Undoubtedly, the future of media industries and the decisions about what to produce are tied up with algorithmic calculation and social media intercourse. For instance, research has shown how engagement with content via online media can augment the power of the messaging when users interact by sharing and commenting favourably on social media platforms.[9] Indeed, it is a key strategy of marketers to get rapid exposure through social media platforms. Can we therefore extrapolate online media practices, sharing, commenting and retweeting with cultural soft power?

Soft power questioned

As noted throughout this book, one of the most cited indicators of national reputation is soft power. As discussed in Chapter 1, soft power derives from the work of Joseph Nye. The concept was adopted by President Hu Jintao in 2007, a time when Chinese policy makers realized the nation needed to 'go global' in the cultural domain. Scholars responded rapidly to the cause. A recent study of Chinese soft power reveals that 'The number of Chinese articles in social science journals that reference soft power in their title jumped to 826 in 2008 and continued to rise steadily in subsequent years, reaching a peak of 1,134 articles in 2012.'[10] Many Chinese scholars meanwhile have taken issue with the calculation of soft power rankings which are an attempt to quantify and codify attitudes. In the US-based Portland Soft Power index China came in at 27 in 2019. Other surveys have offered alternative power differentials: the Lowy Institute in Australia, for instance, proposes an Asian Cultural Power index, which puts China second behind the United States and ahead of Japan and South Korea.[11]

Many of the findings are based on comparative data that can be pulled together, but which is often de-contextualized from actual lived experience. Most measurements reveal little about the emotional or subjective response of audiences to cultural products or their engagement with the political institutions that shape national image. In the current volatile political climate both the United States and China's soft power rankings are likely to change, although much depends on how the 'discourse wars' play out globally. Some commentators have argued that China's soft power and social progress rankings would be far higher if they were measured according to values endorsed by the Chinese government rather than by the more liberal norms of Organisation for Economic Co-operation and Development (OECD) institutions. We discuss some of the other models of research in China below. Clearly however, as researchers it is important to pay more attention to qualitative rather than just readily accessible quantitative research if we wish to know how and why audiences engage with a particular country's cultural outputs. Hence the results of our focus groups in Chapters 6, 7 and 8 provide a useful complement.

Before delving into media reception and the challenges posed by online consumption, it is worth considering how soft power is conventionally ranked. As discussed in Chapter 1, soft power is a twentieth-century addition to the many lists and indexes that have in the past purported to rank nations and regions. As Portugal notes, such listings, indexes, measurements and rankings are associated with the evolution of the economic press, the consolidation of mercantilism and the development of financial capitalism in Europe from the sixteenth to eighteenth centuries.[12] Scoring well can elevate a nation, or a region's reputation and standing. Rankings are probably the most pertinent to cities, which are subject to competition for talent and investment. The most visible ranking in recent times is Richard Florida's creative city index, which uses three key indices: talent, tolerance and technology.[13] One of the more provocative descriptors is a 'gay index', signifying a high proportion of creative types. Even more interesting is that the Canadian-based Martin Prosperity Institute headed by Florida offers a range of suggestions for analysing Chinese creative cities, substituting a 'hukou index' (also known as the household registration quotient) as an alternative indicator for openness rather than the 'gay index', which presumably was difficult to quantify.[14]

The most pertinent global index to consider with respect to China's media and cultural influence is the Portland Soft Power 30 index, although as we will indicate below it has little of value to tell us about actual media consumption. It is important because it is frequently cited, despite having flaws when it comes to evaluating cultural outputs and reception. A joint initiative between the strategic communications consultancy Portland and the University of Southern California's Centre on Public Diplomacy, Portland Soft Power 30 index is often mentioned disparagingly in China and because of China's lowly position on this index its findings are often disputed. The survey captures data from 60 nations, including respondents' 'impressions' of the appeal of nations in categories including cuisine, tech products, friendliness, culture, luxury goods, foreign policy and liveability. With regard to assessing culture Portland offers a 'culture sub-index'. However, it is not media industry products disseminated or reception of media that counts (as one might expect) but the annual number of international tourists, the global success of a country's music industry and a nation's international sporting prowess; hence New Zealand 'punches above its weight' thanks to the prowess of the All Blacks rugby team. As many have noted, indicators are often arbitrary and biased towards Western nations. Zhang Chang and Wu Ruiqing discuss how the addition of the number of Michelin star restaurants to the index in 2017 biased the results towards European nations and particularly France. The Michelin Guide did not even make its way into China until 2016. In the Portland index China came in at number 27 in 2019, well behind other East Asian nations including Japan (5), South Korea (20) and Singapore (21).[15]

Alternatively, there are other ways of gathering information that purports to identify perceptions. One of the most cited within China is the Q&A platform Quora.com. This kind of crowd-sourced model is widely recognized but hardly rigorous. Registered users of Quora may either view or provide an answer to the questions. Users can upvote, downvote or comment. Most users only 'upvote' and the upvotes are almost always greater than the number of comments. Therefore, the quantity of upvotes for answers can be regarded as an index of how popular the answer is, similar to the 'like' functionality of Facebook. Following this process, the results are positive for China's soft power. According to a study of users of Quora.com and China's influence, Chinese culture is ranked fourth in terms of the percentage of positive answers. The category includes traditional Chinese culture, modern Chinese culture, Chinese food, Chinese media and Chinese sports. Interestingly, the attitude towards Chinese culture in general was 34 per cent positive, 16 per cent negative and 50 per cent neutral.[16] If this is the case, then one wonders why China has such difficulty exporting its media culture to the world and 'telling its stories well'.

The Lowy Institute, a privately funded think tank in Australia, publishes its own Asia Power index. It advertises itself as an online analytical tool, what it calls an 'innovative calculator' for sharpening debate on power in the Asia-Pacific. Lowy researchers selected 25 countries and regions. The index proposes eight key 'power indicators': namely, economic resources, diplomatic influence, military capability, economic relationships, resilience, defence networks, future trends and cultural influence. Certainly, the Lowy Institute has claimed the high ground of debate in Australia although its analysis of cultural influence, like Portland's, is problematic. In early 2020, the Cultural Influence category listed the top five countries/regions as United States (86.7), China (58.3), India (49), Japan (50.4) and South Korea (33.8). No doubt its findings would be celebrated profusely in Beijing if not for the fact that the index separates Taiwan from the PRC. Significantly China's ranking, which is trending upward, is almost three times that of Russia (20.1) and almost twice that of Australia (26.7).

Cultural influence breaks down into three sub-themes: Cultural Projection (weighting of 40%); Information Flows (weighting of 40%) and People Exchange (weighting of 20%), which are composites of secondary data mostly harvested from Google or existing databases. 'Cultural Projection', for instance, uses the following indicators: (i) Google interest (representing the average Google search over a 12-month period); (ii) the percentage of cultural exports in the UNESCO statistics; (iii) number of brands in the Global 500 directory; (iv) number of buildings above 150 metres in the financial capital (presumably this is Beijing with reference to China); (v) the number of countries that a person can travel to visa-free; and (vi) the number of UNESCO listed World Heritage Sites. In the People Exchange category China is the benchmark with 100, which pushes China to second overall; however, how People Exchange actually translates into influence, and particularly cultural influence, is somewhat unclear. The fact that China sends its students internationally to get an education, far more than India at 68.4, and the reality that many people of Chinese nationality choose to live outside the PRC could be seen as a sign of relative weakness.

Another barometer of perception is the Pew Research Centre Global Attitude and Trends, and here again China appears to score well compared with Portland. Attitudes towards China across 34 countries show over 40 per cent 'favourable', compared with 41 per cent 'not favourable', with the highest unfavourable being in Japan (85%) and the highest favourable being Russia at 71 per cent. However, this indicator is fairly volatile, with recent surges in 'not favourable' in Canada and the United States no doubt associated with trade tensions and the arrest of Huawei's CFO Meng Wanzhou. Other surveys that show high levels of confidence in government in China compared to that of the United States and other Western nations are often used by the Chinese media and Chinese nationalists to argue that China is a harmonious society.

What is not highlighted, however, is the fact that people in China have no choice to elect a leader or a political party. In the West people will distrust a government because they didn't vote for a particular political party. Western distrust in authority devolves from philosophy according to Julian Baggini, who writes, 'The problems of Western democracy are a kind of allegory for the problems of Western philosophy. Its pursuit of the clear distinction between true and false creates a default either/or mindset.'[17] Support for government is usually split between conservatives and progressives and such polarization is reflected in polling. It is also evident in the kinds of audiovisual content that producers are allowed to make. For instance, in the realm of audiovisual culture, the West can produce a film such as *Absolute Power* (directed by Clint Eastwood) about a corrupt US president and an incompetent administration. Similarly, successful films have been made about the role of investigative media in the Watergate incident that led to the impeachment of President Nixon in 1974. China does have audiovisual content about government corruption but it is corruption well down the line and far away from Beijing – the so-called 'flies' instead of 'tigers'. China's media are the guard dog of the Chinese government not the watchdog of the people.

Because of the ability to elect government, Western cultural soft power is arguably more robust, that is, it is more trustworthy. This is somewhat ironic if we take the point about Western distrust of leaders. But Stanley Rosen argues that US soft power is successful because it is *not* linked to the US government, a fact that allows people to dissociate negative views of the US government, for instance, its foreign policy, with American culture and society: 'whereas Chinese soft power hardly exists apart from the efforts of its government'.[18] Moreover, while many Chinese content makers lament the failure of Chinese content to achieve global recognition, often blaming a lack of film-making nous or an inability to make universal themes, the problem lies elsewhere. And data analytics can't solve it. If a Chinese director were to make a story that exposed the problems in the system at a high political level, audiences globally might take notice. While some content makers do try, it is generally about allegorizing, historicizing and circumventing dangerous political issues. More often than not the point is lost in translation.

Although China does not have a dedicated instrument like the Portland Soft Power 30 index, a number of projects have challenged the Western-centric soft power measurement and ranking.[19] These include: 'The Report on International Competitiveness of China's Cultural Industry' in 2004 by Qi Shuyu of the Chinese Academy of Governance; a qualitative and comparative study of Chinese and American soft power led by Yan Xuetong of Tsinghua University in 2008; other longitudinal studies that include a report called 'China's Soft Power through International Communication' compiled by researchers at Beijing University in 2011, 2015 and 2017; the 'Global Report on China's National Branding' produced by the International Communications Research Centre of China International Publishing in 2012, 2013, 2014 and 2015; and finally the 'Evaluation on Effect of Chinese Culture Going Global' led by Li Huailiang of Chinese University of Communication in 2013 and 2018. Elsewhere, Yu Dan, director of the Beijing Institute of Culture Innovation and Communication, and author of the soporific *Confucius from the Heart*, mounted a survey in 2015 to assess people's understanding of Chinese culture, with respondents from the United States, UK, France, Australia, Japan and South Korea. Pandas, green tea and tai chi topped the list.

Chinese media and its uneven reputation

When it comes to assessing China's media influence, the lens become murkier. One of the inherent problems with reporting of China's media 'going out' is a lack of rigour. China's official media has often inflated its geographical reach (e.g. celebrating number of CCTV foreign language channels) while bemoaning its lack of influence in the world of ideas. How then do we best measure the success of China's culture as it goes out to the world? How should one differentiate between Made-in-China content for domestic consumption and content that is produced in China for international consumption, for instance, productions such as *Crouching Tiger Hidden Dragon*, *Mao's Last Dancer* or the 2019 US-Chinese film *The Farewell*? We know what is successful in China, but what constitutes real success outside China? Is global box office a reliable indicator?

Cross-cultural reception is not straightforward and is complicated by uneven distribution, cultural misunderstandings and a legacy of anti-PRC media commentary. Only in the past three decades has China's media become commercially oriented. In an important theoretical contribution to the debate about reception of Chinese audiovisual content outside the PRC, Yingchi Chu says, 'Media producers in the national arena are able to steer the expectations of their audience in a way that is not possible across cultural divides, where there is neither a shared history of values nor the benefit provided by ratings and audience feedback.'[20] This is not to say that Chinese audiences in the PRC are homogeneous or read texts the same way – Chu is careful to note the history of media reception studies – but that certain symbolic motifs are embedded and these activate cultural memories. Symbolic motifs are less understood, and can even be misunderstood, by 'foreign' audiences.

In his 2012 study of East Asian pop culture Chua Beng-Huat identifies three possible audience positions. The first position is where the audience watches a locally produced programme. Identification with the themes comes naturally. Chua says 'there is an excess of knowledge that can be drawn upon to judge the "accuracy" and "truth" of the programme content and "critical" reflections can be based on this knowledge'.[21] A second position according to Chua might be the diasporic subject watching a narrative that references the homeland. The programme may be made in homeland, for instance, the PRC, or by foreign producers. Examples are the PRC blockbuster *Wolf Warrior 2* (directed by Wu Jing), the Australian-directed Hollywood film *Mao's Last Dancer* (directed by Bruce Beresford) and the US-produced independent film *The Farewell* (directed by the Chinese American Lulu Wang). Indeed, Chua suggests that an additional nationalist element can arise if the programme is foreign produced: there is a tendency on the part of native audiences to see the overseas made film as less true, for instance, the case of *Mao's Last Dancer*, which was filmed mostly in China but not released in China due to political sensitivities. Another reading position is when the audience is watching an imported programme. In this case, the film, television programme or animation crosses cultural boundaries and the message is mediated through a cultural filter – horizons of expectation – that may be shaped by events in the world, for instance, the spectre of a 'China threat', or by the dominant cultural values of the receiving society, for example, the contrasting evaluations of the reality TV show *If You Are the One (feicheng wurao)* in China and in Australia, to be discussed in Chapter 8.

Undoubtedly, one can find more data about reception within China than outside China. Significant amounts of industry data exist and dedicated Blue Books (*lanpi shu*) compete to compile statistics of internal consumption indicating year by year fluctuations. Usually the data is derived from internal sources and this makes it hard to verify. Fine-grained data about Chinese media 'going out' is not usually a part of these reports, most likely due to the problem of accounting for it – such data is usually not released by the industry players – and the fact that results don't exactly make good reading. Chinese media has of course been quite happy to report on the number of Chinese media outlets available globally and some propaganda accounts have seen fit to publish articles about how African audiences are disposed to viewing Chinese TV dramas although the evidence remains mostly anecdotal. Vivien Marsh has examined how China Central TV has built institutional capacity in Kenya, how it employs locals in its news editorial offices and how editorial decisions are made regarding representations of China for consumption by African audiences, including for instance, a lack of reporting on the 'problems' of China's expanding presence in Africa compared with other international media outlets including the BBC or CNN.[22]

Complicating the process of reception is the effect of social media. Some assessments of China's media and culture going out have taken a quantitative solution, sidestepping the more complicated question of how they are actually received. One report cites the 2015 Chinese historical drama serial *Nirvana in Fire* as receiving a phenomenal 13 billion views globally.[23] The fact that the serial had multiple episodes, combined with e-word of mouth, may have contributed to this phenomenon. But what does an online 'view' actually entail? Does it mean a person watched an episode or did they just 'click' on the service? Elsewhere, reports claimed 3.3 billion views on iQiyi, China's version of Netflix, by the end of the serial. Another dynastic serial *Yanxi Palace* is reported to have received the even more fantastical figure of 15 billion streams in 2018 on iQiyi, an interesting and timely release of industry data when one considers that the Western streaming platform Netflix does not release such figures.[24] Of course, reception is problematic when the number of hits online is used as proxy of success. Use of 'hit' data by Facebook to pitch their site to advertising has come under criticism.[25] Similarly, equating the global reach of China Global TV Network (CGTN) as tangible evidence of China's soft power is equally flawed. Chinese TV channels do reach overseas Chinese audiences of course, but the fact is that the presence of CCTV channels in international hotels and resorts frequented by Chinese tourists is more symbolic than real. A 2009 survey on CCTV-9, formerly CCTV International, showed that the channel struggled to get significant audience traction even among the Chinese diaspora.[26]

Part of the problem with recognition of Chinese content outside the PRC is reviews. Whereas a film, TV series or online video may go viral among online communities, racking up millions of hits and shares in a few days, this does not correlate with commercial or critical success outside China. Some films garner good fan reviews and the social web can easily muster up the numbers to 'upvote'. Reviews, such as those found on sites like IMDB, Rotten Tomatoes, or Douban and Maoyan in China, and personal recommendations from friends, do help in generating interest. But when it comes to actually paying for professional content, many consumers are persuaded by critical industry reviews. Patriotic blockbusters such as the aforementioned *Wolf Warrior 2* and the science fiction offering *The Wandering Earth* ignited Chinese social media and seemed to signal a significant breakthrough for China's film industry. Yet their commercial success failed to correlate with critical acclaim. In particular, the much-vaunted production *The Wandering Earth* (directed by Frant Gwo), while having the honour of being the highest grossing picture in China, failed to light up outside the mainland, with one critic labelling it as 'unwatchable'.[27] Another notable example is *The Great Wall* (2017), a co-production with Hollywood and China. Universal Studios reportedly spent over $80 million on promotion.[28] When industry and fan reviews surfaced the film sank into oblivion like a dark star, leading industry observers to speculate that this might be the end of the Sino-Hollywood love affair.[29]

A report on Chinese film consumption in the United States and Canada by a team at the Beijing Normal University has provided some useful insights into consumption of Chinese films outside the PRC.[30] Using a professional survey company to ensure the survey was as demographically broad as possible, the research collected 1208 and 312 responses in the United States and Canada respectively. Nominated ethnic groups were 'white', Asian, African-American and 'other ethnic group'; 68.4 per cent of the respondents self-identified as 'white', which on the surface would seem be a problematic racial category. Whites were found to consume less kung fu than 'blacks', although possibly this could be equated with income and education but that variable wasn't investigated. The report concluded that movies were a better way to transmit understandings of China's national image than mainstream media or even the internet. The survey found that overall 79.1 per cent of people had watched one or more Chinese movies in the past three years with 43.3 per cent reporting they had watched five or more. Aside from the problematic methodology of ascribing racial profiling to viewing habits, the report made no distinction regarding 'Made-in-PRC' movies and those made in adjacent territories, or even co-productions; that is, it assumed that the respondents can identify a Chinese movie because it features Chinese actors and producers, including those from Hong Kong and Taiwan.

Evaluating China's messaging in the Asia-Pacific

The Beijing Normal University survey did not seek to ascertain how people watch movies, for instance, in cinemas or at home, using DVDs, streaming or video-on-demand. As with international media industries, China's audio-visual sector has been disrupted by the advent of online platforms. The key platforms with stakes in the audiovisual content sectors are Baidu, Alibaba and Tencent, although the global phenomenon of the user-generated content video site TikTok is worth considering as an indicator of China's overseas success. Tencent Video provides audiences with exclusive copyright content from industry-leading companies like HBO and Time Warner. Baidu's iQiyi is well known for its professionally generated content (PGC) and high-premium self-made content and has entered into collaborations with Netflix. Alibaba, which owns the platform Youku, also has its film production assets, known as Alibaba Pictures.

In order to ascertain if digital platforms are more effective in carrying China's message than traditional media, in 2018 and 2019 we conducted a series of focus groups and online surveys. The analysis was part of a three-year research project called 'Digital China: from Cultural Presence to Innovation Nation' funded by the Australian Research Council. The target was the Asia-Pacific and the countries and regions surveyed included Singapore, Hong Kong, Taiwan, South Korea and Australia, although response came from several other geographical areas outside the Asia-Pacific (these were discounted). The focus groups and surveys were authorized by Curtin University's Human Ethics Research Committee to ensure confidentiality and anonymity. The focus groups were conducted at the same time as the survey and used a method of prompting participants with visual cues such as images of leading brands and logos. This is discussed in more detail in Chapters 6, 7 and 8.

Survey respondents were contacted by advertisements posted on Facebook and WeChat as well as through local community organizations. On the survey introduction page (see Appendix), we specifically directed attention to 'Made-in-China' audiovisual content; we were aware that some respondents might conflate Hong Kong and Taiwanese Chinese language content or even Jackie Chan's English language Hollywood movies with PRC Chinese audiovisual content. Part of our interest was identifying platforms that distributed narrative forms of content, that is, we did not investigate user-generated platforms, for example, TikTok in the first two surveys, as this platform had not become well known outside China at the time. All of the surveys conducted sought to discover the motivations for seeking out and viewing 'Made-in-China' entertainment products. We therefore needed to emphasize that we were not referring to Hong Kong cinema or Taiwanese drama, although we anticipated and accounted for some category confusion. We hypothesized that a person might seek out Chinese content, and even pay for access if they had some personal connection, that is, friends or family members who were Chinese, or if they had visited China or had studied Chinese. This proved to be the case. The survey was opt-in (i.e. persons choose to participate). Overall, the results confirmed that Chinese audiovisual content is engaging with persons who have an existing interest. From the combined results of three surveys, it was difficult to show conclusively that Chinese audiovisual content was winning new audiences.

The first survey was made available in Chinese, Malay, Indonesian and Japanese in April 2018 using Qualtrics software. The focus in this survey was on how respondents understood soft power and this was then followed by a question about their perception of China's soft power. People nominated what they believed was the 'most familiar indicator of soft power' (a single choice only). Among 258 valid responses, 63.95 per cent selected 'a nation's cultural and creative output', followed by 'a nation's political standing and leadership in the global community' (21.32%). The two other choices available were 'a nation's reputation as technologically innovative' and 'a nation's foreign aid'. The results appeared to confirm the significance of cultural and creative products, at least in the minds of our respondents. Of course, the naming of this survey as 'China's cultural influence' may have predisposed some people to answer the question this way. The survey also asked respondents to rank in descending order eight countries' soft power. Among 262 valid responses, the United States was ranked first by most people while PR China was ranked first by only 6.97 per cent. In this survey 39 per cent of respondents self-identified as Chinese citizens. From these results, albeit limited, we might conclude that there is a lack of confidence among Chinese citizens in their nation's soft power status internationally. Many respondents avoided questions about soft power in the 2018 survey. This may be attributed to the lack of understanding or certainty of the meaning of 'soft power'. We subsequently developed a second survey in which we changed soft power to 'influence.' In addition, we sought to ascertain where people were now living, not just their passport nationality. In September 2018, we launched the second iteration, eliciting 1,063 valid answers within a month. Due to one of the platform distribution methods used (WeChat), a large number of respondents came from PR China, which indicated an interest in sharing the survey within the WeChat community. Among the respondents, 47.98 per cent expressed Chinese nationality. While this was a large demographic, 24.7 per cent of these respondents were not living in the PRC, which was of particular interest to us, as we were seeking to ascertain perceptions of China's media content outside the PRC. Our surveys revealed that YouTube is the major platform for people living in Australia, Hong Kong, Indonesia, Malaysia, Singapore, Taiwan and South Korea to access Chinese audiovisual contents, while iQiyi and Tencent video are familiar among Hong Kong and Taiwan audiences. The Chinese video-sharing websites iQiyi and Bilibili are well known to audiences in Singapore and Malaysia.

Cognizant of the fact that most respondents in the second survey identified as coming from the PRC, we initiated a third and final survey in August 2019 and promoted it among non-Chinese nationals living outside China (see Appendix). This survey attracted 520 valid responses. The behemoth known as TikTok had by now appeared on the radar of possibilities. This survey and its finding are discussed more in Chapters 6, 7 and 8. Overall, iQiyi performed well with 47.2 per cent of respondents from Malaysia and 40.5 per cent of respondents from Taiwan nominating it as the 'Chinese platform of choice'; 51.4 per cent of Hong Kong respondents chose Bilibili. However, the survey confirmed our earlier finding that the free 'Western' platform YouTube is used the most in Australia, Hong Kong, Malaysia, PR China, Singapore and Taiwan to access Chinese entertainment content.

Concluding remarks: Regional variance and public diplomacy

China has great stories worth telling. But are the stories hitting the intended targets? Overall, the results – metrics or data – do not make good reporting, aside from the breakout of Chinese social media platforms such as TikTok. Certainly, many Chinese films score well in international film festivals but such films are often not endorsed by the government in Beijing and hence are not widely screened in China. Patriotic films resonate with overseas Chinese audiences but fall flat with non-Chinese audiences. Historic epics do better in the region because there is more shared cultural knowledge of China. The Asia-Pacific, where the Chinese diaspora is most concentrated, therefore offers the best hope for a Chinese cultural rejuvenation. Meanwhile, the creative migration of artists and film personnel from Hong Kong, Taiwan, South Korea and Singapore to the Chinese mainland augurs well for the professionalization of Chinese media.

The rejuvenation, however, is a work-in-progress. Having a large domestic audience and a massive diaspora creates an impression that Chinese culture is reaching out, and depending on what metrics one uses, the cultural trade deficit no longer exists. Big budget films like the 2019 science fiction project *The Wandering Earth* show that China's artists have the capacity to break into new genres and go global yet the problem remains the mode of storytelling. The perceptions of China and its cultural products remain uneven in the various countries in the region, as we will show in the following chapters.

Chapter 6

EAST ASIA: HONG KONG AND TAIWAN

Culturally and geographically proximate to the Chinese mainland, Hong Kong Special Autonomous Region (HKSAR) and Taiwan have many reasons to tap into the developments unleashed by Internet +. Whereas three decades ago Hong Kong and Taiwan were the economic drivers of a region referred to by some economists as The China Circle, 'mainland China' has rapidly ascended as an economic powerhouse.[1] Both Hong Kong and Taiwan face increasing economic uncertainties and these uncertainties provide many incentives to integrate with the powerful mainland. However, with the growing politicization of society in the mainland under the Xi regime, the term 'integration' takes on different nuances.

This chapter explores how digital platforms from mainland China are expanding into Hong Kong and Taiwan. The examples come from video-streaming providers iQiyi and LeTV, which offer professionally produced content, as well as the short-form video-sharing app TikTok, which aggregates non-professional content. While political advocacy in mainland China has seen the 'going-out' strategy gaining momentum since the early 2000s, commercial imperatives provide an even stronger motivation for market expansion. Hong Kong and Taiwan are prime markets with Chinese-speaking populations ready-made for expansion. Moreover, internet infrastructures in these territories are highly developed. Users can access high-speed internet at relatively low cost. Users' potential willingness to pay for content adds further to the commercial appeal of these markets.

The introductory section considers the disappearance – and reappearance – of identity in these territories as the mainland exerts increasing political control. Over the past two decades Hong Kong and Taiwan have 'told Chinese stories well', that is, according to audiences.[2] But will future audiences be as receptive to Chinese stories embellished with the creative skills of professionals from Hong Kong and Taiwan? The online video platform owned by Baidu, iQiyi, provides an illustrative example of how a mainland China-based service provider has sought to circumvent regulatory barriers in Taiwan and how it has subsequently modified its content offerings, taking advantage of the increasing professionalization of mainland entertainment shows and television formats featuring celebrities from both Hong Kong and Taiwan. We discuss LeTV's high-profile entry into Hong Kong, its attempts to partner with local incumbents and its subsequent demise. We then look at how the short video-sharing platform TikTok has become embroiled in issues of censorship pertaining to nationalism and identity politics. In the final section the chapter draws on survey data that shows an ambivalent attitude towards Chinese platforms in these territories, with YouTube leading the pack in terms of popular use.

Contested identities

While Hong Kong SAR has long been an entrepôt, a vibrant commercial hub, its pre-eminent position in the global system is waning, a casualty of political turmoil and uncertainty about the former British colony's autonomy. In the 1980s, Hong Kong had become an important conduit for foreign investment into the PRC. In early 2019, the Chinese government unveiled its Greater Bay Area plan to foster innovation and productivity in the Pearl River Delta region by driving closer economic integration of the industrial powerhouse regions of Guangdong, Hong Kong and Macau.

In contrast to Hong Kong's close economic relationships with the PRC, direct economic exchanges between Taiwan and the mainland did not begin until after the mid-1990s, although a proposal called the Three Links (of postal, commercial and transportation) across the Taiwan Strait was initiated in 1979. Cross-strait economic activities have seen further growth since the full restoration of direct air, sea transport and postal services in 2008.

Since the 1980s, both Hong Kong and Taiwan have been part of a larger entity, sometimes called Greater China. The term emphasizes closer economic ties although it brings with it political and cultural complexities. Greater China indicates the potential of a common cultural-linguistic market, rechannelling and redirecting global cultural flows at a regional level.[3] The democratic entities of Hong Kong and Taiwan do not block Goggle and Facebook for instance, while WhatsApp is the preferred online messaging service. The Chinese government's signing of the Closer Economic Partnership Agreement (CEPA) with Hong Kong SAR in 2003 and the Economic Cooperation Framework Agreement (ECFA) with Taiwan in 2010 further accelerated economic integration. The growing integration of the two territories with mainland China is illustrated in new vocabularies, trade agreements, policy initiatives and, as we will show, new tensions.

China's so-called great rejuvenation – the Chinese Dream – complicates questions of national identification. In Taiwan and Hong Kong national identification is intertwined with political orientation.[4] Ien Ang has poignantly framed the problem of Chinese identity, 'If I am inescapably Chinese by *descent*, I am only sometimes Chinese by *consent*. When and how is a matter of politics.'[5] In Hong Kong the immediate post-handover differentiation between a 'political China' and a 'cultural-economic China' has rapidly evolved into political resentment. This has spilled over into popular resistance to PRC-style culture.[6]

On the cusp of the handover of sovereignty over Hong Kong from Britain to China at the end of the last millennium, Ackbar Abbas argued that Hong Kong was manifesting a 'culture of disappearance' when faced with the threat of its imminent integration.[7] Compared with the 1980s and 1990s, mainland Chinese cultural influence in the post-1997 era saw a waning of Hong Kong's popular cultural influence. Now, Hong Kong is a contested space. Competing ideas of identity, politics and culture are inspiring a 'culture of reappearance'.[8] In the wake of protests against extradition laws, many people in Hong Kong are expressing their political aspirations and dissent through artistic expressions: as Anthony Daparin writes, they 'consciously integrate art and spectacle into their actions as a means of capturing public and media attention'.[9]

The people of Hong Kong have proven to be more resilient than the Chinese government had imagined. And that makes it a more interesting space, where competing ideas of identity and culture will continue to inspire new and exciting forms of artistic expression and where competing platforms and services of Chinese, American and regional backgrounds will continue to vie for middle-class consumers of Hong Kong and surrounding areas. Hong Kong may have begun its post-handover life under the shadow of its own disappearance, but 20 years later, it unequivocally enjoys a similar culture of reappearance. This is key to our understanding of the city's vitality and agency in the shadow of China's overwhelming presence.

Taiwan, on the other hand, is an example of a 'compressed modernity' due to the island's historical and contemporary entanglements with multiple cultural and ideological influences. 'Compressed modernity', according to Chang Kyung-Sup, describes 'a civilizational condition in which economic, political, social and/or cultural changes occur in an extremely condensed manner in respect to both time and space'.[10] Like Hong Kong, Taiwan exists in the entangled zone of influence of multiple powers and exerts its influence in turn. The economic and cultural connections with the mainland are evolving amid broader regional dynamics. In predominantly Mandarin-speaking Taiwan, there has been a significant upsurge in local identity due to Taiwanese renaissance policies and what is called the New Taiwanese movement. However, perceptions of Taiwan's national status, its growing security concerns and the rising Chinese economy have activated a dual or even schizophrenic identity.[11]

Evolving connections: From high-tech to culture

Taiwan and Hong Kong's economic importance in East Asian production chains and trade is evident in technology industries. Both harbour the ambition to become high-tech hubs, connecting market players in and beyond the region. The rapid development of the consumer electronics industry has been a major driver of Taiwan's economic success over the past decades. With the Taiwanese government sparing no effort in promoting technology industries, industrial bases in Taiwan have attracted many OEM (original equipment manufacturing) and ODM (original design manufacturing) contracts from world-leading brands since the 1990s. Meanwhile, Taiwanese suppliers have been quick to exploit the profit growth opportunities arising from low labour costs in mainland China.

Hong Kong, as a global trade hub, shares the ambition to elevate its global standing in the information and technology sector. In 1998, Hong Kong SAR government put forward a developmental strategy to turn the city into a global high-tech hub. A crucial project under the strategy is Cyberport, which was designed to attract and nurture start-ups, facilitate collaboration and accelerate innovation of new technologies, applications, services and content. Noticeably, the project marked Hong Kong SAR government's departure from its laissez-faire approach in the past. The broader picture of Hong Kong's quest for the leadership in high-tech is deeply embedded in the political economy of post-colonial Hong Kong's state–society relationship.

In the cultural and creative industries, both Taiwan and Hong Kong have enjoyed a long-standing reputation, particularly in film and TV production. From idol dramas to variety shows to kung fu cinema, both markets have produced memorable classics; this output led in the 1990s to a composite term, *gangtai* culture, with the PRC more often the receiver of culture than the sender.[12] *Gangtai* includes official exports and informal trade; for instance, products not showing up in official statistics travel by alternative routes, via street vendors of pirate disks, satellite spillover or peer-to-peer networks.[13] Moreover, both Taiwan and Hong Kong have been crucial sites of inspiration for producers in PRC with growing collaborations between market players.

Since the Asian Financial Crisis in 1997, Taiwan has witnessed a slowly declining television industry. Hong Kong too has lost its position as a leader in film and TV production.[14] Over the past decade the PRC has begun to attract the creative workforce from Taiwan and Hong Kong, generating hybrid cultural products and new forms of collaboration.[15] Bilateral trade agreements (e.g. CEPA and ECFA as mentioned earlier) have provided incentives for collaboration; for example, the relaxation of trade restrictions allows Hong Kong and Taiwan films to receive exemption from China's film import quota. Preferential access to the mainland Chinese market has propelled co-productions with the mainland.[16] As mainland China further opens the door of its huge market, it absorbs investments, talent, content and technologies, which strengthen its cultural and media industries.

More recently, Taiwan and Hong Kong have become desirable target markets for digital enterprises from mainland China as they expand across borders. As China's postcolonial other, Hong Kong is both a contested place and a testing ground for Chinese media and cultural industries to go global. Writing about film industries, Darrell Davis says, 'Hong Kong's colonial background is important [...] as its long history as British territory offers private property, common law, English language contracts and corporate bona fides. Also, now part of the PRC, it can sell itself (again) as comprador, being both (China) and neither, positioned between two colonizers.'[17] Taiwan, although having more political uncertainties and policy restrictions, also serves as an ideal test market for digital enterprises from the mainland seeking to serve the diaspora population. As we illustrate in the next section, market entry can be a tricky process for mainland content-hosting platforms seeking expansion into Taiwan more than those eyeing Hong Kong. This however does not deter the aspiring market players.

Chinese platforms gain entrance

Over the past two decades video streaming in mainland China has witnessed rapid growth and major shake-ups. As discussed in Chapter 3, the once piracy-ridden mainland market has moved towards formalization under market forces and state regulation. Surviving service providers from the market shake-ups in 2008 have escalated investment in licensed content and increasingly make their presence felt in original content production. Many have launched initiatives to identify and nurture emerging creative talent, playing a key role in professionalization of amateur production.[18] While some players have gained a bigger market share through mergers and acquisitions, others struggled to maintain the momentum and were eventually pushed out of the market. Against this backdrop of disruption, internet giants from mainland China made capital investments in the maturing pan-Asian market. Leading contenders have included iQiyi, which is backed by Baidu; Youku Tudou by Alibaba; and Tencent Video launched by Tencent. LeTV (later LeEco) made a brief foray but lost its position. TikTok, while late to the game, has become a dominant player as a video-sharing platform.

Both Hong Kong and Taiwan are crowded markets with multiple international service providers vying for market share. These include global leading brands such as YouTube and Netflix. While not all major Chinese streaming market players have expanded into Hong Kong and Taiwan, many viewers in these regions have found ways of circumventing geoblocking in order to access content. The platform choices made by consumers in Taiwan and Hong Kong are therefore pertinent to understanding how content made in mainland China fares, considering there are few linguistic barriers. Another factor to bear in mind is the convoluted political interplays and tensions in the regions: this is indicated by choice of messaging apps, as we will discuss later. In mid-2019, Hong Kong SAR was disrupted by anti-mainland protests and this has continued to play out. Protests spilled over to democratic Taiwan with many fearing that a future tied to the PRC would be a future that would deprive citizens of their basic freedoms.

iQiyi was the first video-streaming platform to venture beyond mainland China. As an early step in its expansion plan, iQiyi chose Taiwan as the first regional market to tackle. With Baidu as its majority shareholder, iQiyi was established in 2010. Unlike many of its predecessors in the video-streaming market, iQiyi did not initially choose to become a video-sharing platform. Instead, in building up its content library, iQiyi focused on licensed TV and films and made a growing investment in original production since 2011. It gained initial traction in the mainland with the advertising-supported model, quickly followed by the introduction of the subscription model.

iQiyi officially launched its service in Taiwan in March 2016. The Taiwan site offers a variety of genres including movies, variety shows, animation, comedy, children, documentaries and iQiyi productions. As an attempt to gain more subscribers, the platform offers a three-tier subscription plan of various duration. A monthly subscription costs NT$239 (roughly 48 RMB), slightly cheaper than the NT$270 charged by Netflix in the same market. Paying subscribers have the privilege of accessing a broader range of content, viewing certain popular content ahead of non-paying users, and skipping advertising.

A local intermediary was crucial to iQiyi in its attempt to break into the Taiwanese market. iQiyi set up operations via the local agency OTT Entertainment Ltd. on a revenue-sharing basis. A major regulatory roadblock emerged when Taiwan's Investment Commission under the Ministry of Economic Affairs, in consultation with the Ministry of Culture and Mainland Affairs Council, rejected iQiyi's application to establish a subsidiary in Taiwan. According to Taiwan's Investment Commission, iQiyi submitted an application to establish a subsidiary as an 'electronic information service provider', but it actually operates as an over-the-top (OTT) service for broadcasting entertainment content; in this domain mainland Chinese investment is not allowed in Taiwan according to the *Regulations Governing Permission for People from the Mainland Area to Invest in Taiwan*.[19]

Conceptual frames have regulatory implications. While platform is a widely used term in the industry, not only by service providers but also by those with whom they engage, it has multiple connotations. Gillespie has noted the politics of platforms, whereby they need to carefully position themselves to various users and policy makers.[20] Despite market players' embrace of the term, some services are better conceptualized as portals,[21] functioning as a gateway to a library of television programmes. iQiyi is positioned as both a portal and platform and functions to 'integrate, as well as fragment, a mass audience'.[22] While there is no current regulatory framework regarding streaming services in Taiwan, the authorities have so far decided to treat iQiyi as a content provider. In this sense, iQiyi's positioning as a neutral service provider in dealing with the government is negated. By regulating the platform as a broadcaster, the authorities closed the door on iQiyi's proposed establishment of a subsidiary.

Behind the regulatory decision is a long-standing debate among political parties in Taiwan. The debate speaks to diverging views regarding cross-strait relations. The regulatory challenge over market entry of a streaming service both reflected and intensified the political debate. For the ruling Democratic Progressive Party, key concerns centre around Beijing's cultural and political influence.[23] Incoming platforms from the mainland, perceived as carriers of such influences, could be a threat, echoing some of the political concerns seen in Australia and New Zealand (Chapter 8). Potential collaboration in the broader context of Beijing's policy initiatives of 'using economy to steer politics' and 'using economy to promote unification' is thus viewed with suspicion.

So far, the regulatory move has not killed the possibility of market entry for iQiyi. At the time of writing, it still operates in Taiwan via its local agent. When commenting on the rejected application to set up a subsidiary, an iQiyi spokesman stressed that the company has no intention to withdraw from the Taiwanese market, and it will purchase more premium content to serve the Taiwanese audience.[24] In order to enhance its appeal to the audience in Taiwan, iQiyi, much like a broadcaster, endeavours to enhance and promote its content offerings. This will be elaborated further in the following section.

While the outcome is not completely settled, Tencent Video has chosen to follow iQiyi's approach. It entered the Taiwan market via its Hong Kong investment subsidiary Image Future Investment HK in May 2019. In this gambit Hong Kong is a launching pad and a detour to Taiwan. Users can download the subscription-based video-streaming app WeTV from Taiwan's

App Store or Google Play. Subscription costs NTD 190 (USD 6) per month or NTD 560 per quarter. This is priced higher than the service in the mainland market but lower than iQiyi and Netflix in Taiwan. So far, the two leading streaming service providers from mainland China have already deployed market presence in Taiwan amid regulatory uncertainties, eyeing for a share of the market.

Like Taiwan, Hong Kong is a market where pay TV is popular. However, online streaming has significantly disrupted this industry sector. As in Taiwan, the regulatory void saw an influx of platforms foraying into the local market. LeTV (later LeEco), which started its online video-streaming business in mainland China as early as 2004, was a front runner in exploring the Hong Kong market. In 2014, it set up a subsidiary in Hong Kong, the first destination in its overseas expansion. Touting a free market and a majority population of ethnic Chinese, Hong Kong served as a strategic testing ground in the company's global expansion plan, which was aimed first at capturing diasporic Chinese. The company rebranded itself in 2016 into LeEco, short for Le Ecosystem, to reflect its comprehensive business strategy. In this vertically integrated ecosystem, according to the vision, proprietary content plays on its own online portal and it provides hardware from smart TV to smart cars. Partnering up with telecom operators is a key strategy to grow the user base. LeEco's collaboration with Hong Kong Broadband Network Ltd offers affordable package deals of broadband and content.

Fierce competition in regional telecom services is crucial in driving such collaborative dynamics. Since the late 1990s, the market has seen increasing liberalization and growing competition. This has consolidated Hong Kong's role as a regional telecom hub in Asia. It becomes crucial for telecom operators to offer added value to customers. Beyond technological capacity, content offerings in service packages provide incentives for users. For telecom operators, partnership with streaming platforms provides such added value; for streaming service providers, alliance with telecom operators not only supports optimal viewing experience but also provides a gateway to user acquisition. The densely populated city touts the world-leading fixed broadband speed, second only to Singapore. The rapid broadband speed provided by telecom operators offers further advantages in delivering a smooth streaming experience of ultra-high-definition content.

Content acquisition and nurturing for market expansion

Landing in the target market is only the first step in expanding across the border. Competitive content offerings are crucial in acquiring and maintaining users.

In the context of financialization powered up by global capital markets,[25] streaming portals have accelerated investment in curating content libraries. This involves both licensing and original content production. Licensing is a major approach adopted and, when deployed strategically, lends significant competitive advantages to service providers. Original production is a further strategy to differentiate against competitors and enhance content libraries.

Collaboration with local content partners serves as an efficient strategy to address local tastes. For example, in the attempt to appeal to viewers in Taiwan, iQiyi partnered with local broadcasters including Gala Television (GTV), Eastern Broadcasting Company (EBC) and Taiwan Television (TTV) to secure simultaneous screening of popular content in the local market. This approach collapses the broadcasting logic and provides audiences with nonlinear access to local content. iQiyi is quick to spot and acquire quality productions emerging from the local scene. Its acquisition of *Q series* (*zhi juchang*) is an illustrative example. At a time when revitalizing the local cultural industry is of utmost importance in Taiwan, *Q series* is a project subsidized by Taiwan's Ministry of Culture. Launched by the local start-up Q Place Creative Inc. together with TTV, GTV and Public Television Service (PTS), the project comprises eight series ranging from romantic drama to suspense and terror, each containing six to seven episodes. iQiyi acquired the rights to these series and negotiated a close-to-simultaneous streaming deal, offering access to content only two hours behind the first screening and leading other broadcasters by days or months. Several series in the project won awards or nominations at Taiwan's Golden Bell Awards in 2017 and 2018. In contrast to iQiyi's move, Netflix only came to acquire the series in 2017 one year later than the former. The approach to acquiring local content explains why iQiyi performs much stronger than Netflix in Taiwan.

Prior to its entry into the Taiwanese market, iQiyi had already formed a number of creative partnerships. Indeed, recent years have witnessed integration of Taiwanese creatives into the screen entertainment industries in the mainland. The sheer size of the mainland market and the growing investment in licensed content and original production, particularly on the digital frontier, have become a magnet for creative talent in Taiwan.[26] Such crossovers of talent are conducive to iQiyi's attempts to reach audiences in Taiwan with a local approach. In a similar move to acquire local content, LeEco announced an investment of 300 million yuan to attract viewers in Hong Kong[27] with moves to acquire rights to a massive selection of TV series and movies.

In addition to local content, mainland productions are available on iQiyi's Taiwan site. Variety shows and costume drama hold great appeal in Taiwan. The ascendance of variety shows is situated in the broader context of TV format trade.²⁸ In recent years, Taiwan is losing its aura as a knowledge broker in entertainment production for the mainland as global TV format trade accelerates cultural technology transfer.²⁹ Creative teams in the mainland absorb ideas to create adaptations not only through formal licensing but also via informal borrowing. Bold investment and thus high production quality further add value to content appeal. Moreover, according to our survey, casting is a major motivation for viewers in Taiwan to watch content produced in mainland China, with the drawing power comparable to positive reviews. A notable title offered by iQiyi in Taiwan is Season 4 of the highly popular variety show *I Am a Singer* (*woshi geshou*) (Hunan Satellite TV). Inspired by the Korean format, the show lined up professional singers to enter a singing competition, with celebrities from Taiwan and Hong Kong to enhance its appeal not only in the mainland but also in neighbouring markets. At the 27th Golden Melody Awards instituted by the Ministry of Culture in Taiwan, Julia Peng won the Best Mandarin Female Singer award. She attributed her success to the show which effectively revived her career.

While Chinese export of variety shows is a relatively recent phenomenon, costume drama from mainland China has a long-standing reputation in the region. As our survey findings show, appealing storylines and Chinese cultural elements are top reasons for viewers in Taiwan to watch content produced in mainland China. *The Legend of Zhenhuan* (*zhenhuan zhuan*) is a prominent title, which has been screened repeatedly on several broadcasters in Taiwan in recent years. Notable titles offered by iQiyi Taiwan include the martial arts drama series *Nirvana in Fire* (*langyabang*) and the period drama *Story of Yanxi Palace* (*yanxi gonglue*).

Further, content with regional appeal is a crucial driver in the growing subscriber base for streaming service providers. *Hallyu* is a strong manifestation of transnational cultural phenomenon in recent years. K-dramas, as a part of Korean wave sweeping across East Asia, appeal to regional, including Chinese, audiences with culturally relevant themes.³⁰ For iQiyi, the simultaneous screening of the Korean drama *Descendants of the Sun* (*taiyang de houyi*) on its site and the Korean broadcaster KBS lent a significant advantage to the platform in the Taiwan market. It was not until several months later that the local broadcaster ETTV started to screen the drama in Taiwan. The imperative to overcome the temporal window is a strong incentive for many fans in Taiwan to become paying subscribers. Through cultural trade on the digital front, the incoming service provider manages to supply powerful regional content to local audiences. In this sense, the Chinese platform acts as an intermediary in producing a transborder popular culture and builds up its presence in the local market. Riding on the Korean wave thus enhances the power of the platform as a distributor.

Beyond drama series and variety shows, sport has attracted growing attention in the rights market. It is a mainstay of screen content consumption. In the post-broadcast era streaming service providers have joined in the bidding for premium sports content. LeEco stood out on this front. In 2014, LeEco established its sports streaming division LeTV Sports Culture Develop Ltd. and since then has made aggressive moves to obtain premier sports coverage rights in Hong Kong. Most notably, LeTV Sports snapped up the rights to the English Premier League (EPL) for three seasons from 2016 to 2019, outbidding other contenders including Netflix, Alibaba and Wanda. The cost reportedly ran over US$400 million, more than doubling what the previous rights holder PCCW's Now TV paid for a similar three-year deal.[31] As the most watched sports league in the world, EPL benefits from increasingly lucrative sales of broadcasting rights to international markets.[32] In Hong Kong, prior to the deal with LeTV Sports, the rights to broadcast EPL had seen fierce competitions between two local pay TV operators, namely i-Cable and Now TV.

As a result, fans migrated between these platforms depending on who secured the rights. Clearly, LeTV Sports expected the deal to aid its ambition to grow its subscriber base in Hong Kong. Subscribers could access content on LeTV's smart TV, or via LeTV box, the LeSports.com website or the mobile app; this included not only live matches but also a spectrum of original content featuring highlights or comments from well-known pundits. In a similar vein, LeTV Sports acquired the Hong Kong rights to National Basketball Association games in the United States (2016–21) and World Cup soccer games (2016–18).

Despite the aspiration to lure subscribers with premium sports content across multiple screens, LeEco soon found itself facing a financial crunch. Its hefty investment turned out to be unsustainable and the vision of a vertically integrated ecosystem fell through. In 2017, LeEco filed for liquidation to Hong Kong's High Court following acute financial troubles which led to multiple lawsuits from creditors. It eventually shut down its operations in Hong Kong in 2018. LeSports Hong Kong also had to close its business in the same year. The dream of going global had hit a wall.

While rights acquisition continues to gather force, with varying levels of effectiveness, streaming service providers have exploited original content production. Original production has subsequently evolved from 'filler content' to quality productions along with increasing investment in mainland China.[33] iQiyi is a leading player in original content production, especially in drama series and variety shows. Since entering Taiwan, iQiyi has offered its consumers original drama productions including the crime series *Burning Ice* (*wuzheng zhizui*) and the thriller *Tientsin Mystic* (*he shen*). Both are adapted from online literature work, by Chen Zijin and Zhang Muye respectively. Online literature is a field witnessing booming creativity from emerging writers in mainland China.[34] These writers are becoming increasingly entrepreneurial with the formalization of the internet literature market where screen adaptation is now a driving force behind commercialization.[35] These fast-paced stories with intricate plots have proved appealing to viewers. This is consistent with the findings of our survey, where participants nominated appealing stories as the top reason to choose to watch entertainment content from mainland China.

As well as exporting its original content produced in mainland China, iQiyi has established a drama series production unit under its Taiwan agent. Liao Jianxing, a veteran producer in the local industry, oversees this unit. Before joining OTT Entertainment, Liao acted as a producer for the previously discussed *Q series*. In 2018, OTT Entertainment launched four 24× 45-minute original drama series, including *Meet Me@1006*, *Befriend*, *Plant Goddess* and *Replay*. These series span the genres of fantasy, suspense, romance and comedy. They were first streamed on iQiyi, followed by broadcast at TTV and EBC. By working with local creative talent, iQiyi not only obtains the first screening rights but also serves as a platform of opportunities for local creative talent. The latter enhances the platform appeal at a time when both market players and the government are eager to reinvigorate the local industry.

Unlike LeTV and iQiyi, TikTok, which is a short-form video-sharing platform, does not concern itself with content acquisition strategies. Market expansion relies much on content nurturing. Data aggregation and algorithmic-driven distribution play a decisive role. For the platform, viewing data is a crucial indicator of audience preference. This then informs, partially, how the platform promotes certain content over others. Algorithmic logic of content nurturing, however, is a complex beast. Much of content moderation goes on with little transparency to the public. This creates challenges to the platform, which hopes to establish a playful and harmless image. The following section will elaborate more on this.

Governance amid the intersection of entertainment and politics

As streaming service providers boost content offerings to enhance competitiveness, content policing is high on the agenda of governance especially when geopolitical tensions continue to brew. The entanglement of entertainment and politics becomes accentuated as border-crossing digital platforms exert policing power over content. This reflects the concern raised by regulators, content creators as well as the broader audience in the target market. In

2017, iQiyi withdrew the mini-series *Days We Stared at the Sun II*, directed by Cheng Yu-chieh and funded by the Taiwanese PTS. It is the sequel to the award-winning mini-series which debuted in 2010, telling stories of a group of teenagers as they enter adulthood. While the platform cited service differentiation as the reason behind the decision, it is widely perceived that the platform censored the content due to political sensitiveness.[36] In a similar vein, the platform triggered controversy when a live-streamed concert of Taiwanese singer Cyndi Wang was cut to a commercial when the national flag of Taiwan appeared in the background.

These instances attest to the longer history where content suppliers and transnational stars become implicated in geopolitics.[37] In the context of China's ongoing nation-building projects and nationalism moving online, multiple stakeholders including the state, digital enterprises and users shape the complicated terrain of digital nationalism as demonstrated by Florian Schneider.[38] This remains a contested field as Chinese digital enterprises expand across the border, which in turn impact local audience perception towards the incoming service providers. According to our survey, while not the top reason, censorship is an important issue that turns away respondents in Hong Kong and Taiwan from entertainment content produced in mainland China.

Another example that has created waves is *The Rap of China* (*zhongguo you xiha*) which is produced by iQiyi. *The Rap of China* has gained a large following in Taiwan, where hip-hop culture has been popularized since the early 2000s. The rap contest featured Taiwanese judges Kris Wu, Will Pan, MC HotDog and Chang Chenyue. The appeal in Taiwan is evident in online search and discussions among viewers.[39] The show has attracted questions regarding the ethos of rap culture in mainland China, and it has issued challenges to the regulators of content. iQiyi exercised extreme caution in self-censorship in order to keep the show on stage, by deciding who or which part of the lyrics can be shown or heard. 'Do you freestyle', a question frequently asked by Kris Wu as a selection criterion in the competition, quickly became an internet meme. Freestyle, an important characteristic of rap culture, showcases the capacity of the rappers to improvise rhymes and flows on the spot. This triggered heated discussions over whether Chinese rappers can be truly creative. Audiences also questioned the role of the platform in moderating the visibility of such creativity.

Before iQiyi had staged the show, the Ministry of Culture in China banned 120 songs, mostly rap, that were circulating on the internet in 2015.[40] This ban included songs of MC HotDog and Chang Chenyue. Interestingly, the ban did not prevent them from acting as judges in *The Rap of China*. This conundrum illustrates the governance approach by the state, which involves moulding popular culture for the purpose of the state, promoting so-called positive energy while purging unwanted creativity; in other words, to stay within boundaries. With *The Rap of China* bringing underground culture into the spotlight, rap music has further come into the remit of state governance. The winner of the show, Zhou Yan, better known as GAI, started to dispense positive energy via his lyrics. As discussed in the chapter on Culture +, the development of online media industries is closely intertwined with the imperative to distribute positive energy.

For platforms that host user-generated content, the regulation of online content presents more severe challenges. The history of online video platforms in China is a reminder of how user creativity can trigger problems for advertisers and in turn for the hosting platforms.[41] The unpredictability of user creativity and the accompanying governance challenges is also partly a reason for some platforms to shift strategies towards licensing professional content.

Currently, TikTok is facing the challenge of content regulation. With its algorithm-driven content distribution, TikTok aims to get users hooked. A large pool of data generated by user activities informs an ever-evolving experiment in content recommendation. The learning capacity of algorithms is further enhanced by human moderators who follow corporate guidelines and train algorithms. As in the case of other digital platforms that rely on user-generated content, TikTok faces challenges in handling risks associated with misinformation, hate speech and political content. Geopolitical tensions add to the regulatory challenges. While TikTok identifies itself as essentially providing entertainment, albeit much of it banal and quickly forgettable, entertainment is closely bound up with the politics of nationalism. In Hong Kong and Taiwan, political tensions and competing ideologies with mainland China in the postcolonial context bring the connection between entertainment and politics into sharp focus. Considering that algorithmic logic is notoriously opaque to the public, the issue of how to gain public trust remains unclear.

Unsurprisingly, in Hong Kong and Taiwan questions have been raised about platform regulation with regard to content and data security. One prominent case is the scepticism provoked by apparent scarce content related to the pro-democracy protests in Hong Kong on TikTok.[42] The company denied the suspicion that it censors 'inconvenient content' for Beijing. Rather, it stressed the platform was a place for entertainment instead of politics, which is a plausible explanation for the significantly smaller presence of politically inconvenient content for Beijing when compared to other free world global platforms such as Twitter. Another possible explanation, however, lies in trust deficit, which was not brought up by the platform. Specifically, users will choose other social media platforms as they expect that certain content will be out of bounds on TikTok, or they avoid TikTok out of privacy concerns. In this sense, TikTok shares the fortune of WeChat, which was avoided by activists in Hong Kong.

Survey findings

Between August 2019 and February 2020, coincident with the ongoing unrest, we conducted an online survey to ascertain which online video service providers in Hong Kong and Taiwan were most used for accessing entertainment content produced in mainland China. The methods used for the survey are discussed in detail in Chapter 5 (see also the Appendix). In one survey we received responses from 150 participants in Hong Kong and 43 in Taiwan. Over 90 per cent of participants in Hong Kong were aged between 18 and 28, and 58 per cent of respondents in Taiwan were between 40 and 50 years, with the rest in their 30s and 50s. Among these participants, 54 per cent in Hong Kong had high school education and 32.7 per cent had a bachelor's degree. Participants in Taiwan had a noticeably higher education level, with almost 70 per cent possessing a master's or higher degree. Around 69.5 per cent of participants in Hong Kong and over 93 per cent in Taiwan said they were native Mandarin Chinese speakers or had native proficiency. Participants holding Chinese passports were less than 30 per cent in both places.

The survey responses confirm that YouTube is the most popular online video service provider for participants in both Hong Kong (54.7%) and Taiwan (46.5%) to access Made-in-China entertainment content. Among service providers focusing on subscription-based streaming, iQiyi leads in both markets as the top choice for consumption of entertainment content produced in mainland China. Youku and Tencent Video have appeal to local viewers, particularly in Taiwan. In Hong Kong, around one in five participants chose iQiyi (24%) and Youku (17.3%). Tencent Video claimed just 7.3 per cent of respondents. Netflix with 19 per cent of respondents is a middle-rank player; however, it should be noted that Netflix does not have much Chinese language content in comparison with its competitors. In Taiwan, iQiyi shows its leading edge, closely following YouTube with almost 40 per cent of respondents using it to access content produced in mainland China. Youku and Tencent Video are the next popular in Taiwan, claiming more users among the respondents than Netflix when it comes to Chinese content. Overall, apart from the free platform YouTube, iQiyi performs strongly in both Taiwan and Hong Kong. TikTok, which exploded in late 2019 lagged in our survey with only 10 per cent of respondents in Hong Kong and 20 per cent in Taiwan. TikTok revealed more than 3 million monthly active users in Taiwan by the end of 2018.[43] The penetration rate has since increased.

According to our survey, over 85 per cent of respondents in Hong Kong used WhatsApp 'daily' and close to 50 per cent said they 'never' used WeChat. In Taiwan, 87.5 per cent of the total respondents use Line 'daily', and less than 50 per cent used WeChat 'sometimes'. All this highlights the uneasy spaces Chinese digital tech giants have to carefully navigate in their expansion across borders. The survey results are interesting in the context of rising anti-PRC sentiment. Did the events of mid-2019 and the fallout over the ensuing months have an impact on people's answers? Unfortunately, we were unable to ascertain this answer, although we did note a spike in responses in Hong Kong, indicating a tendency to 'avoid content that was censored' (27.3% in Hong Kong and 16.3% in Taiwan).

Concluding discussion

This chapter has charted the expansion of Chinese digital platforms, represented by streaming service providers, into the territories of Hong Kong SAR and Taiwan. While digital enterprises as well as the Chinese government are partners in a grand vision of 'going out' and empire building, market entry has encountered initial challenges. Local partners, as seen from the above discussion, are crucial. Intermediary-mediated entrance is particularly instrumental amid regulatory uncertainties. Alliances along the line of vertical integration attract local collaborators while delivering mutual growth.

Once achieving market entry, a reliable content library is central to consolidation and expansion. How these service providers position themselves in the new territories ultimately has an impact on their content offerings. In the context of a booming content licensing market, rights acquisition is a widely adopted strategy. Localization, particularly through purchase of local content, features prominently on Chinese platforms as they move into new markets. Content with regional appeal is high on the menu of acquisition, as evidenced by the will to ride on the energy of the Korean wave. Streaming rights of high-profile sporting events with global appeal attract bold investment by the digital players. Such investment could be risky at the same time. Sustainability of the model is still in question.

For Chinese streaming service providers, their approaches to content policing constitute potential challenges to popularity in target markets. As entertainment and politics inevitably intersect, even more so amid geopolitical tensions in the postcolonial context and complicated politics of nationalism, expanding digital enterprises from the Chinese mainland have to tread more carefully. Governance challenges become more critical for video-sharing platforms, particularly where users are actively engaging in content creation. When algorithm-powered content distribution attracts users, it could trigger new regulatory responses, which in turn impact on platform presence, operations and appeal. Locating local partners, weighing local audience appetite and negotiating with evolving regulatory environment and public trust is therefore a constant exercise for expanding digital champions.

As Chinese digital platforms such as iQiyi and Tencent Video expand their consumer markets in Greater China there are implications for the cultural identities of people living in Hong Kong and Taiwan. Residents of these regions have an affinity with Chinese stories 'told well'. Both regions have been emblematic of a vibrant, cosmopolitan Chinese identity, modern and unapologetically critical of power. With mainland China absorbing many of the best creative artists, directors, producers and animators from Hong Kong and Taiwan, the cultural power of mainland China is augmented and the critical power of artists is diminished. Mainlandization may be the future for many who opt to take the opportunities on offer but Hong Kong and Taiwan will most likely remain important wellsprings of creative imagination.

Chapter 7

SOUTH EAST ASIA: SINGAPORE AND MALAYSIA

The earliest Chinese arrivals in Singapore and Malaysia were sojourners from mainland China. Few of those who arrived to trade or find employment intended to stay long in Nanyang (the Southeast) although many eventually settled after World War II. Despite the familial links to China, affective, geographical and generational distances have increased over the decades. With the PRC now moving confidently on the world political stage, making territorial claims in the South China Sea and expanding its power in the Asia-Pacific region, governments and people in the region are facing unprecedented challenges.

This chapter examines China's digital presence in Singapore and Malaysia. It begins with a brief explanation of the juxtapositions of national and cultural identity in these states, peoples' identification with Chinese culture and language dialects and the growing presence of the nation-state of China, including an influx of PRC migration. The term 'PRC migrants' is used here to distinguish between post-1980s migrants from mainland China and earlier pre-1980s generations of migrants. We note an ambivalence and sometimes resistance to Chinese investment despite its potential for development. In Singapore where the ethnic Chinese dominate, the arrival of PRC foreign capital, businesses and people has further deepened delineations. Malaysia, with less ethnic Chinese among its population, is similarly ambivalent, with Chinese language remaining a barrier to acceptance.

We then consider China's digital presence. In doing this we draw from a series of semi-structured interviews held in Singapore and Malaysia in 2019. Ambivalence to China, and Chinese products and services, appears in some of the responses.[1] Fifteen interviews were conducted with the help of images featuring digital corporation logos, figureheads of the digital corporations and promotional advertisements for pop cultural content: lengthier conversations developed from these visual prompts, including questions about Chinese products, services, platforms and brands. There is no intention to claim statistical significance but we do construe the interviews as first-hand accounts of and insights into how well China's cultural presence is faring.

Chinese presence in Singapore and Malaysia

Singapore today is one of the few Chinese-majority societies in the world. It is often regarded as a part of Greater China. Singapore's image, and the citizenry's view of Singapore, is first and foremost as a place of business. In fact, Singapore is today consistently voted one of the best places to start and run a business.[2] Capital is welcomed. Singapore's ruthlessly efficient technocratic government focuses on policies that deliver results and the population is thankful for this kind of approach. The city-state's prosperity, its high standards of living, the value of the Singapore dollar and the ease of travel when using the Singapore passport all rest on the city-state's reputation as an international centre that deals efficiently with the hustle and bustle of trade.

The Singaporean government plays a crucial role, determining polices on business and utilizing huge sums from state-owned sovereign funds for investments. The government also sets up special zones from time to time and provides exemptions that facilitate specific industries. In many ways the government is the intermediary that brokers relationships between local and foreign businesses. Capital and businesses from the PRC are as welcome as those from anywhere else. Culturally, it is worth noting that all students of Chinese descent in Singapore are required to take Mandarin Chinese as a second language. While all Singaporean Chinese are literate in Chinese, few actually have the same fluency with Mandarin as migrants and visitors from the PRC. English or Singlish (a mix of English with words and phrases borrowed from Malay, Chinese languages and Tamil) is the everyday language of all Singaporeans, including the Malay, Indian and Other minorities.[3]

The cultural landscape is very different in Malaysia, not least because the ethnic Chinese and Indians are minorities in Malay-majority Malaysia. Unless parents have deliberately placed their children in what is known as 'vernacular schools' – where depending on the school the medium of instruction is either Mandarin or Tamil – many Malaysian Chinese do not speak Mandarin. Still, although many Malaysian Chinese do not read the Chinese script, they do speak other Chinese languages such as Cantonese, Hokkien (Fujianese), Teochew (Chaozhou) at home. The national language of Malaysia is Bahasa Melayu and it acts as the basis of common identity among Malaysians whatever their ethnicity, culture and religion.

Like the Singaporean Chinese, Malaysian Chinese are careful to differentiate themselves from the contemporary Chinese of mainland China. Like Singapore, the Malaysian government is often the intermediary of business and has been responsible for creating conditions conducive for foreign businesses and investors who wish to establish businesses. However, recent capital and trade from China have met with resistance. For example, when former prime minister Najib Razak visited China in 2016 and secured US$34 billion in trade deals, there were some who feared being overwhelmed by cash-rich PRC companies and the perceived PRC preference for working with Malaysian Chinese businesses.[4] Many of the deals referred to were infrastructural and included the construction of the East Coast Rail Line, the High-Speed Rail linking the capital of southernmost state, Johor Bahru, to Singapore and the Malaysia–China Kuantan Industrial Park. Even the national marque, Proton, one of two Malaysian car manufacturers, is now partially owned by Geely, a PRC automaker.[5]

Digital China today

The number of Chinese digital platforms in Singapore and Malaysia changes rapidly. Digital platforms and services face few barriers to entry except where regulatory issues and licences arise. Generally speaking, consumers in South East Asia have a broad choice; they can (linguistically and culturally) access digital products developed in the East and the West. For example, while Taobao is available in the region and frequently offers good value for money, other e-commerce platforms such as Amazon, eBay, Lazada, Shopee, Qoo10 and newer regional entrants such as Indonesia's Tokopedia provide keen competition for local custom. Consumers in Singapore and Malaysia are price-sensitive and enjoy the array of platforms from which they can pick and choose. As the following paragraphs will show, trust and consumers' own ability to navigate user interfaces are the major stumbling blocks to greater adoption of Chinese e-commerce platforms.

In Malaysia the government's reception to digital projects developed by Chinese tech corporations such as Alibaba, Huawei and Ant Financial in China have been warm. This is also true among the populace and most evident in the welcome extended to Alibaba's Jack Ma when he was appointed digital economy advisor to Malaysia in 2016 and then when he launched the Digital Free Trade Zone (DFTZ) in 2017.[6] The same was obvious when Ma launched Alibaba's Malaysia office the same year. The DFTZ is a node of the eWTP (Electronic World Trade Platform) that was initiated by Ma. Malaysia's DFTZ is the first eWTP site outside of mainland China. Additionally, Alibaba's office in Kuala Lumpur (KL), the capital of Malaysia, is its first within South East Asia and KL is the first foreign city to implement Alibaba's City Brain system.

In many ways China's digital platforms are equally alien to all Malaysians, especially since a sizeable proportion are not familiar with the Chinese written script, being able neither to read nor identify with it. E-commerce platforms are the most well-known among the Malaysians we interviewed, although not being able to recognize the Chinese characters in some cases and for others, the machine-translated English product descriptions pose a hurdle. Take, for example, Maxine, an ethnic Chinese professional in her 40s, who describes the obstacles she faces and the convoluted workaround she has devised in order to complete her online transactions on Taobao (Alibaba's e-commerce platform):

> I surf Taobao a lot but I have not bought anything (directly) [...] My sister uses a lot of Taobao, if I want to buy anything that I like through Taobao, I will send her the link and she will then tell me whether can buy or cannot buy because Taobao relies a lot on reviews [...] so she will read for me and she will tell me whether this supplier has good review(s) and the people have said this particular dress is [...] If I really like it then I'll ask my sister to pay for me because she holds a Taobao account. I'm just lazy to register with Taobao and the registration page is all in Mandarin so I dislike [...] even surfing is very difficult at times [...] so if I want a midi dress but I don't know what it is called but lately I have learnt (*zhongchang*) [...] is the term used.

To be clear, the difficulties Maxine describes are only partly caused by poor skills in Mandarin. Considering the importance of reviews in social shopping, these are not insignificant difficulties and Maxine's workaround is only possible because of her sister's linguistic abilities. The other gaps, as Maxine's last quip reveals, are the localized phraseology unique to users and sellers in China. This makes both product sourcing and reviews unnecessarily onerous. In other words, the labour involved in commencing a relationship with a mainly Chinese e-commerce platform, browsing for, assessing and then completing the transactions is complicated for those individuals who, like Maxine, are not entirely fluent in Mandarin.

The situation is somewhat different in Singapore where there are many who read both English and Mandarin. One of our oldest informants, Frank, is a chemical engineer who trained in the UK. Frank's home is filled with antiques from China and tall vases stuffed with peonies adorn almost every corner. Chinese culture and links to his ancestral roots are central to Frank and his family. Now in his mid-60s and semi-retired, Frank is an enthusiast of China and professes to be a regular and frequent customer of AliExpress. However, as he also confessed later, all his purchases, major and minor, are handled by one of his assistants at his behest. Unlike Maxine, Frank has no need to wrestle with the e-commerce interface or trouble himself with multiple transactions even if he does do 'extensive research' between the various e-commerce platforms before deciding where to make a purchase. Although trilingual in English, Mandarin and Malay, he failed to recognize the Taobao logo when it was shown to him and of the 20 images shown, Frank only identified one. That was the photo of Jack Ma, at which he exclaimed 'Jack Ma! Jack Ma! Alibaba! Everybody knows Jack Ma! He says he can change the world, which I believe.' Frank's enthusiastic avowal of Ma finds its companion in Andy's (Malaysian interviewee, in his 30s) view of Ma as an Asian icon: 'Alibaba is famous, I think because of Jack Ma [...]. I'm not sure how influential he is in China but international [sic] he is seen as (an icon) [...] I wouldn't compare him with [...] Steve Jobs because he is from Asia. [...] [A]n icon from the East, he's beyond Asia.'

May, another informant from Singapore, is an undergraduate in her early 20s who is fluent in Mandarin and English. An exponent of the Chinese string instrument, the pipa, many would expect May to be at least somewhat enamoured with PRC culture, products and services. Yet, during the interview when asked if she would differentiate between Chinese culture and Singaporean Chinese culture, May's answer speaks of a strong sense of the hybridity of Singaporean Chinese culture, which according to her 'incorporates a lot of the Western ideas also. Maybe Singapore culture would be a bit of a diluted version of the China Chinese culture'. While the cultural debt is acknowledged, May's take on day-to-day purchasing decisions via digital platforms is somewhat more hard-nosed:

> Carousell is safer [...] it's Singapore led and, in that sense, you can't escape from Singapore, the chances of you being scammed is pretty low, whereas if you buy from Taobao, you buy 10 things maybe 3 of the things turn out alright and the other 7 are [...] I experienced once and a couple of my friends did too. [...] For me personally, I bought a pair of shorts and the measurements were off and they didn't cut in the buttonhole. So, I couldn't put it on and the material shrunk in the washing machine [...] I think the more epic story is one of my friends [...] bought this really nice rug to put on the floor and it turned about to be a print of the rug. She got a shock.

A Singapore-based platform, Carousell is designed to facilitate the online reselling of things people own but no longer want. When asked if anyone she knows has sought refunds for their Taobao purchases, May explains,

> it's just about impossible to get a refund. Taobao is really, really cheap so for you to get a refund, to get it they want you to send back the item, which is going to cost [...] So, my overall impression of Taobao is not

that great, ah but [...] Taobao is good for facial washes and things like that [...] they actually come through for most of the products.

Horror stories of the dubious products sold on China's e-commerce sites are rife, as are advice columns on how to avoid being victims of AliExpress scams.[7] Some buyer experiences between expectations and reality are so far apart they have even become memes. Our youngest interviewees from Singapore, Sharon and Kate, provide further elaboration. The two are sisters who asked to be interviewed together. Kate is two years older than Sharon and dominates the interview but the younger Sharon chips in throughout the interviews. The two agree that Shopee (a South East Asian e-commerce platform) and Carousell are much better options for online shopping. Queried why, Kate somewhat apologetically elaborates, 'it's about quality. We're not being racist, but when the product is cheap the standard is not very good. Not up to our standard.'

During the interviews with our younger informants, May, Kate and Sharon, mobile gaming inevitably came up. Strikingly, when shown the Honor of Kings game logo, all three remarked that it resembled Mobile Legends: Bang (*wújìn duìjué*) another China-made product. Although neither of the younger pair plays Mobile Legends, they very quickly whipped out their mobile phones to show us a game they do play, Rules of Survival, that all among their circle of friends are addicted to. It was with some surprise that they greeted the information that the maker of Rules of Survival, NetEase (Wangyi), is based in China. Sharon's response was: 'Oh really? We didn't know. No wonder the new guns always come out first on the China server.' May, who does play Mobile Legends, insisted, 'yup I play this game (Honor of Kings) but the English version'. Later she elaborates, 'this is the English version, the characters, you will be able to tell the similarities [...] the powers and skills of the characters are equivalent in this game. If I play this [Honour of Kings] I would be able to choose the characters easily.' We then asked if she would believe if we told her Honour of Kings was China made and her response was: 'yes, because the English is very bad.' The opinion common to all three is that individuals from PRC either do not speak English or do so rather poorly.

Of course, this is a stereotypical fallacy but it seems to be important as a characteristic by which Singaporeans distinguish themselves from individuals of PRC origin. Throughout our interview May showed little recognition of the visual cues shown and even QQ's penguin logo is mis-recognized as Pingu, a British Swiss children's animated comedy. Interestingly, shown a screenshot of *Empresses in the Palace* (hougong zhenhuan zhuan, a China-made drama series with a big following in South East Asia), she excitedly responded, 'I love these kinds of shows [...] *gudaixi* (ancient dramas)', which she watches via

Netflix but without recollection of their titles, only their theme songs. Having said that there are certain media formats such as China's version of *Running Man*, originally of Korean origin, that May has viewed where she reckons the production quality is 'just as good' although 'the games are not as creative' (as those thought up by Korean producers).

The perception of inferior quality, especially when held up against products from the West, was quite common among our informants. Perhaps more importantly with respect to China's cultural presence vis-à-vis its digital technologies and corporations, Singaporeans and Malaysians are developing a preference for localized alternatives whenever they are available rather than China's digital platforms. For example, in Malaysia GrabPay is used daily by thousands to pay for items as diverse as lunch deliveries and prepaid reloads to hotel bookings. In an eerie repetition of patterns in China, where internet users have for various reasons, including their ban from use in China, not taken at all to Western-based platforms and turned instead to local alternatives, Malaysians and Singaporeans are also favouring local apps.

Specifically, although WeChat may be a ubiquitous super app in China, the likelihood of it becoming similarly popular in Singapore or Malaysia at this point is low to nil. What that means in terms of our question of whether China's digital presence improves its cultural influence remains unclear but it does argue that new devices, whether discursive, material or symbolic, may well be necessary for China's reputation as an innovative nation to gain a foothold in the South East Asian nations of Singapore and Malaysia. So far, the answer to our question of China's digital cultural presence seems to be largely negative, but there are indications that things may be changing and not necessarily from the expected quarters.

Despite preconceptions of doubtful quality and the linguistic obstacles between sellers and service providers from China and buyers in Singapore and Malaysia who are not native Mandarin speakers, the view of Chinese digital platforms and products seems to be changing. On this front Maxine from Malaysia relates a telling anecdote that speaks of the conflicts between the canny shopper's eye for a good bargain, doubts about China-made products/platforms and deeply held familial biases that inform her view of China's digital presence:

> My perception has changed but there are certain things that I still don't trust China that much [...] My impression is changing now that I have used iPhone and non-Apple phones. [...] Before Huawei P20 I was using iPhone 5. [...] but see, with iPhone every feature that I use I am very sure I have the confidence whereas in [...] I am not entirely sure because they ask you for a lot of your data: do you want to, do you agree

> to share your contacts, your details in your phone [...] iPhone will never do that! [...] among my family members there are still a lot of umm [...] the confidence level of China products is still not very good and I think I've inherited that but I'm experiencing a certain change in perception. It's quite amazing that I started shopping in Taobao and I bought a dress from Taobao and the quality is very good compared to what I buy. For example, I usually buy UK brands [...] the quality is getting worse and it's very expensive, whereas Taobao the quality is very good and the price is like less than half [...] the service is excellent and the packaging is excellent and the speed is excellent!

Direct experiential knowledge is evidence that is difficult for any consumer to argue with. Maxine's change of perception is, however, not an isolated example. Andy, the other interviewee from Malaysia, too speaks of how his rather low expectations were confounded:

> I'm surprised, with that price I pay I thought I would get poor workmanship but when it came, when it arrived it was like, OMG, this is good. And I think it was because I do quite a lot of research to see not just the price but also the reviews [...] Quite an interesting approach to buying. I never envisioned buying sofa, my rack, even by cycling duffle bag that cost half or even less than half than I could get in the shops here [...] The expectation of low quality was because 'I was buying from China'.

Although Andy can converse in Mandarin he cannot read the Chinese script. So he relies on online translation services to make decisions about purchases and obtain a bargain. As any retailer or producer will tell you, the combination of great products paired with competitive pricing and excellent service is an absolute winning formula – even when consumers are not wholly convinced when first embarking on their purchases. In this contest between goods from the West (UK) and goods from the East (China), it seems the minor risk of paying for a dud is worthwhile compared to the exorbitant prices one would otherwise pay.

Good, yet still apart

None of our interviewees were able to deny the powerful presence of China in their daily lives. As the common saying goes, 'everything is made in China'. Even our youngest interviewees, sisters Sharon and Kate, acknowledge that China is the most powerful nation in the world 'because it's rich' and, as Sharon observes, 'China is smart that's why Singapore wants to be like them.' China's digital platforms may not as yet have significantly and positively influenced China's cultural presence in Singapore or Malaysia but there is no lack of awareness of their presence in South East Asia. Simon (trained art curator, late 40s to early 50s) is similarly awed by the pace and power of China – 'if they put their minds to it, they can solve almost any problems'.

Yet Kate makes clear that she distinguishes between Chinese culture and China's culture. For her, 'China is a country and Chinese is a race […] China's culture is what goes on in their country, Chinese culture is, in general the race culture.' Asked for an example she points to the heavy censorship that occurs in the PRC. The separation between Chinese and China culture is unclear but the sentiment is not. As Sharon puts it, 'we don't follow the Chinese culture, we're not from China'. Later on, she adds, 'We are bilingual. They only speak one language. We learn things differently, we study differently. We study two languages, they study one language only.' The dis/connection to China's culture for May is rooted in the past, with the ancient cultures of the Chinese empires viewed from a temporal distance and with the Confucian ideals of filial piety and emphasis on the 'roundness' (unity and completeness) of Chinese families via interactions with her Hainanese grandfather.

May seems to have a divided view of contemporary China: as a respectable repository of Singapore Chinese culture and as the source of affordable but less than trustworthy online purveyors. As the head of a centre that focuses on Singaporean Chinese culture, Simon is sensitive to the nuances that separate the Chinese in Singapore from those elsewhere: 'because we've developed differently, the things we do, the food we eat, the language that we use must also develop differently'. Asked to name some of these traits Simon, like the other interviewees in Singapore, counted bilingualism (English and Chinese) as first, 'the ability to understand or empathize or appreciate cultural difference' as second and a 'developing this sense of Singaporean identity' as third. In Malaysia, Andy's understanding is similar but broader: 'I understand Chinese culture as *nanyang* culture. Chinese people that actually are in Southeast Asia. So, there is no Chinese culture per se but I only knew Nanyang is referring to the Chinese who adopt the culture from China and actually embrace it and perhaps they have undergone changes and localized it.'

This suggests that one consequence of China's overwhelming presence in the region is the pushback from South East Asian nations through the assertion of their own identities, reputations and cultures. Furthermore, whether China itself distinguishes between its digital and non-digital products and services, for South East Asians it is an increasingly obvious divide. They associate Chinese culture with ancient China and China's digital platforms with contemporary China.[8] Ancient China, historical customs and ways are held closer than contemporary mainland Chinese cultures. Still, that does not mean they necessarily identify with ancient Chinese culture. Andy speaks for many of his fellow South East Asians who are increasingly confident and bold about their nations, their cultures and identity when he says, 'I do not see my roots as being associated with the Chinese in China. I see it as a separate identity. My identity is as Nanyang Chinese not China Chinese. I am the second-generation Malaysian Chinese.'

Further, South East Asians' habitual ease with English as lingua franca is not going to be forsaken for Mandarin anytime soon. The obstacles to doing so are formidable and include writing and reproducing the Chinese script in both its modern and traditional form at speed, typing on QWERTY keyboards patently ill-suited to the language and the difficulty of reading what can be highly idiosyncratic styles of writing when done by hand. Voice-activated smart speakers and instant accurate translation enabled by artificial intelligence and machine learning may one day shift the predilection for English as the language of business by totally removing linguistic barriers. Until then, so long as the day-to-day use and connection to the English language survives, China's objective of increasing its cultural presence in Singapore and Malaysia remains a work-in-progress and an uphill one at that.

The gulf that isolates China from South East Asia is not only a concern to China. All the individuals we interviewed were acutely aware of the marching tides of change that a more powerful, more vibrant China will bring to the region. And each in their own way is trying to assess, prepare and act upon their understanding of the changes that will occur. In this endeavour they are joined by their national institutions. While Singapore has for many decades required schoolchildren of Chinese ancestry to undergo Mandarin lessons throughout their education, Malaysians are not far behind. Indeed, many are keenly aware that Mandarin language skills and Chinese ways of communicating and doing business will eventually be widespread, if not global. To that end they try, as many South East Asians have in the past, to absorb and adapt the incoming cultural influences into their lives. The gallant Maxine details here the struggles she undergoes in order to use Baidu, China's largest search engine, and her reasons for doing so:

> Baidu, if I (have I used Baidu?) [...] I think it have through Google [...] but everything is in Mandarin and it takes a long time to read [...] and whenever I come across this it's because my daughter needed something in Mandarin [...] especially I think there is a Baidu Encyclopaedia that I use quite a bit. My daughter, when she studies Chinese there's a lot of things she asks me but I cannot answer her so I do a translation through Google and it will link me to Baidu Baike [...]. I can read Chinese [...] but my reading is very very slow, much slower than I do in English [...]

I hate reading Mandarin not that I cannot read but it takes me a very very long time because I do word for word and a lot of words I cannot recognise them any more so when I have to explain to her I cut and paste and via Google Translate [the machine translation service developed by Google] translate it into English and she reads it for herself. I love Google Translate, otherwise I will not survive. Because I have to do three languages and she only knows English.

Digital China, however, seems to be a different creature. Its might and power are widely acknowledged but only celebrated by our older informants. Some of the middle age informants like Maxine and Andy profess to slowly changing attitudes towards Made-in-China products. Of course, there are links between how well China's rise is celebrated and attitudinal changes towards products made in China, which is why the distinctions in how they are perceived are worth pursuing further. For example, most of the interviewees from the youngest at 18 to the oldest in their 70s (except Maxine), recognized Jack Ma's photo and associated him with Alibaba without fail. Even when Maxine failed to identify Ma by his photograph, she did not fail to recognize him by reputation. Ma's fame is only partly explained by the records broken and buzz created when Alibaba went public in 2014, after all Pony Ma (Ma Huateng, Chairman of Tencent) is arguably just as innovative and probably wealthier.

As is the way of digital corporations, every founder of the BAT triumvirate (Baidu, Alibaba and Tencent) has had a crucial role in shaping the direction of their firms from the get-go.[9] This suggests the high recognition factor vis-à-vis Pony Ma and Robin Li (the two other founder photos shown) to have something to do with Ma's visibility on the world stage and his engagement with the broader (read Western) world: speaking at the World Economic Forum, conversing with President Donald Trump, being part of the Bloomberg Global Business Form and being nominated as digital/e-commerce economy advisor to not just one country (Malaysia) but two countries (Indonesia) in South East Asia. As Simon, our art historian, put it, 'you make Alibaba as admired as Apple, that's one big hurdle, that's one quantum leap', emphasizing once again that the American/Western cultural hegemon remains the yardstick against which all the rest are measured. When pressed to rank China's reputation within the South East Asian region, Simon places it (for now) just below the United States but carefully sums it up thus:

> I get the sense that the digital field is progressing extremely rapidly in China [...] how fast they rollout products and how fast it is being adopted or adapted by the Chinese public. So I'm very impressed by the pace of development. I can't say I'm a fan of any technological product

that came out of China, I just have an impression that the technological front is doing very well in China.

Such awareness is driven in part by the acknowledgement of China's technological prowess, the very large sums made and exchanged by Chinese firms wheeling and dealing, acquiring significant shares in companies across the world, as well as paradoxically, the paranoia whipped up by the United States over China's 5G capability. It is close to impossible to avoid China's digital technologies and corporations today, but it remains unclear how much their presence adds to China's image as an innovative nation.

For the siblings in Singapore, Sharon and Kate, their instantaneous recognition of the Weibo, WeChat and TikTok logos accord with their age group but as neither uses any of them, their connection to China's digital platforms and China's cultural influence is minor at best. Both avid fans of Korean dramas, Kate shares that she feels 'American and Korean culture are taking over the world. Homogenizing, fast food, entertainment, K-pop […].' She struggles somewhat with expressing her thoughts but continues, 'I feel like China is very isolated. You see, right, even though it's very big' […] 'because they are communist, they are isolated because everyone else is a democracy. Like these, right […] (she gestures toward the apps listed on the visual cues) no one knows them and no one uses them.' At this point, Sharon pipes in, 'they are always in their own group. In their own world. It's like […] we just care about ourselves. They're making their own apps, their own everything, they're not connected to the world, no sharing, stuck in their own world', and Kate continues, 'even those games and movies they build and finance, they're in English, they're just sponsoring it, there's still American influence in it'.

China's isolation, partially self-imposed and partially foisted upon it, even, or perhaps especially, in the digital sphere is not lost on others. Why, for example, could China's citizens not use WhatsApp or Facebook Messenger, much like the rest of the world, instead of WeChat? Why not Twitter instead of Weibo? Yes, China-origin apps such as TikTok and Didi Chuxing are increasingly used outside China but they have seldom attained the enormous user bases they have at home. Of course, scholars of the West would argue that it is the action of a government that wants to shield its citizens from open discussion, the US cultural hegemon, the corruptive influences of the West, constrict the level of dissent in the country and thereby maintain order among its 1.4 billion population. The language barrier is, after all, a useful political barrier. It keeps the curious but linguistically less well versed from learning and knowing more. Conveniently, it also keeps the English-speaking Western world looking in from the outside at the Middle Kingdom. Still, China must also be aware that the more its reputation and power ascends in the region, the more outsiders ranging from co-ethnic foreigners from South East Asia to less similar but eager suitors of all stripes and colour will want to converse, enter and know the country. Going global or 'going out' (*zou chuqu*), as China's state machine puts it, inevitably entails some coming in. Neither trade nor culture works successfully on its own. The question is, Is China ready to loosen its grip sufficiently to allow the free-flowing exchanges necessary to its march into the region?

Social +?

Finally, the story of Forrest Li Xiaodong, founder of Shopee, suggests another way by which China's digital presence is establishing itself in South East Asia. The e-commerce company, Shopee was launched in July of 2015 and is today a popular alternative to Lazada, Amazon and Taobao in the region. The company Li founded, Garena, began as an online gaming platform.[10] Later renamed SEA, the tech unicorn is based in Singapore and counts China's Tencent as one of its minority shareholders and mentor.[11] A native of Tianjin, China, and a graduate of Shanghai Jiaotong University, Li is today a citizen of Singapore and runs his tech unicorn from the city-state. It is Li's rise to fame in the start-up world that provides additional insight into how China's digital presence in the Asia-Pacific could take a different route.

As related by Li, his epiphany began when he was attending his then girlfriend's graduation ceremony at Stanford in 2005. This was when Steve Jobs, co-founder of Apple Computer, delivered his now famous commencement address. Li drew inspiration from Jobs' exhortation to 'stay hungry, stay foolish'[12] and after completing his MBA at Stanford, went on eventually to found Garena in 2009. American-style entrepreneurship continues to inspire not just the décor of SEA's corporate headquarters but also the range of perks enjoyed by employees. Li's first and most crucial angel investors included the son-in-law of Malaysian billionaire Robert Kuok, Skype co-founder Tovio Annus and Kuok Khoon Hong, CEO of palm oil major, Wilmar. By Li's own admission, all three were introduced via the vast and powerful Stanford Alumni network.[13] SEA was successfully listed on the New York Stock Exchange in 2017, making Li a billionaire and, in 2019, placing the 42-year-old among the 50 richest in Singapore.[14]

In contrast to Alibaba's method of acquiring shares in successful local start-ups such as Lazada, SEA's and its founder's route presents an intriguing alternative. What Forrest Li's journey illustrates is the role that a Chinese-majority country like Singapore plays as a landing pad for China's digital presence in the Asia-Pacific. The strength of the hybrid approach is borne out by how Li was able to combine the influence of Silicon Valley, draw on the networks of Stanford's international alumni and mimic Tencent's model to create a success story. As Nick Nash, former group president of SEA, put it: 'We've learned the recipe, but we've made it Peranakan [Straits-born cuisine with both Chinese and Malay influences]. In some ways, we're the Peranakan version of Tencent.'[15]

Conclusion

This chapter has explored China's digital presence in relation to its cultural influence in Singapore and Malaysia. It has tried to answer the question, Have China's digital platforms and products significantly improved China's cultural presence in these two countries? With the help of our interviewees and the examination of reception to the discourses surrounding the PRC's digital technologies and platforms, the short answer is: not yet. Although what the interviews also reveal is that Alibaba, via Taobao, is increasingly making China's digital presence felt in both Singapore and Malaysia. The first issue that needs to be addressed if Singaporeans and Malaysians are to equate their positive experiences of digital platforms and technologies discussed here with China is the perception of Made-in-China products and services as being of dubious quality. This obstacle to China's increased cultural presence is, as our interviewees relate, one that time and experience can overcome. As price differentials drive more consumers from Singapore and Malaysia to consider products and services from China, their actual quality will correct or cement perceptions.

The second issue is one of recognition. If users are not aware of, or misrecognize the PRC origins of a digital product or platform, recognition or failure to recognize products as products of China is part of what enabled the games' and platforms' popularity for now, the second issue goes right to the heart of cultural differences. Technologically speaking, the digital platforms and products from China are comparable, if not better than those that originate from elsewhere. However, despite Singapore and Malaysia both being Asian countries with improving fluency in Mandarin among citizens, there is still an important cultural and linguistic gap between South East Asian users and PRC platform owners/sellers in terms of phraseology and colloquialisms and buying preferences. Research elsewhere has already established the PRC internet as distinct from the broader Chinese internet.[16] This is without even taking into account those who do not read the Chinese script at all. Until these cultural differences are sufficiently well translated for Singaporeans and Malaysians of all races and creeds to grasp easily, China's cultural presence in these two countries will remain limited.

In its push to boost its reputation in the region, China needs to recognize that conditions, culturally, socially, politically and economically, in South

East Asia are changing rapidly. Additionally, the broader region of Asia is also undergoing tremendous change. As Khanna points out in *The Future Is Asian: Global Order in the Twenty-First Century*, '[o]f Asia's nearly 5 billion people, 3.5 billion are *not* Chinese'.[17] He then goes on to explain: 'China has only one-third of Asia's population, less than half of Asia's GDP, about half of its outward investment, and less than half of its inbound investment. Asia is therefore much more than just "China plus". Asia's future is thus much more than whatever China wants.' Indeed. While China imagines itself to be battling the US hegemon, there are other forces at play. Khanna boldly predicts a future where Asian institutions and norms will stand side by side with Western ones, out of which a fusion will grow into a global norm.[18] This portrait of the future does not exclude China but it does reduce its role to one among many parts of Asia. It also does not accord in any way with China's vision of its own future on the world stage. Yet Khanna has posited a scenario that remains a distinct possibility. The rise of the European Union as a bloc, working to leverage its economic, political, cultural and social capital for its own advantage, is one example of how collective power can be exercised by nations, big and small.

Finally, while China might regard the ethnic Chinese diasporas in South East Asia as cultural insiders because of their ancestral roots, South East Asians seem increasingly certain that their identities and their destinies are separate to that of the People's Republic of China. As far as this chapter and bridge-building goes, the distance between Singapore, Malaysia and China might be less than compared to that, say, between Australia and China, but the gulf is possibly deeper than realized. The new world that China seeks to influence in South East Asia is a modern hybrid, with constituents bred by their postcolonial struggles of nation formation and toughened by the need of the smaller countries to survive the turbulence of the twentieth century. Neither Chinese nor Western, Singaporeans and Malaysians see themselves as modern Asians who are developing and holding their own in the twenty-first century. In this regard, the example of SEA's Forrest Li suggests that another way to further China's digital and cultural presence in the region is to embrace the innate hybridity of South East Asia. Although future manifestations of such hybridity will surely vary, by incorporating myriad influences from South East Asia itself, melding it with America's Silicon Valley style and leveraging on China's tech giants' capital and expertise, SEA's recipe for success might be one worthy of emulation by China's many digital corporations.

Chapter 8

OCEANIA: AUSTRALIA AND NEW ZEALAND

Australia and New Zealand are predominantly English-speaking Western countries with a historic connection to the United Kingdom and many parts of Europe. While both nations are examples of successful experiments with the modern ideal of a multicultural society, both have experienced tensions around migration. Both Australia and New Zealand are home to many native Chinese speakers; historically most spoke the Cantonese dialect but that has changed in the past two decades with more Mandarin-speaking Chinese taking up residence.[1]

But perhaps the greater change is in attitudes towards assimilation. Rather than being naturalized (willingly or not), as once was the case, Chinese migrants can remain culturally connected to the PRC via digital platforms.[2] In recent years the number of digital platforms linking families, friends and businesses has multiplied substantially, from the earlier instant messaging platforms QQ and WeChat to the latest short video platforms such as Bilibili and Douyin (or its international version TikTok outside the PRC). With ubiquitous connectivity, keeping in touch with familiar cultural practices poses few problems; in fact, many persons from China inhabit 'cultural filter bubbles'.[3] Home country news services including CCTV, *The Global Times*, *Xinhua News* and *Toutiao* provide alternative commentaries to the media institutions of their host countries. The social media app WeChat in particular carries links to many of these services. Parallel universes have thus formed among Chinese migrant communities, sometimes between migrant communities and the mainstream Anglosphere population.

With this in mind the challenge is to understand how Chinese media fares in the antipodes and to gauge changing perceptions of China. The chapter begins with some background to the history of Chinese settlement in Australia and New Zealand as well as noting the political repercussions of 'Chinese influence', a term that is mostly negatively charged. Because of the large numbers of PRC arrivals over the past two decades, the dynamics of Chinese-language media in Australia and New Zealand have changed.

In short, simplified characters and Mandarin-language media have increased their presence. Where the overseas Chinese media market was once predominantly Hong Kong and Taiwanese owned and operated, PRC government-linked entrepreneurs have moved to assert greater control; this ultimately has ramifications for the kinds of opinions that can be aired in the media. We also note cultural diplomacy through Chinese cultural performances and exhibitions in Australia and New Zealand that have generated controversy.

Overall, we see a growing web presence in both countries, often aided by resources from the PRC. We consider Chinese print and digital media forays into Australia and some unsuccessful attempts by Australian media entrepreneurs to position themselves in the PRC. We then look at Chinese film co-productions with Australia and New Zealand, and we show examples of television location shooting. The chapter also draws on a study of reception of Chinese film in New Zealand that shows an increase in distribution of made-in-PRC films through theatres in Auckland and Wellington but a corresponding decrease in the distribution of Chinese independent cinema.

While the media consumption habits of the Chinese diaspora are part of the puzzle, our intention is to delve even further with regard to cultural influence. To ascertain if China is telling its stories well in Australian and New Zealand, we need to go beyond the Chinese diaspora. The more significant question therefore is, To what extent are non-PRC persons living in Australia and New Zealand attracted to seek out Chinese media? By using the term 'non-PRC' we are cognizant that we are constructing a politicized and racialized frame of enquiry that may be problematic in a multicultural society; however, we endeavour to justify this through the results.

Furthermore, we are interested in assessing media narratives that can transfer across cultural boundaries. In order to gain some understanding of the extent of Australian familiarity with Chinese culture we conducted focus groups among 'non-Chinese' (i.e. people of other nationalities) in March 2020, the results of which were cross-referenced with findings from surveys conducted in 2019, where we also managed to reach out to a significant number of people living in Australia. The survey respondents included people with little or no Chinese cultural literacy, for instance, native Australians, and those who have Chinese heritage, including second- and third-generation Chinese, international students and recent migrants from Hong Kong SAR, Taiwan and South East Asia. We look at some of the key findings of the focus groups and survey in the final section of the chapter.

A brief cultural history of exchange

In 1972, Australia became the first Western developed nation to diplomatically recognize the PRC, predating the United States by seven years. China–Australia relationships have in the main been positive, although one does not have to dig deep to find evidence of racism. One of the most famous cultural intermediaries in China was the Australian adventurer George Morrison, known as Morrison of China. Morrison served as a journalist and was a political advisor to the Republic of China at the Treaty of Versailles in 1919. Intercultural relations, meanwhile, were less cordial at home. The White Australia Policy, instituted on 23 December 1901, is often cited as historical evidence of anti-Chinese sentiment, along with stories of Chinese workers being ostracized in the Australian gold fields during the late nineteenth century.

The threat of an Asian invasion grew in the years after World War II, paralleling McCarthyism in the United States, and was mostly construed in racialized terminology as the 'yellow peril', themes that pre-existed in pulp fiction in the 1920s. The White Australia Policy was eventually consigned to history in 1973 as Australia set its direction to becoming a modern multicultural society.[4] The invasion rhetoric, however, lingered and was reactivated in late 1996 by a conservative politician called Pauline Hanson, who formed a fledgling political party provocatively entitled One Nation. The key political message of One Nation was that 'Asians' were invading and taking Australian jobs and that they should 'go back to where they came from'.[5] It has since become a vehicle for nationalist and far-right policies that include strict immigration restriction.

The story of New Zealand's encounter with Chinese people and China shares similarities with that of Australia. Chinese workers, mostly from Fujian, had come to the goldfields of Otago in the 1860s, and as was the case in Australia they suffered racial discrimination. New Zealand's cultural intermediary with China was Rewi Alley, a writer and freedom fighter who became a member of the CCP and lived for a time in China in high esteem after the Revolution of 1949. Like Australia, New Zealand struggled to reconcile its colonial history defined by white supremacy with multi-ethnic democracy. It adopted exclusionary immigration policies as early as 1881 with its legislation to restrict Chinese immigrants; in 1907, it instituted the Chinese Immigrants Amendment Act, following the 1899 Immigration Restriction Act, to limit Chinese arrivals and keep them out; then an official 'White New Zealand' policy was installed in 1920 with the Immigration Restriction Amendment Act, which was not abolished until the early 1970s.[6] In December 1972, New Zealand quickly followed Australia in recognizing the PRC. In 2008, New

Zealand became the first developed nation to enter into a free trade agreement with China.

An increase in the rate of PRC migration to Australia during the 1990s was precipitated by the Tiananmen Square incident in June 1989. The Australian government granted special humanitarian residential visas to overseas students from the PRC, a dispensation that led to family reunions; this increased the quota of Mandarin-speaking Chinese and business migrants of the affluent class.[7] During this time Chinese people in Australia received considerable support in the media as they were often seen in a similar light as refugees. Attitudes towards China in Australia since then have gravitated from sympathy for political dissidents to paranoia, particularly from right-wing politicians about the extent of Chinese Communist Party influence. New Zealand likewise has experienced its share of anti-Chinese sentiment. The pendulum swings both ways. China is both good and bad depending on one's positioning. Business groups are cautious about upsetting the Chinese government and Chinese people, both in China and in the diaspora. Both Australia and New Zealand are heavily dependent on China economically and both nations take thousands of fee-paying students. In 2019, 260,000 Chinese students were enrolled in tertiary education in Australia.[8] The number in New Zealand is far less, with over 22,000 Chinese students.[9]

Attitudes have become strained in recent years as Beijing continues to exert territorial influence in the Asia-Pacific and particularly within the Pacific Island states. China's far-reaching Belt and Road Initiative together with its clandestine United Front activities have activated alarms down under. In New Zealand, Prof Anne-Marie Brady, a political scientist from the University of Canterbury, has been vocal about Chinese political influence in New Zealand, citing the activities of the United Front and their ties to surveillance networks.[10] A number of academics in Australia have loudly criticized the Chinese government's handling of human rights. The idea that a 'China threat' was imminent received a boost when Clive Hamilton published a book called *Silent Invasion* in 2018, decrying how PRC operatives were allegedly manipulating the Chinese communities in Australia.[11]

The right-wing think tank, Australian Strategic Policy Institute, has been forthright in pursuing enquiries into alleged Chinese interference.[12] Anti-China sentiment was exacerbated by the Chinese government's detention of a long-time critic of the regime, the political scientist Feng Chongyi, in 2017. In early 2020, Australia further infuriated Beijing when its Prime Minister Scott Morison called for an international independent inquiry into the origins of COVID-19. Tensions about Huawei's operations in Australia, combined with alarms about Chinese surveillance, have fanned the fires of suspicion, with the Chinese company banned from participating in Australia's 5G infrastructure.[13] Huawei, like Alibaba, has worked to establish a presence in Australia since 2016, hiring Australian executives and employees and setting up branch offices. Jack Ma, the former boss of Alibaba, even claims that his road to becoming an internet entrepreneur was made possible by a personal friendship with an Australian electrical engineer and a visit to Australia in 1985.[14] Still, Alibaba, with its core business in e-commerce and cloud computing, is viewed with a degree of suspicion in the current political tensions between China and Australia.

Chinese communities meanwhile are conflicted about the influence of the PRC, many having migrated to Australia and New Zealand to enjoy the freedoms of an open society. Linda Jaivin writes about how the Asia-Pacific Triennial of Performing Art's 2017 performance in Melbourne of *The Red Detachment of Women*, a revolutionary opera from the Cultural Revolution, aroused the ire of protesters, many of whom had fled Chinese persecution.[15] Jaivin also notes the unanticipated success of the 1993 exhibition called 'Mao Goes Pop' at Sydney's Museum of Contemporary Art and the National Gallery of Victoria's 2016 exhibition 'Andy Warhol/Ai Weiwei', the latter attracting nearly 400,000 visitors. In 2009, the Melbourne Film Festival screened a controversial documentary called the *Ten Conditions of Love* about the conditions of China's minority population, the Uyghurs, who mostly live in Xinjiang Province and who have undergone, according to the film-maker and many independent reports, degrees of cultural genocide and persecution. The Film Festival's website was hacked by 'patriotic' Australian Chinese trying to prevent ticket sales.[16]

It is therefore difficult to generalize about cultural understandings of China within Australia. A general awareness of both China and Asia exists among Australians, but it is mostly superficial because of stereotypical media coverage, the dominance of Anglo heritage and Australia's cultural ties to the UK, North America and Europe; this is particularly evident within the political system. Some commentators argue that a lack of nuanced understanding of China – what one might call low China literacy – is a key reason for (often) misguided policy responses to the rise of China.[17] This is compounded by Australia's ambiguous identity in the Asia-Pacific region. In a perceptive article by the Singaporean scholar Sarah Teo entitled 'Can Australia Be One of Us?' the author argues that while Australia may be a valuable member of the Asia-Pacific region, it is harder to make the case that it is currently seen as an Asian country within Asia itself. She says, 'Perhaps we should accept that Australia's identity and place in the region are characterized by ambiguity and ambivalence.'[18] In the context of this ambiguity about Australia's identity, the allegiance of Australia's Chinese-speaking migrants, now numbering

1.2 million and making up around 4 per cent of the national population, has come under increasing scrutiny.

Chinese print, screen and digital media culture in Australia

Understandably, media is a focal point in public discussion about Chinese influence. The content of China's state media often appears in Australia's ethnic Chinese-language media. Contributors include the increasing number of offshore correspondents for major state media organizations such as Xinhua, the *People's Daily* and the China Global TV Network (CGTN). In recent years there has been an expansion of the scope of partnerships and content-sharing arrangements with Chinese migrant media – mostly the traditional print media. China's state media has also had some success in securing business deals with mainstream English-language media organizations to carry Chinese state media content (e.g. with the Fairfax organization to carry *China Daily* content and the *Australian Financial Review* to carry the content of Caixin). A major commissioned report written by Wanning Sun has documented these developments.[19]

The report points to the growing impact of a new online Chinese-language media sector, thanks to the super app WeChat owned by China's tech giant Tencent. WeChat is central to the interpersonal and public communication practices of Chinese migrants all over the world. It has played a key role in political communication and citizenship education among Chinese migrants. The power of WeChat was evident in the 2019 Australian federal election when candidates of major parties vied for Chinese Australian voters, particularly in marginal seats. Both Chinese- and Anglo-Australian candidates and Chinese Australian voters interacted in civic education and citizen-making processes, albeit not without the usual claims of fake news as the election intensified.[20]

As Sun points out in her research on WeChat in Australia, it is vital to the debate on Chinese influence in Australia that we understand crucial distinction between WeChat as a *platform* and the *content* that it carries, between WeChat as a target of the Chinese authority's censorship practices and its use as an instrument of the CCP's propaganda.[21] In other words, Chinese social media platforms and the content they carry are subject to regulations and scrutiny of the Chinese government, but they are not necessarily designated tools to toe the party line in their overseas operations and for overseas consumers. Both WeChat and TikTok are fundamentally business entities responding to transnational financial and advertising markets, as well as the regulatory frameworks of their country of origin (China).

While WeChat has successfully expanded overseas, following Chinese migrants, visitors and students to Australia and New Zealand – and has continued to be an essential part of the everyday life of the Chinese population 'down under' – TikTok has rapidly expanded its overseas market beyond the Chinese population. By early 2020, there were 1.4 million monthly active users of TikTok in Australia and New Zealand, making up about 2 per cent of TikTok's worldwide users.[22] Despite a relatively small market, it is so far the only Chinese digital video platform that has landed successfully in the mainstream Australian market. Many Australians and Australian businesses have become visible on the app. As discussed in Chapter 4, TikTok has struck a chord with younger audiences, who care less about the 'Made-in-China' nature of the platform than what it enables them to do. This is illustrated by our surveys among focus groups in Australia, to be discussed in the next section.

The paranoia about 'Chinese' influence and United Front Work activities intensified after the Australian Broadcasting Commission's (ABC) Four Corners exposé 'Power and Influence' in 2017.[23] Before the Chinese influence debate broke out, many saw China's media industries as an opportunity to enhance collaborations. Early media collaborations with China were mostly conducted in the spheres of print media, satellite TV and film along with some sporadic initiatives in television. Australia was the first foreign nation to have a private investment in China's state-owned media. The Seven Network, one of three key commercial media corporations in Australia, initiated a collaborative venture with the *Shanghai Daily* in 2008. This relationship, which was brokered by the media magnate Kerry Stokes, was intended to help the Shanghai Daily become more 'Western' in its editorial outlook. The challenge of toeing the line with the regulators in China eventually proved too difficult and Stokes withdrew the company's media involvement, although his company maintained a presence in other areas including agricultural equipment. Even earlier than Stokes, News Corporation CEO Rupert Murdoch had opened his satellite TV campaign in the region, buying the Asian-based Star TV in 1993.[24] Murdoch went on to establish a television production company in 2006 in Shanghai. Canxing (literally 'shiny stars'), as it was called, co-produced Mandarin-language television content for Star TV. The Chinese production company later played a key role in licensing and developing popular reality TV formats, including *The Voice of China*.[25]

Film production, distribution and festivals are other important areas of collaboration. China has a strong demand for high-level skills in post-production, sound, music and visual effects business. Australia, like many other nations, has eyed the world's biggest screen industry, now with the largest number of studios and highest box office revenues. The Chinese screen presence in Australia is however uneven, often invisible to most Australians. Many Chinese-language films are screened in cinemas and at film festivals (via the International Chinese Film Festival and Golden Koala Chinese Festival, for example) as well as suburban cinemas where Chinese-speaking populations are dominant (Sunnybank in Brisbane or Box Hill in Melbourne, for example). Likewise, in New Zealand the distribution chains Event Cinemas and Hoyts regularly feature mainstream Chinese films with the majority of the screenings in Auckland, which accounts for 69 per cent of New Zealand's Chinese population.[26]

China and Australia signed a film co-production Memorandum of Understanding Treaty in 2007 but by 2020 only four films had been completed. One of these, *Children of the Silk Road*, was actually completed before the treaty was signed. Two others were produced in 2011: *The Dragon Pearl* (directed by Mario Andreccio) and *33 Postcards* (directed by Pauline Chan).[27] None have achieved any noteworthy box office success in either Australia or China. An Australian production without Chinese investment, *Mao's Last Dancer* (2009, directed by Bruce Beresford) was shot in China and was critically acclaimed internationally. It earned US$5 million in the United States and over US$22 million worldwide, which according to Stan Rosen compared favourably with most Chinese films internationally.[28] Another film that achieved a somewhat unexpected success is *Bait* 3D, a cheap 3D thriller about a rogue shark in a flooded supermarket. This was made under the Australia–Singapore film treaty, together with Chinese investment and distribution assistance. The film earned over AU$40 million at cinemas worldwide, and was successful in the Chinese market, generating AU$27 million.[29]

The film co-production pathway is rarely smooth and success is often hard to gauge, depending on where the target market is. A number of projects have never got past the concept stage. While Chinese film personnel are willing to come to Australia to sound out projects, a large part of the problem is script development. Storyboards about Chinese lost in remote Australia, unable to communicate or searching for gold illustrate a kind of reserve exoticism. Similarly, Australian co-productions set in China such as *The Dragon Pearl* and *Guardians of the Tomb* are likewise built around cultural stereotypes such as lost treasures or ancient labyrinths. Chinese producers, and presumably audiences, see Australia as a primitive country. In 2016, the Chinese TV reality show *Where Are We Going Dad?*, in which fathers and their one-child offspring go off together to experience nature, filmed several episodes in the cosmopolitan wine-growing region of Margaret River, 240 kilometres south of Perth in Western Australia. The storyline was sold to Chinese audiences as 'back to the stone age'. It's evidently easier to pitch projects with Chinese film-makers than complete them, and the difficulties include not only cultural stereotypes but running the gauntlet of censors. New Zealand followed Australia in signing a film co-production treaty in 2010 and although no projects have yet to be finalized, there was a great deal of media enthusiasm for an animated movie called *Beast of Burden* in 2016.

Increased demand in Australia for Chinese audiovisual content followed the influx of migration from the PRC. Prior to the digital age much of the content came from Chinatowns in the major cities. Within a decade after 1989 and following a rapid increase of PRC migrants via family reunions, audiovisual services were increasingly provided by mainland Chinese entrepreneurs. Video cassettes and DVDs could be rented at Chinatown outlets. Video stores would either stock Mainland Chinese videos, mostly China Central TV serials, or deal with Hong Kong distributors, for instance ATV and TVB Cantonese entertainment.[30] Initially CCTV operated as a distribution platform for Mandarin content, but this has diversified with multiple players competing for the spoils. In fact, Chinese communities were among the first to purchase satellite receivers to receive media signals from home; by the mid-2000s set-top boxes were available and packaged content, including entertainment and variety, was readily accessible.

Chinese content is also supplied by the Australian federal government-funded multicultural Special Broadcasting Service (SBS). Services provided by SBS include the national CCTV news bulletin, a smattering of Chinese movies especially around the Chinese spring and autumn holiday seasons and the Chinese dating show *If You Are the One (feicheng wurao)*. The last of these is especially noteworthy as it goes against the popular belief that Chinese-language content is unmarketable in Anglophone domains. The show, or at least the format for the show, originated in Australia in 2008, where it was developed by the Seven Network as *Taken Out*. The idea behind the format is that one heterosexual male has the chance to choose a date from among 24 female contestants on a panel, as long as the female contestant leaves their light on, indicating willingness. A panellist who doesn't leave the light on might still be chosen by the male contestant. The format was sold to Fremantle Media in the UK and rebranded as *Take Me Out*, then sold back to Hunan Satellite TV, before it was copied by Jiangsu Satellite TV.[31]

In Australia *If You Are the One* succeeded beyond expectations, after its initial screening on SBS since 2014. Wanning Sun and Jing Han identify an interesting cultural conundrum, namely, a scornful attitude among Chinese academics and elites to the show's success.[32] The Chinese central government has in the main adjudicated the benchmark of Chinese cultural products worthy of representing the nation. According to Sun and Han, the perception in China is that this show plays no role in lifting China's image. Audiences overseas have begged to differ. According to one of the producers responsible for editing and subtitling, 'Chinese culture is exposed, not lectured on.'[33] Many viewers watch *If You Are the One* to learn Chinese; others are curious about life in China. One might then be forgiven for asking, Is this programme 'telling China's stories well'?

In the wake of the success of *If You Are the One*, SBS was approached by Jiangsu Satellite TV to take another show called *The Strongest Brain* (*zuiqiang danao*) which was very popular in China at the time and featured contestants who demonstrated incredible feats of memory recall rather than banal commentaries of talk show hosts and pubescent adolescents seeking commitment. *The Strongest Brain* had a very brief run on SBS. Other shows that have attempted to emulate the success of *If You Are the One* on SBS, such as *Where Are We Going Dad?*, *Meet the Parents* and *Dating with Parents*, have not fared well, although they can be found on YouTube. In these kinds of shows the family plays a decisive role. While the popularity of *If You Are the One* suggests that dating culture in China has commonalities with Australia, the introduction of the family introduces an element of cultural dissonance. But there is recognition of similarity, compared with distrust that exists in other media forms. Some segments of Chinese culture are evidently changing and for want of a better word, modernizing to the extent that non-PRC viewers can empathize, while other segments of Chinese culture such as family relationships and social hierarchies remain alien to non-PRC societies.

Much of the show's success among non-PRC audiences is due to English subtitles provided by SBS. A good question to consider is what is lost in translation, or alternatively, How does subtitling smooth over cultural differences? Sun and Han write about this very problem. They say that innocuous expressions in Chinese can acquire a different meaning when directly translated into English; for instance, phrases like 'living with your parents in-law' or 'handing over your salary to your wife'.[34] Likewise, the occupational and aspirational proclivities of the Chinese contestants appear to be very materialistic, and not what one might expect of a developing country with a recent history of egalitarian communism. The attraction for viewers who are bilingual may be the gaps in translation but by the same token, literal translations are likely to evoke bemusement among native Australian audiences.

Reception of Chinese cultural content in Australia and New Zealand

Chinese audiovisual content is invariably targeted at Chinese-speaking audiences in Australia and New Zealand. Subtitled content is most likely to be found on SBS or in movies shown as part of film festivals. The question is, How effective is Chinese cultural content in communicating with non-Chinese-speaking communities in the antipodes? Research has shown that apart from linguistic and digital competency, political orientation and cultural stereotypes are factors that impact on the consumption and reception of Chinese cultural content.

For many people residing in Australia and New Zealand, Taiwan is not seen as part of China and Hong Kong is reluctantly part of the PRC. It is surprising therefore that *Crouching Tiger Hidden Dragon*, directed by a Taiwanese and produced by a consortium of companies including Sony Pictures and Columbia Pictures Asia, is regularly mentioned as a Chinese film. Of course, China does claim this film as one of its own. Yet Ang Lee is ostensibly a Western-style director, using Western storytelling frames. But herein lies the issue of cultural recognition. Many people can't differentiate when they see Chinese stories and Chinese actors. China is simultaneously complex and stereotypical in peoples' imaginations. Documentaries about China occasionally find their way on to SBS in Australia as well as the other national public broadcaster, the ABC. Current affairs feature news stories about the PRC, mostly in regard to negative depictions of the Chinese government. Commercial networks do not broadcast Chinese-language films or indeed any other foreign language films in Australia. For people unfamiliar with Chinese culture, Chinese cinema can present a considerable cognitive challenge. Political tensions between nations as well as cultural stereotypes frequently impact on reception.

A study of reception among non-Chinese audiences that factors in political events was conducted in Melbourne in September 2017 and October 2018 by Nicole Talmacs.[35] Thirty-one participants (16 female and 15 male) living in Australia with a range of cultural backgrounds were shown one or more of five films: these ranged from a teenage romance *Forever Young* (2015, directed by He Jiong), a Chinese-Hollywood co-production *The Great Wall* (2016, directed by Zhang Yimou) and two official Sino-Australian co-productions *33 Postcards* (2011, directed by Pauline Chan) and the adventure film *Guardians of the Tomb* (2018, directed by Kimble Rendell). The final film shown was the comedy *Goodbye Mr Loser* (2017, directed by Damo Peng and Fei Yan). None of the selected audience expressed familiarity with Chinese cinema, with only a few mentioning Ang Lee's *Crouching Tiger Hidden Dragon* as a Chinese film of note while three persons admitted having previously seen films by Zhang Yimou. The audience were surveyed before and after about attitudes to China, for instance, questions such as knowing who the leader of China is, but also regarding social issues and the threat, imagined or real, of China. The main problem of the research, however, is the nature of the films surveyed, which aside from *The Great Wall*, don't convey ideas about a rising China, which purportedly is the premise of the research project, considering the amount of 'priming' of the audiences.[36] In fact, what is evident in this study is the high degree of confirmation bias: people see what they believe. Respondents saw evidence of a rising China and 'recognized' the foregrounding of propaganda in the films. The overall impressions were not favourable. The priming no doubt contributed to activating bias.[37]

Another study conducted in New Zealand in 2019 reveals interesting findings of the consumption of Chinese cinema, noting that New Zealand has significant theatrical release of Chinese blockbusters via Hoyts and Event Cinemas, particularly in Auckland and Wellington where there are large communities of Chinese and where these chains largely operate.[38] In addition to theatrical release, the research takes into account releases on the film festival circuit, namely the New Zealand International Film Festival (NZIFF), the biennial Chinese film festival known as CFFNZ and film events organized by the Confucius Institute at the University of Wellington. Box office results for theatrical releases showed that the animation *Ne Zha* (directed by Yu Yang), the sci-fi blockbuster *The Wandering Earth* (directed by Frant Gwo) and the patriotic documentary *My People, My Country* (directed by Chen Kaige and others, made to celebrate the 70th anniversary of the PRC) filled the top three places. They were followed by the US–Chinese production *The Farewell* (directed by Lulu Wang). There was, however, a significant drop in revenue from 3rd to 4th, despite the fact that *The Farewell* was released in 28 theatres and had significant media exposure on commercial media outlets. What this seems to reveal is that while *The Farewell* played well across cinematic communities in Auckland, its message of caring for family didn't connect as well with Chinese diasporic audiences.[39]

Moreover, although *Ne Zha* was confined to just 12 cinemas, these cinemas were proximate to the distribution of Chinese communities; in its opening week the film averaged 18 daily screenings in Auckland. The independent film *Ash Is Purest White*, directed by the independent film-maker Jia Zhangke, did not get a mainstream theatrical release although it was chosen by the Confucius Institute's director on the pretext that it gave an important insight into contemporary China. It is also interesting that most of the films that did feature in theatrical releases and which ranked highly had Hong Kong directors, either as Hong Kong/China co-production films or Made-in-China. Huffer concludes that the popularity of blockbusters servicing the overseas Chinese community has had the effect of marginalizing Chinese independent cinema, even reducing its presence in film festivals.[40]

Reluctant consumers

To better understand how Chinese media fared in Australia we initially conducted two focus groups in Perth: the first one in early February 2020 comprised seven people, of whom three were of Anglo heritage, three were first-generation Asian-Australians and one was a recent migrant from the PRC. The youngest among this group was in her 20s and the rest ranged from late 30s to early 50s. The second group in late February 2020 numbered 24 participants, all of whom were undertaking Masters degrees by coursework at Curtin University. They were aged mostly in their late 20s, with the youngest in early 20s but mostly falling in the range of 30–50 years. Among the 31 participants in Perth, there were 11 males and 20 females, while 5 were international students from Nepal, Africa, India and Dubai. The focus groups in Melbourne and Sydney were conducted in early March, with 17 participants in Melbourne (12 males; 5 females) and 19 in Sydney (4 males; 15 females) and their age ranging from the early 20s to late 50s and composing of people in tertiary education and full-time employment.

The focus group participants were shown 21 slides to elicit cultural recognition, misrecognition or degrees of familiarity. The moderator began by showing logos of Chinese digital tech companies and their products – for example, Sina Weibo, WeChat, TikTok, Taobao, AliPay, Baidu, Ant Financial and Tencent. This was followed by slides of promotional images of some well-known Chinese-language content including some that might be recognized as having non-PRC elements; for instance, the 2013 Hong Kong kung fu movie, *The Grandmaster* (directed by Wong Kar-Wai), and the 2011 TV serial *Empresses in the Palace*, which featured actresses from Taiwan. In the Melbourne and Sydney groups we replaced *The Grandmaster* with the blockbuster *Wolf Warrior 2* (2015, directed by Wu Jing) and added two hybrid items, co-produced by Western companies, that is, *Mulan*[41] and *Kung Fu Panda*.

Other images included head shots of the founder-CEOs of the BAT, all well-known figures in China: Jack Ma (Ma Yun), Robin Li (Li Yanhong) and Pony Ma (Ma Huateng). Discussion prompts included: 'name three things you know about China'; 'name three things you know about Chinese culture'; 'name three brands/ products/films you know of, admire, like or use'; 'what are the three words that come to mind when you see the words "Made in China"?'; and 'do you shop online, and if you do, what platform do you use?'

Chinese films like *The Wolf Warrior* (2015) and its sequel (2017) that literally exploded in China were hugely popular among Chinese students and migrants in Australia. The patriotic Chinese Rambo portrayed in the movie, although resonating strongly with people of PRC background, had little or no influence, however, on non-Chinese population. Our focus group discussions revealed that the vast majority could not recognize the Chinese blockbuster, despite posters conspicuously displayed in the CBD of Sydney and Melbourne at the times of their Australia screenings. Nor could non-Chinese participants recognize the popular Chinese TV serial *Empresses in the Palace*.

This lack of recognition stands in contrast to familiarity with Disney's *Mulan* and DreamWorks' *Kung Fu Panda*: almost all participants in Sydney and Melbourne recognized the images from the two movies immediately. This shows how cultural assimilation – of Chinese cultural elements (kung fu and folk stories) by the US film industry – works in using foreign tales to tell Western-styled stories. *Kung Fu Panda* is, to use a Chinese scholar's words, 'an American panda in Chinese clothing'.[42] The transculturalization of Chinese stories by global Hollywood and the hybridization process are not merely about mixing, blending, borrowing or synthesizing, but involve intricate processes of 'deculturalization', 'acculturalization', and 'reculturalization' to make ethnic cultural elements universally appealing, to both the Western and non-Western markets.[43] Cross-cultural communication is never just about what one says (persuasion) but about influencing perceptions; it is achieved through content reception and impact as well as distribution and reach. We will return to this important point soon.

Our focus group surveys found that age rather than gender matters when it comes to people's familiarity with Chinese cultural content. To the small number of middle-aged participants (aged 45–65) across the three sites, everything we showed was new, completely alien, almost a parallel universe. Their recognition of the Chinese digital platform logos and faces of BAT founders was extremely low. TikTok was the only platform recognized, only by a few, and largely because younger family members had mentioned it in their hearing. None among this older group, however, was aware that TikTok is the global version of Douyin, nor did they seem to care when so informed. Yet, even when Anglo-Australians in the group could not identify Jack Ma from his photo, his reputation as a digital titan from China meant that his name itself met with instant recognition.

The younger cohort, in contrast, is more cosmopolitan in their media consumption habits. Many recognized WeChat, Weibo, TikTok, Huawei, Alipay and Jack Ma (called by some 'the Alibaba guy') straightaway. A few have been on TikTok; a very small number have WeChat on their phones, only to communicate with their Chinese acquaintances. Among the younger cohorts were a number of Asian-Australians and Asian students from South East Asia. Unsurprisingly, they show how *the degree* of cultural proximity and familiarity with China and Chinese culture matters in the reception of Chinese cultural content. For the Asian-Australian participants, particularly those of Chinese heritage from South East Asia, there was the expected in-betweenness but also some surprising gaps in knowledge or recognition of the visual clues on content, digital brands, e-wallets, games and e-commerce platforms. Many not only recognized logos and Jack Ma like the young cohort (irrespective of race and cultural background) but they also knew of the posters of Chinese movies and TV shows, although they were not able to tell the exact titles; that is, they remembered seeing the posters somewhere.

Cultural familiarity often leads to curiosity and a willingness to know about other cultures and their political systems. This is not limited to Asian-Australians. One Australian student in Perth who said she had spent time in China on an exchange programme had seen Jiang Wen's film *In the Heat of the Sun* (1994) and Feng Xiaogang's *Youth* (2017) and admitted to enjoying the former. This was interesting in that both films were about the Cultural Revolution, a topic that is of marginal appeal to mainstream Chinese audiences.

Overall, the recognition of China's presence was alarmingly superficial considering these young cohorts were graduates and postgraduates in Australian universities, where they would have had exposure to China, including Chinese students, on campus and in their classrooms. The consumption of Made-in-China cultural products among the Anglo university participants was minimal or non-existent. WeChat fared somewhat better, with half of our focus group participants (of all ages) recognizing the logo with a few saying they had used it (although none were regular users). WeChat was sometimes confused with WhatsApp, which is widely used in South East Asia. Sometimes respondents misspelled the brand, indicating vague awareness. Where brand symbols were similar, respondents demonstrated a stronger awareness of Western brands, which was expected. For example, when presented with the Tencent QQ messenger brand logo featuring a Penguin, most respondents mistook it for Club Penguin, a Disney-owned massively popular multiplayer online role-playing game in which all the characters are penguins. When there was a low level of recognition, some respondents tended to use the descriptor 'Chinese' before naming a Western brand; 'Chinese twitter', for example, was the answer given by a third-year undergraduate student on the sight of the Alipay logo, but not Sina Weibo. The colour blue is used by both Alibaba and Twitter, which may have prompted the response.

TikTok, on the other hand, was known by almost all the younger groups, but most did not know it was a Chinese brand. The example of TikTok illustrates the reality that many Chinese products and services can succeed when they are stripped of much of their unique Chinese elements either through offering an international version or presenting themselves as more neutral, for instance, Western-like or hybridized. The Chinese consumer electronics brands that were most recognized included Huawei, Lenovo and Asus.

This can probably be attributed to their presence in the local retail stores as well as advertising exposure. Over half of the respondents shop online, where most popular destinations are Amazon, eBay, Etsy and official websites of the chosen brands. Nobody, however, mentioned Taobao and only one person mentioned AliExpress; both are owned by Chinese e-commerce and tech giant Alibaba.

From the responses, albeit limited, it appears that many of China's digital products and services are unnoticed. Yet Chinese products are widely available. They are mostly cheaper android phones including Oppo, Huawei and Xiaomi. While everyone seemed to agree that 'everything is made in China', few agreed that this makes them Chinese brands or products. Although participants tried to recall when prompted, there was nothing like the recognition they would have for Facebook, Instagram, Twitter, Amazon, eBay, the latest movie from Netflix, or games like Overwatch by Blizzard entertainment.

The overall impression among the groups was that Chinese digital companies offer similar services as their Western counterparts, which means Chinese users have a similar digital lifestyle as people in Australia do. However, as the case of mistaking Alipay with Chinese Twitter shows, the respondents did not know much about specific features of the Chinese products and could not point out the differences from the comparable Western brands. While it is perhaps usual for people to develop understanding about unfamiliar products or services by drawing on their existing knowledge of comparable ones, by equating the two, some respondents hinted that Chinese digital companies were copying from the 'original'.

This perception of Chinese brands as copycats emerged again when participants were asked about their impression of 'Made in China'. Apart from associating this concept with 'the world's factory', characterized by mass production and cheap prices, many respondents were under the impression that fake, pirated or grey-market products are pervasive. This perception was also found in responses to the politically sensitive topics concerning China. For example, the topic of Huawei's struggles and alleged spying was mentioned by one person surprisingly as an example of their familiarity with Chinese stories (one of the question cues); others picked up on this cue and linked it to maltreatment of Uyghurs in Xinjiang and China's surveillance state. The issue of labour exploitation and the geopolitical implications of China in the global value chain were prominent in participants' responses. One person commented, 'I don't know or use any Chinese products that I'm aware of […] Apple products are manufactured there so I suppose that counts?' Another person mentioned 'questionable quality, short durability, and cheap labour' as their response to the question on 'the first three words that come to mind when you see the words "Made in China"?'. There was a sense of unfamiliarity with

Chinese products and a somewhat dubious attitude, if not deep-seated distrust, towards 'Made-in-China' products and content. In this sense, China's attempt to upgrade the image associated with 'Made in China' still has a long way to go among middle-class consumers in Australia.

When it came down to perceptions of China and Chinese culture with the question, 'What do you know about China?', the immediate responses were long history/civilization, large population, food, authoritarianism/communism, control/censorship (e.g. people mentioning facial recognition, persecution of Uyghurs, Mao and Xi Jinping) and diversity (linguistic and geographic). Others mentioned Confucianism, the 5G problem with Huawei, labour abuse (sweatshops) and the Great Wall of China. With regard to naming Chinese culture, responses included tradition (including superstition about numbers), traditional festivals (e.g. the Spring Festival and Dragon Boat Festival), traditional culture (kung fu, importance of family, lion dance), tea and food (dumplings, mooncakes and strange food), architecture (e.g. the Great Wall of China) and avant-garde art. Only a couple of people from the younger cohort groups mentioned Chinese high-tech products like Huawei, Xiaomi and Lenovo.

With regard to Chinese films, drama series and games, recognition saw a sharp decline. A small number of respondents demonstrated surface knowledge about Chinese celebrities, although this was often mismatched. These are typically Chinese stars who have gained reputation in Hollywood, such as Jackie Chan and Zhang Ziyi. *Crazy Rich Asian, If You Are the One, The Grandmaster, Kung Fu Panda* are some titles that received sporadic mentions. Traditional culture and internet censorship featured prominently in participants' response to their overall knowledge about Chinese culture and China more broadly. Sometimes, internet censorship is mentioned in close connection with the political system. It seems that Chinese culture is most well-known for its traditions, forms of culture such as traditional opera, calligraphy, kung fu, Spring Festival and not surprisingly Chinese food. As mentioned earlier, digital entrepreneurs in China were hardly recognized with the exception of Jack Ma. Of course, Ma has been actively engaging with world economic events ranging from interviews at the WTO, multiple press interviews and appearances at the World Economic Forum and commencement speeches at universities. In other words, as with the interviewees from Malaysia and Singapore (Chapter 7), recognition of Jack Ma stems from his exposure in Westernized media and societies rather than China-driven, -produced or -exported media. Ma is by all account's China's most prominent influencer outside the PRC. What this suggests then is that for China's digital platforms, entrepreneurs and cultural products to gain broader recognition among non-PRC societies, they need first to attract the attention, if not the support, of media based in the West.

As noted in Chapter 5, we conducted a third survey in August 2019 that attracted 520 valid responses. The total number of respondents living in Australia at the time of the survey was 241.[44] This represented a significant cohort to compare with the focus groups. Findings from the online surveys shed light on the variegated nature of consumption and understanding of Chinese media. In particular it was evident that having some cultural connection with China was almost a precondition to want to explore Chinese media and culture, or even to opt in to do the survey. The focus groups had revealed minimal interest in China and Chinese stories, which is of course a worry for the Chinese government as it seeks to 'tell its stories well'. In contrast with the focus groups which were more random selections of participants, the respondents to the survey had a reason for participating. The survey was sent via email and social media (Facebook, Messenger, WeChat) and via contacts. People were asked 'what is your connection with China?' Most people who responded claimed an 'existing connection'. The question allowed only one response. A relatively high number (23.4%) had Chinese heritage, a further 7.1 per cent has a family member of Chinese heritage, 5.3 per cent had a spouse of Chinese background, 21.6 per cent had Chinese friends, 14.5 per cent had learned some Chinese language, 22.5 per cent said they had no connection.

For the Australian respondents Facebook Messenger was the dominant daily messaging service (79.3% used it daily or sometimes whereas the comparable data for WeChat use was 32.4%). Tellingly, the most cited response for not watching entertainment content produced in China by Australian respondents was 'The story is not appealing', much higher (41.7%) than comparable responses in Hong Kong and Taiwan (30.0% and 30.2%, respectively). The most popular platforms for accessing Chinese content were Netflix and YouTube (36.5% and 45.5% respectively). TikTok just managed double figures (10.3%) and Youku was 13.5 per cent. Other Chinese streaming platforms were hardly mentioned, although respondents had a long list to choose from including Bilibili, Tencent Video, Viki, Vue and iQiyi.

Conclusion

This chapter has explored cultural interactions over the past century between China and Australia and New Zealand and has analysed contemporary perceptions of Chinese cultural products in Australia through focus group studies and surveys. Our research goes beyond the normal focus on the Chinese diaspora and their media consumption habits[45] to examine the responses of non-PRC migrant persons in Australia to Chinese cultural content and digital platforms. We have attempted to find out if media narratives can transfer across cultural boundaries and whether Chinese public diplomacy through the transnational flow of popular cultural products and digital platforms can achieve the country's soft power goals.

It is evident that Chinese culture is understood and received very differently among overseas consumers. Yet a diverse range of industry intermediaries, content brokers, digital platforms and many other informal channels such as influencers are helping to disseminate Chinese content. Collectively they can contribute to increasing Chinese cultural influence in the antipodes, among and beyond the Chinese-speaking population. Chinese digital platforms have a long way to go to challenge the hegemony of Facebook, Google, YouTube and Messenger. But this is entirely expected. The Chinese living in Australia and New Zealand, however, have a choice of platforms. They can be patriotic or 'qualified' on WeChat moments or Douyin but adopt a different persona on Instagram or TikTok. They are better positioned than people in China (including non-Chinese nationals), who are contained and insulated by the 'walled' Chinese internet, to bridge the gaps in cross-cultural communication between China and the rest of the world. Their agency, and its limits, should be explored in future research.

Chapter 9

FROM CULTURAL PRESENCE TO INNOVATIVE NATION

A theatre of war during the period of China's great 'People's Revolution', the Asia-Pacific region is now embroiled in a cold war developing between the forces of Western liberalism and an emboldened PRC. Indeed, the rise of China and its global ambitions have caused tension among its rivals and partners alike. President Xi Jinping has extolled the benefits of globalization even as China's propaganda forces engage in a 'discourse war'. Xi's signature project, the Belt and Road Initiative (BRI), which has been viewed with suspicion by the United States and some of its allies, is an example of the build-up of Chinese power in Asia in the twenty-first century.[1] Meanwhile, several Western-allied nations have erected physical and logistical barriers to the entry of Chinese digital companies; for instance, bans have been imposed on the 5G network infrastructure services of China's national champion Huawei by the United States, Australia, New Zealand, Japan and Taiwan.[2]

Chinese presence is everywhere in the world, from Chinatowns to international students to branded digital devices, but does this presence translate into cultural power? Drawing on the discussions in the previous three chapters, this final chapter summarizes some of the challenges that Chinese digital platforms face as they navigate a path into the Asia-Pacific and beyond. The findings from our study of Chinese digital platforms in the Asia-Pacific may offer a glimpse of the future of Chinese influence and cross-cultural relations.

In a recent work entitled *China and the West*, Peter Nolan writes effusively about the achievements of Chinese civilization and culture. Whereas the West has wrought terrible environmental damage on the world, not to mention centuries of colonialism, Nolan says that the Chinese government seeks to achieve mutual benefits for all countries.[3] Martin Jacques, a fellow admirer of the China Model, proposes that China is a civilizational state,[4] a view heavily promoted by Chinese Communist Party propaganda apparatchiks such as Zhang Weiwei, author of several books including *The China Horizon: Glory and Dreams of a Civilizational State*. Speaking about his experiences of 'going out',

Zhang says, 'Going abroad makes one feel more patriotic. This is far more effective than the Party's political education.'[5]

Hugo de Burgh is likewise optimistic about China's global image. He writes, 'The Chinese model of development is admired and it is very probable that in many areas of the world, when doing business and politics, it is Chinese norms that now determine how things should be done rather than Anglophone ones.'[6] Where these areas are, however, is not specified, possibly somewhere in the Asia-Pacific or along the Belt and Road. Furthermore, it should be noted that people in Singapore, Malaysia, Hong Kong, Taiwan, Australia and New Zealand, the subjects of our analysis, are very much disposed towards 'Anglophone' norms when doing business, for instance, regarding intellectual property, freedom of information and rule of law.

Research on how Chinese companies are going out and where Chinese companies are going has increased markedly.[7] In particular, market analysts have sought to document the footprints of Chinese overseas investments, projects and markets, as well as noting opportunities and challenges. A plethora of industry information is available and governments outside China have rushed to broker free trade deals, often turning a blind eye to human rights issues. Start-up communities in the Asia-Pacific have oriented themselves eastwards or in the case of Australia and New Zealand northwards, noting the technological gains made in China in such a short time, as well as the potential of using China as a springboard into emerging markets, for instance, those found along the Belt and Road.

A key theme of this book has been the integration of culture and technology. China's cultural industries were launched in 2001, the same year that China joined the WTO. As noted in Chapter 1, in the following decade the focus was on extending material culture: theme parks, production bases, paintings, artefacts and movies. By the time Web 2.0 allowed people in China to join in the online creative carnival, Chinese officials had to confront the problem of other cultures penetrating its territory by stealth. Foreign media was relentless; it was much different from the staid and formulaic production of domestic main melody TV dramas and patriotic films; and it was finding 'devious' ways to enter the Chinese cyberspace. The Chinese government used firewalls and quotas to hold back the waves, buying time for China to develop its own digital media industry champions. By the end of the decade Chinese platforms such as iQiyi and Tencent Video were sending cultural content abroad, finding grateful audiences in the Asia-Pacific. Significantly, moreover, many people in the diaspora were accessing Made-in-China content on YouTube.

In the field of the internet and digital platforms, it is now second-generation start-ups that are helping Chinese soft power to become visible beyond the Chinese-speaking world. As noted in our field work, in many cases people are blissfully unaware that they are using Made-in-China platforms or are participating in the Chinese sharing economy. They may be using TikTok or the ride-hailing service Didi but the association with authoritarianism found in media content is absent. China's new generation of tech company CEOs meanwhile are entangled in a complex web of global financial capitalists, corporate interests, governmental policies, international politics and public opinion. They attend international tech festivals as special guests and parade their innovations, often flamboyantly as in the case of Jack Ma, China's self-appointed influencer.

Apart from the differences in cultural contexts, technological standards and regulatory and legal systems governing the internet, the biggest challenge outside the PRC is arguably the suspicion, if not hostility, from Western countries towards Chinese investment in key infrastructure and cyberspace governance projects. Chinese digital platforms are often caught in the crossfire between the US-led Western alliance and the protectionist policies of nation-states. The Sino-US relation, in particular, is a key challenge to tech platforms that are 'Made in China'. How Chinese platforms respond to the geopolitical–economic dynamics across the Pacific will be a key indicator of their market performance.

Within China itself, the nation's ambitions to go out are caught up in philosophical debates about a great civilization returning to former glory – playing to the national rejuvenation discourse. One of the most cited justifications for China's rise is the short history of Western liberalism, only 200 years – it is bound to fail, whereas the communitarian model of China has stood the test of time. Of course, it was only 60 years ago during the Cultural Revolution that China's tradition was viewed by Mao Zedong as 'a cultural lodestone'.[8] But as China rises, once again the theme is people. In 2015, the Chinese government launched an aspirational concept called the 'community of shared future' (*renlei mingyun gongtongti*), an idea extracted from the Chinese philosophical adage 'all under heaven' (*tianxia*), referring to a moral civilizational order unbounded by geography or ethnicity. If Chinese cultural officials were to pen a script for a sci-fiction movie, one suspects it would be based on Chinese philosophical tenets, spiced with lashings of ethno-nationalism and geographical certitude. In fact, such a film was produced in 2018. In *Wandering Earth*, a Chinese team working with Russian and third-world comrades save planet Earth and human civilization by the use of incredible technological ingenuity.

For many observers situated outside the People's Republic of China the image of a shared future presided over by benign technocrats does not square with messages conveyed by Western media, which have in the modern era cast China's leadership as untrustworthy and its people as brainwashed victims. A sci-fi film about China, if Hollywood were to risk upsetting the Chinese government and Chinese nationalists, might include dystopian images of surveillance, mind control and even cultural genocide. Unsurprisingly, China's leading cadres rehearse Comrade Xi's Chinese Dream mantra, which extols a glorious unbroken civilization. However, as Gregory Lee points out, the inherent contradiction of the depiction of an ancient civilization is that 'China is now fully integrated into economic, technological, spectacular global modernity'.[9] The problem with the community of shared future, moreover, is that the vision is yet to be widely endorsed or shared beyond China. This politicization, combined with a somewhat irrational fear of large numbers (China has the world's largest population), has an impact on the image of China and the reception of its culture abroad.

Before returning to consider China's image outside China, it's worth asking: How does technology within China make people feel about their nation and their culture? Connectivity certainly allows people within the PRC to construct a far different imaginary of their nation than one normally sees outside the PRC, or in Western media. The mainstream media celebration of China's technological and material achievements has greatly boosted nationalism among Chinese people within the PRC.[10] Many do not and cannot understand the international distrust and hostility towards their motherland, even when they have left China. What they see is the shining armour of Chinese authoritarianism in managing China's massive population and restoring its pride after over a century of national humiliation.[11]

With the theme of rejuvenation ringing loudly, celebratory accounts of China's four 'new inventions' appeared in the Chinese media: these 'inventions' are high-speed rail, e-commerce, dockless shared bicycles and mobile payments. As travellers to China attest, China is far more advanced in many areas of its economy than 'foreigners' are led to believe. Shenzhen, a city of ten million people in south China, situated adjacent to Hong Kong in what is now called the Greater Bay, illustrates the new image of China for many. Shenzhen has grown from a fishing village in the 1980s to a dynamic modern city. In the 2000s, the city was known for its copy culture, attracting criticism for crass imitation. Lacking in the kind of cultural memory that marks cities like Beijing, Nanjing and Shanghai, Shenzhen developed artificial culture: theme parks with names like Window on the World that replicated global landmarks and an oil painting village where one could buy a fake Rembrandt or Van Gogh. Fast forward a decade and Shenzhen is the world's centre of artificial intelligence and home to some of the leading technology companies in China including Tencent, ZTE and Huawei. Billboards featuring virtual reality, makerspaces, drones and robotics sit alongside party propaganda for ecological and spiritual civilization.

According to government reports in China, the future of China will be greener, cleaner, beautiful and more creative.[12] 'Digital' and 'Beautiful China' projects are increasing; 'smart cities' are on the drawing board; existing cities are being upgraded (*shengji*); and $15 billion has reportedly been invested by the state in a China New Era Technology Fund to assist start-ups.[13] Projects targeted at delivering sustainable development and grassroots entrepreneurship are central to future thinking. Taobao (e-commerce) villages have allowed rural regions to tap into the booming digital economy. The ambitious Greater Bay Project in Guangdong Province in south China linking Shenzhen, Hong Kong, Macau, Foshan and Guangzhou exploits the region's leadership in technology.

In the cultural domain, the digitization of the past, such as the Mogao Grottoes in Dunhuang and Beijing's Forbidden Palace, attracts financial and technical support from internet companies including Tencent and Alibaba. Every year since 2018, a state-sponsored forum, which promotes itself as a Future Think Tank, brings together Chinese and international innovators from the creative community and from the fields of technology and science.[14] A forum called 2050 sponsored by Hangzhou Yunqi Science and Technology Innovation Foundation, with links to the internet giant Alibaba, advertises itself an international platform for knowledge sharing and technological advancement. The vision presented is of a digitally enhanced future where people are free to create, design, share and collaborate, a future in which virtual reality, 3D printing and artificial intelligence will provide solutions to social problems.

However, outside China, the political baggage of the authoritarian state weighs down China's ambitions to go global, whether this mission is to just 'tell its stories well' or for its enterprises to be regarded as successful international business entities. Ideological suspicion is never far away in the Western media, where a liberal world order has held sway for the past 200 years. Most Western media promote the view that their Chinese counterparts are instruments of control and are subject to draconian control. China's media globalization thus faces a crisis of credibility despite China's refurbished reputation as an innovative nation and a technologically advanced society.

In recent years bitter debates have taken place over the influence of Chinese tech companies, amid the rise of tech cold war.[15] This extends globally and is exacerbated by controversies over the Chinese telecommunications giant Huawei which purports to be a Chinese-style company with its workers as shareholders. Huawei's CEO Ren Zhengfei is on record as saying to the BBC: 'Huawei is a business organisation and we are rarely involved in politics.'[16] Of course, 'rarely' doesn't mean the same as 'never'. This is further complicated when China, Chinese, Chinese government and the CCP are conflated in public statements and narratives.[17] A recent report from a UK think tank asserts: '"China" today means the Chinese Communist Party (CCP)' [...] before clarifying with this statement: 'China is more complicated, as the threat is more subtle and the opportunity much greater.'[18] Conservative critics in Australia, like Clive Hamilton, author of *Silent Invasion*, have offered a more direct perspective: it is the government of China, not the Chinese people that is the core problem.[19] With regard to Chinese people, the former CEO of Hewlett Packard and unsuccessful Republican candidate, Carly Fiorina, maintained in 2015, 'the Chinese are not entrepreneurial, they don't innovate, and this is why they are stealing our intellectual property'.[20] This kind of racialization and stereotyping is the burden that Chinese digital enterprises carry when going overseas.

From disputes over Huawei's foreign influence, Alibaba's technology transfer and intellectual property rights,[21] to TikTok over its control of data, Chinese ideas of expansion are viewed as a serious threat to Western democracy. While most of the Chinese tech firms now expanding abroad are private entities and wear the masks of corporate capital, they cannot entirely distance themselves from politics when they are ostensibly responding to the state's BRI. Indeed, many start-ups align strongly with the infrastructural ambitions of the Chinese authorities, the techno-nationalist vision of an AI superpower, aiming to leapfrog collectively into an advanced technological future. Such techno-nationalist sentiments and discourse have dominated the trade war between the United States and China.[22] It is widely believed that Chinese digital platforms have not escaped the powerful influence of the Chinese Communist Party across many businesses, from content regulation to market prioritization.[23]

Tencent's WeChat, for example, is the most popular social media platform among the Chinese diasporas. Yet, it is regarded as a security risk by foreign government agencies and a highly censored space for individual users. The problem here is that it is widely used outside of mainland China, and for this reason it is regarded by media pundits and policy hawks as a channel for the dissemination of propaganda and as a tool of influence among the Chinese diaspora.[24]

TikTok is also viewed by some as 'a vector for censorship and surveillance'.[25] Its advanced AI-powered algorithm is believed to put the CCP and the CCP-led state in a vantage position to control and shape overseas Chinese-language media and export its surveillance authoritarianism overseas. In the United States, lawmakers are worried about how TikTok handles the data it gathers on its US-based users,[26] and what the Chinese company would do to help the Chinese government's broader AI and data ambitions to conquer the world. The claim that ByteDance is advancing Chinese foreign policy objectives abroad through TikTok is echoed in Australia. TikTok is under scrutiny for its ties to China, with some of Australia's 'top cyber and national security minds warning the app could potentially be used by Beijing authorities to influence and monitor millions of Australian users'.[27]

The exponential growth of TikTok in the United States poses a significant challenge to the Facebook empire. In 2019, it beat out Instagram and Facebook, and was only second to Facebook-owned WhatsApp in total downloads in 2019. Mark Zuckerberg fired a shot across the bows of TikTok, claiming the rise of Chinese internet enterprises was a threat to American democracy and freedom of speech. He warned, 'While our services, like WhatsApp, are used by protesters and activists everywhere due to strong encryption and privacy protections, on TikTok, the Chinese app growing quickly around the world, mentions of these protests are censored, even in the U.S. […] Is that the internet we want?'[28] Despite the denial by TikTok (among other Chinese companies) of any Chinese government influence over their content moderation policies, it seems that what will make or break a platform in the current context of the tech cold war are not just cutting-edge technologies or innovative features but the global public opinion that is shaped by soft power. To mitigate such accusations and suspicions of its China linkage, TikTok is considering moving its headquarters outside China.[29]

The growing pains of Chinese transnational digital companies are becoming more evident. One example is their leading role as content aggregators, especially when inappropriate user-generated content is allowed to circulate. This is a problem experienced by a number of leading global digital platforms. Facebook has been subject to increasing scrutiny for allowing fake news and inappropriate content and Zuckerberg has sought to rectify these issues. As Luzhou Li shows, the irony is that while Chinese media companies are heavily monitored within the PRC, outside the state's national boundaries they are more 'liberal' than Western companies.[30] It seems they are unprepared for free speech. BAT and BMT have all paid fines for pornographic or blasphemous content, fraudulent ads or breach of IPR in the United States, India and Indonesia. In response these companies have adopted creative solutions, including establishing local marketing teams, in-country moderators and public relations team based on local regulations and cultural values. Some have implemented a combination of AI and human censorship to filter inappropriate content.

At the end of the day, like most transnational media platforms, China's digital champions (including WeChat and TikTok) are driven by a capitalist expansionist logic. They source and distribute fast-moving content, much of which is fashionable and user generated. As we have seen in the focus groups and surveys, perception counts when it comes to consumption of foreign products, although the association with authoritarian China matters less when the products and services are no longer perceived as speaking for the Chinese state. Nevertheless, while the bulk of what is produced is purely commercial, ideology is embedded in products and services, often subliminally. Younger consumers are more likely to identify with the content than the ideology lurking in the shadows. Many platforms have deliberately de-sinicized in order to 'go out', making them more 'culturally odourless'.[31] The danger, however, is that in the future the state may choose to intervene in their overseas commercial activities, to utilize their success to insert its message of a rising China more directly, and if this happens China's digital champions will be caught between a rock and a hard place (*zuo you wei nan*). The political burden of the technocratic state is in turn further exacerbated by the close scrutiny of media and cultural content and the top-down approach by the state in international cultural diplomacy.

Having illustrated how Chinese cultural power is extending overseas and the challenges of overcoming 'threat' perceptions, we would like to end with a more positive note about China as an innovative nation. In the last 20 years, China has been transforming from the 'world's factory' to a modern services-led economy, with a focus on technology, innovation and entrepreneurship. Chinese cultural, media and communication industries are burdened by the country's political system and historical legacies; they are constrained by international technological, financial and political norms, standards and expectations; they are at the same time conditioned by contemporary geopolitics, particularly the new cold war.[32] As such, their transnational operation, structure and influence are contingent on a number of factors. The Chinese people are no less resourceful and creative than other peoples. Their ingenuity and pragmatism have seen innovative applications of cutting-edge technologies. However, to become an innovative nation requires more than the application or practical use (*yong*) of technologies, but the essence or superstructure (*ti*) that sustains efforts to seek innovative solutions to structural and systematic problems. Our effort to document and critique China's transformation from cultural power to innovative nation has just begun.

APPENDIX

SURVEY CONDUCTED FROM AUGUST TO DECEMBER 2019

Two previous surveys were conducted by the team in April 2018 and September 2018. This final survey sought to identify the attitudes of persons living outside China towards Made-in-China content and their propensity to use PRC digital platforms.

Thank you for linking to our survey. This survey is part of an Australian Research Council project 'Digital China: from Cultural Presence to Innovative Nation (2017–2019). More information about this project can be found at the Digital China website. The survey is designed for people currently living outside China.

Chinese entertainment content (film, TV, animation, games and online video) refers to content produced in the People's Republic of China including content co-produced in the PRC.

The survey is completely anonymous. Your answers will be treated as confidential and used only for the purposes of this project. The survey asks for information about your perception and consumption of Chinese media, including online media.

The survey will take less than 10 minutes of your time. Please select one answer for each question unless indicated other*wise*.

Your nationality (as it appears on your passport)

- Australia
- Hong Kong SAR
- Indonesia
- Japan
- Malaysia
- New Zealand
- PR China
- Singapore
- South Korea

- Taiwan
- Other (please specify)

Where do you live now?

- Australia
- Hong Kong SAR
- Indonesia
- Japan
- Malaysia
- New Zealand
- PR China
- Singapore
- South Korea
- Taiwan
- Other (please specify)

What is your age?

- Under 18
- 18–28
- 29–39
- 40–50
- 51–61
- Over 61

What is your gender?

- Male
- Female
- Other

Which of the following best describes your educational level? (Choose one answer only)

- Master's or higher degree
- Bachelor's degree
- High school or equivalent
- Below high school
- Other (please specify)

Have you ever viewed entertainment content produced in mainland China (film, TV, animation, games and online video)? (Choose one answer only)

- Yes
- No (please go to answer question 13)
- I've seen Chinese language content but I'm not certain of its origin

Please choose the best statement to describe your connection to China. (Choose one answer only)

- I am a Chinese national (i.e. passport)
- I have Chinese heritage
- My partner/spouse is ethnic Chinese
- Someone in my extended family is of Chinese heritage
- I have Chinese friends
- I have learned some Chinese language
- I have no connection to China
- Other reason, please specify

How would you rate your level of Chinese (including Mandarin, Cantonese and other dialects)? (Choose one answer only)

- Native speaker of Chinese
- Fluent, non-native
- Intermediate
- Basic
- I can't speak or read Chinese

Please select reasons why you might choose to watch entertainment content produced in mainland China. (multiple choices allowed)

- The story is appealing
- It features known stars or celebrities
- It has received positive reviews
- I'm attracted to the cultural elements
- I like the director or producer's work
- Other reason, please specify

Please select reasons why you might NOT view entertainment content produced in mainland China. (multiple choices allowed)

- The story is not appealing
- I'm not interested in viewing content that is censored
- It doesn't feature known stars or celebrities
- It hasn't received positive reviews
- I'm not attracted to the cultural elements
- I don't like the director or producer's work
- Other reason, please specify

Which platforms do you use to access entertainment content produced in mainland China? (multiple choices allowed)

- Bilibili （哔哩哔哩）
- Foxtel
- iQiYi （爱奇艺）
- Naver
- Netflix
- Tencent video （腾讯视频）
- TikTok (抖音)
- Viki
- Vue
- Youku (优酷)
- YouTube
- Other (please specify)

How do you rate the attractiveness (overall viewing appeal) of the following region/countries' entertainment media content?

0 None – 50 middle – 80–100 strong
Mainland China
HK SAR
Singapore
South Korea
Taiwan

APPENDIX

Please describe your use of the following online messaging platforms during a normal week.

	Never	Sometimes	Weekly	Daily
Facebook Messenger				
WhatsApp				
KaKao Talk				
WeChat (微信)				
QQ				
Line				

Please comment on your willingness to use the following online shopping sites/apps:

	I have never heard of it	very unwilling	unwilling	neutral	willing	very willing
Taobao (incl. Tmall)						
Jingdong (JD)						
eBay						
Amazon						
Gumtree						
Daraz						
G-Market						
Lazada						
Shopee						
Qo100						

NOTES

Introduction: A Giant Awakening?

1 Parag Khanna, *Connectography: Mapping the Global Network Revolution* ((London: Orion, Kindle Edition, 2016), Location 485.
2 Douglas Fuller writes about the influence of 'hybrid' ethnic Chinese films with links to Western capital a commitment to driving China's resurgence. For a discussion see Douglas Fuller, *Paper Tigers, Hidden Dragons: Firms and the Political Economy of China's Technological Development* (Oxford: Oxford University Press, 2016).
3 Our study is based on an Australian government-funded Australian Research Council project called Digital China: From Cultural Presence to Innovative nation. This project did not include Japan. The focus was on places and regions where there was existing fertile soil for the reception of Chinese culture. While the project did investigate South Korea, we chose not to include South Korean findings in this book due to time constraints on finalizing, that is the research on South Korea was incomplete.
4 The BRI refers to the 'belt', a maritime route traversing the South China Sea and the Malacca Straits, and an overland 'road', the latter connecting China to central Asia and Europe. The BRI is viewed, mostly by Western-based scholars, as an attempt to secure China's presence in South and Central Asia via physical infrastructure and international trade deals.
5 Michael Keane, Brian Yecies and Terry Flew, *Willing Collaborators: Foreign Partners in Chinese Media* (London: Rowman & Littlefield, 2018).
6 Michael Curtin, *Playing to the World's Biggest Audience: The Globalization of Chinese Film and Television* (Berkeley: University of California Press, 2007).
7 For a discussion of innovation in China and detailed analysis of high-tech policy see Richard Applebaum, Cong Cao, Xueying Han, Rachel Parker, and Denis Simon, *Innovation in China: Challenging the Global Science and Technology System* (London: Polity Press, 2019).
8 For a definition see 'Report of the Work of the Government', Third Session of the 12th National People's Congress, *China Daily*, 5 March 2015. Retrieved from http://www.chinadaily.com.cn/china/2015twosession/2015-03/05/content_19729663.htm.
9 Silvia Lindtner, 'Hackerspaces and the Internet of Things: How Makers Reinvent Industrial Production, Innovation and the Self', in *China's Contested Internet*, ed. Guobin Yang (Copenhagen: NIAS Press, 2015), 44–74.
10 Yuan Yang, 'China Turns Up Heat on Individual Users of Foreign Websites', 7 January 2019 www.ft.com/content/dda957be-1256-11e9-a581-4ff78404524e.
11 For figures on China's internet see Internet Live Stats. Retrieved from https://www.internetlivestats.com/internet-users/china/. Accessed 20 February 2020.

12 Michael Keane, *China's New Creative Clusters: Governance, Human Capital and Investment* (London: Routledge, 2011).
13 Kai-fu Lee, *AI Superpowers: China, Silicon Valley and the New World Order* (Boston: Houghton Mifflin Harcourt, 2018).
14 For a discussion of the field see David Kurt Herold and Gabriele de Seta, 'Through the Looking Glass: Twenty Years of Chinese Internet Research'. *Information Society: An International Journal* 31, no. 1 (2015): 68–82; see Jack Qiu and Joseph Man Chan, 'China Internet Studies: A Review of the Field', in *The Academy and the Internet*, ed. Helen Nissenbaum and Monroe Price (New York: Peter Lang, 2004), 275–307; and Jack L Qiu and Bu Wei, 'China ICT Studies: A Review of the Field, 1989–2012'. *China Review* 13, no. 2 (2013): 123–52.
15 For work in the political economy of the internet see Yuezhi Zhao. 'After Mobile Phones, What? Re-embedding the Social in China's "Digital Revolution"'. *International Journal of Communication* 1 (2007): 92–120 (29). Retrieved from https://ijoc.org/index.php/ijoc/article/view/5. For a variety of research in sociocultural spaces see Ya-Wen Lei, 'The Political Consequences of the Rise of the Internet: Political Beliefs and Practices of Chinese Netizens'. *Political Communication* 28, no. 3 (2011): 291–322; Jia Lu and Yunxi Qiu, 'Microblogging and Social Change in China'. *Asian Perspectives* 37 (2013): 305–31; Guobin Yang, *The Power of the Internet in China* (New York: Columbia University Press, 2009); Guobin Yang, 'Political Contestation in Chinese Digital Spaces: Deepening the Critical Inquiry'. *China Information* 28, no. 2 (2014): 135–44; Haiqing Yu, 'From Active Audience to Media Citizenship: The Case of Post-Mao China'. *Social Semiotics* 16, no. 2 (2006): 302–26; Daniela Stockmann, 'Online Media Publics in China: Who Seeks Information Online?' in *Urban Mobilization and New Media in Contemporary China*, ed. Lisheng Dong, Hanspeter Kriesi, and Daniel Kübler (London: Ashgate, 2015), 19–32; Wilfred Y. Wang, *Digital Media in Urban China: Locating Guangzhou* (London: Rowman & Littlefield, 2019). For surveillance see David Bamman, Brendan O'Connor, and Noah A. Smith, 'Censorship and Deletion Practices in Chinese Social Media'. *First Monday* 17, no. 3 (2012), http://firstmonday.org/article/view/3943/3169; Geoffrey Taubman, 'A Not-so World Wide Web: The Internet, China, and the Challenges to Nondemocratic Rule'. *Political Communication* 15, no. 2 (1998): 255–72; Thomas Chen, 'The Workshop of the World: Censorship and the Internet Novel "Such Is the World"', in *China's Contested Internet*, ed. Guobin Yang (Copenhagen: NIAS Press, 2015), 19–44; and Rongbin Han, *Contesting Cyberspace in China* (New York: Columbia University Press, 2018). For e-governance see Jesper Schlæger, 'Collaboration in China's E-government', in *The Road to Collaborative Governance in China*, ed. Yijia Jing (New York: Palgrave Macmillan, 2015), 123–46; Jesper Schlæger and Min Jiang, 'Official Microblogging and Social Management by Local Government in China', in *China's Contested Internet*, ed. Guobin Yang (Copenhagen: NIAS Press, 2015), 192–226; Steven J. Balla, 'Government Consultation and Political Participation on the Chinese Internet', in *China's Contested Internet*, ed. Guobin Yang (Copenhagen: NIAS Press, 2015), 75–107. For digital divides see Joo-Young Jung, Jack L. Qiu, and Kim Yong-Chan, 'Internet Connectedness and Inequality: Beyond the "Divide"'. *Communication Research* 28, no. 4 (2001): 507–35; Jack L. Qiu, *Working-Class Network Society: Communication Technology and the Information Have-Less in Urban China* (Cambridge, MA: MIT Press, 2009); Ian Weber 'Mobile, Online and Angry: The Rise of China's Middle-Class Civil Society'. *Critical Arts: South-North Cultural and Media Studies* 25, no. 1 (2111): 25–45; and Marcella Szablewicz, 'The "Losers" of China's Internet: Memes

as "Structures of Feeling" for Disillusioned Young Netizens', in *China's Contested Internet*, ed. Guobin Yang (Copenhagen: NIAS Press, 2015), 168–91.

16   For digital infrastructures and capitalization see Yu Hong, *Networking China: The Digital Transformation of the Chinese Economy* (Urbana: University of Illinois Press, 2017); Eric Harwit, *China's Telecommunications Revolution* (New York: Oxford University Press, 2008); Lianrui Jia and Dwayne Winseck, 'The Political Economy of Chinese Internet Companies: Financialization, Concentration, and Capitalization'. *International Communication Gazette* 80, no. 1 (2018): 30–59; Michael Keane and Ying Chen, 'Entrepreneurial Solutionism, Characteristic Cultural Industries and the Chinese Dream'. *International Journal of Cultural Policy* (2019). doi:10.1080/10286632.2017.1374382. For platformization see Jeroen de Kloet, Thomas Poell, Guohua Zeng, and Yiu Fai Chow, 'The Platformization of Chinese Society: Infrastructure, Governance, and Practice'. *Chinese Journal of Communication* 12, no. 3 (2019): 249–56; Elaine Jing Zhao, *Digital China's Informal Circuits: Platforms, Labour and Governance* (London: Routledge, 2019); and Steven J. Balla, 'Government Consultation and Political Participation on the Chinese Internet', in *China's Contested Internet*, ed. Guobin Yang (Copenhagen: NIAS Press, 2015), 75–107.

17   For work on copyright and *shanzhai* see Lucy Montgomery and Eric Priest, 'Copyright in China's Digital Cultural Industries', in *Handbook of Cultural and Creative Industries in China*, ed. Michael Keane (Cheltenham, UK: Edward Elgar, 2016), 339–59; Michael Keane and Elaine Jing Zhao, 'Renegades on the Frontiers of Innovation'. *Eurasian Journal of Economics and Culture* 53, no. 2 (2013): 316–330; Lena Scheen, 'Isn't That Funny? The Unsettling Effect of Shanzhai Products', in *Boredom, Shanzhai, and Digitisation in the Time of Creative China*, ed. Jeroen de Kloet, Yiu Fai Chow, and Lena Scheen (Amsterdam: Amsterdam University Press, 2019), 211–16. For an account of user rights protection and Alibaba see Ming Cheung, 'The E-commerce Revolution: Engendering Trust and Consumer Rights in China', in *Handbook of Cultural and Creative Industries in China*, ed. Michael Keane (Cheltenham: Edward Elgar, 2016), 412–30. For user experience see Lingling Gao, Kerem A. Waechter and Xuesong Bai, 'Understanding Consumers' Continuance Intention towards Mobile Purchase: A Theoretical Framework and Empirical Study – A Case of China', *Computers in Human Behavior* 53 (2015): 249–62.

18   On FinTech, for example, see Xie Ping, Chuanwei Zou, and Haier Liu, *Internet Finance in China* (London: Routledge, 2016); For an account of online philanthropy, see Haiqing Yu, 'Philanthropy on the Move: Mobile Communication and Neoliberal Citizenship in China'. *Communication and the Public* 2, no. 1 (2017): 35–49. A number of books have addressed cybersecurity and cyberpolicy, see Nigel Inkster, *China's Cyber-Power* (London: Routledge, 2016); and Greg Austin, *Cyber Policy in China* (Cambridge: Polity Press, 2014). For cloud computing see Jingzi Zhu, *China Cloud Rising* (New York: Springer, 2014). For makerspaces see Silvia Lindtner, 'Hackerspaces and the Internet of Things: How Makers Reinvent Industrial Production, Innovation and the Self', in *China's Contested Internet*, ed. Guobin Yang (Copenhagen: NIAS Press, 2015), 44–74; Wen Wen, 'Making in China: Is Maker Culture Changing China's Creative Landscape?' *International Journal of Cultural Studies* 20, no. 4 (2017): 343–60, https://doi.org/10.1177/1367877917705154; For the cashless society see Gladys Pak Lei Chong, 'Cashless China: Securitization of Everyday Life through Alipay's Social Credit System – Sesame Credit'. *Chinese Journal of Communication* 12, no. 3 (2019): 290–307.

19 Ge Zhang and Gabrielle de Seta, 'Being "Red" on the Internet: The Craft of Popularity on Chinese Social Media Platforms', in *Microcelebrity around the Globe: Approaches to Cultures of Internet Fame*, ed. Crystal Abidin and Megan Lindsay Brown (Bingley: Emerald, 2018), 57–68; Crystal Abidin, *Internet Celebrity: Understanding Fame Online* (Bingley: Emerald, 2018); Stuart Cunningham, David Craig, and Jian Lin, *Wang Hong: Social Media Entertainment in Global China* (London: Palgrave Macmillan, forthcoming 2021); and Elaine Jing Zhao, 'Professionalization of Amateur Production in Online Screen Entertainment in China: Hopes, Frustrations and Uncertainties', *International Journal of Communication* 10 (2016): 5444–62.

20 For recent accounts of China's expanding internet empire see Michael Keane and Haiqing Yu, 'China's Emerging Platform Capitalists in the Asia Pacific', *International Journal of Communication* 13 (2019): 4624–41; and Hong Shen, 'Building a Digital Silk Road? Situating the Internet in China's Belt and Road Initiative'. *International Journal of Communication* [Online], 12 (2018). Available at https://ijoc.org/index.php/ijoc/article/view/8405.

21 For a discussion of the SCS see Rogier Creemers, 'China's Social Credit System: An Evolving Practice of Control', 9 May 2018. Retrieved from https://ssrn.com/abstract=3175792.

22 Yu Hong, *Networking China*.

23 E.g. Qiu, *Working-Class Network Society*; and Yuezhi Zhao, *Communication in China: Political Economy, Power, and Conflict* (Lanham: Rowman & Littlefield, 2008).

24 At the time of writing Huawei was banned from 5G network infrastructure in a number of Western countries including the United States, Australia and Great Britain.

Chapter 1 Culture +

1 See Orville Schell, 'Foreword', in *China's Influence and American Interests: Promoting Constructive Vigilance*, ed. Larry Diamond and Orville Schell (Stanford, CA: Hoover Institution Press, Kindle Edition, 2019), Location 132.

2 For a discussion of these spectacles see William Callahan, *China Dreams: 20 Visions of the Future* (Oxford: Oxford University Press, 2013); Florian Schneider, *Staging China: The Politics of Mass Spectacle* (Leiden: Leiden University Press, 2019).

3 Gungwu Wang, *China Reconnects: Joining a Deep-Rooted Past to a New World Order* (Singapore: World Scientific, 2019).

4 Sometimes called 'grabism' or *(nalai zhuyi)*.

5 Linda Jaivin, 'Red Detachment: Is Chinese Culture beyond Reach?' *Australian Foreign Affairs* 5 (February 2019): 29–54 (24).

6 Jaivin, 'Red Detachment', 33.

7 While there are variations, it is important to note that Mandarin is the official language and that regional variations are probably less now than during the dynastical period due to the government's concerted attempts over the past 80 years to impose a Chinese national identity.

8 Michael Keane, *Created in China: The Great New Leap Forward* (London: Routledge, 2007); Wuwei Li, 'The Challenges of China's Culture "Going to the World"', in *The Handbook of China's Cultural and Creative Industries*, ed. Michael Keane (Cheltenham: Edward Elgar, 2016), 116–28.

9 Zhang Xiaolu, 'Guide and Support China's Cultural Industries to Go Global under the Conditions of Globalization' (*quanqiuhua tiaojian I xia yindao he zhichi zhongguo wenhua*

chanye zou quchu). China Development Observation, Development Research Center of the State Council. Retrieved from http://theory.people.com.cn/n1/2016/0302/c83865-28165982.html (accessed 22 September 2020).

10   For a discussion of television drama in China in the late 1990s and early 2000s see Ying Zhu, *Television in Post-Reform China: Serial Dramas, Confucian Leadership and the Global Television Market* (London: Routledge, 2008).

11   Michael Keane, *The Chinese Television Industry* (London: BFI Palgrave, 2015).

12   There are many excellent accounts of East Asian pop culture. See Beng-Huat Chua, *Structure, Audience and Soft Power in East Asian Pop Culture* (Hong Kong: Hong Kong University Press, 2012); for an edited volume covering film, television and games see Anthony Fung (ed.), *Asian Popular Culture: The Global (Dis)Continuity* (London: Routledge, 2013).

13   For example, see Michael Keane, Brian Yecies, and Terry Flew (eds), *Willing Collaborators: Foreign Partners in Chinese Media* (London: Rowman & Littlefield, 2018); Dal Yong Jin and Wendy Su (eds), *Asia-Pacific Film Co-Productions: Theory, Industry and Aesthetics* (London: Routledge, 2019).

14   Wendy Su, *China's Encounter with Global Hollywood: Cultural Policy and the Film Industry 1994–2013* (Lexington: University of Kentucky, 2016), 20.

15   Jinping Xi, *The Governance of China* (Beijing: Foreign Languages Press, Kindle Edition, 2014), Location 1083.

16   Yingchi Chu, 'The Politics of Reception. Made in China and Western Critique'. *International Journal of Cultural Studies* 17, no. 2 (2014): 159–73.

17   Nina Lizhou Li, *Zoning China: Online Video, Popular Culture and the State* (Cambridge: MIT Press, 2019), 79–81.

18   See Eric Harwit, *China's Telecommunications Revolution, China's Telecommunications Revolution* (New York: Oxford University Press, 2008), 89.

19   Shujen Wang, *Framing Piracy: Globalization and Film Distribution in Greater China* (Lanham: Rowman & Littlefield, 2003).

20   Elaine Jing Zhao and Michael Keane, 'Between Formal and Informal: The Shakeout in China's Online Video Industry'. *Media Culture and Society* 35, no. 6 (2013): 724–41.

21   See Michael Keane, 'Disconnecting, Connecting, and Reconnecting: How Chinese Television Got Out of the Box'. *International Journal of Communication* 10 (2016): 5426–443.

22   Michael Curtin, *Playing to the World's Biggest Audience: The Globalization of Chinese Film and Television* (Berkeley: University of California Press, 2007), 2.

23   Michael Curtin, 'The New Geography of the Global Blockbuster: Wanda Scales Up', in *Willing Collaborators: Foreign Partners in Chinese Media*, 31–46.

24   Co-production ventures with and in China are a subject of several books, see Aynne Kokas, *Hollywood Made in China* (Berkeley: University of California Press, 2017); Yong Jin and Su (eds), *Asia-Pacific Film Co-Productions*; Keane, Yecies, and Flew (eds), *Willing Collaborators*.

25   Keane, *The Chinese Television Industry*; Wenna Zeng and Colin Sparks, 'Localization as Negotiation: Producing a Korean format in Contemporary China'. *International Journal of Digital Television* 1, no. 8 (2017): 81–98; Arjen Nauta, 'Localizing Korean Television Shows in China: The Practice of Production and Censorship', in *Willing Collaborators: Foreign Partners in Chinese Media*, 171–86; Y. Cho and H. Zhu, 'Interpreting the Television Format Phenomenon between South Korea and China through Inter-Asian Frameworks'. *International Journal of Communication* 11 (2017): 2332–49.

26 Su, *China's Encounter with Global Hollywood*.
27 Susan Leong, 'Prophets of Mass Innovation: The Gospel According to BAT'. *Media Industries Journal* 5, no. 1 (2018). doi:10.3998/mij.15031809.0005.105.
28 Kai-fu Lee, *AI Superpowers: China, Silicon Valley and the New World Order* (Boston: Houghton Mifflin Harcourt, 2018).
29 Zhou Fan, *Zhongguo wenhua chanye sishinian huigu yu zhanwang (1978–2018) [Review and Prospect of China's Cultural Industry in the Past 40 Years (1978–2018)]* (Beijing: Commercial Press, 2019).
30 Fan, *Zhongguo wenhua chanye sishinian huigu yu zhanwang (1978–2018)*, 333.
31 Raymond Tallis, *From Two Cultures to No Culture: C. P. Snow's Two Cultures Lecture Fifty Years On* (Civitas: Institute for the Study of Civil Society, Kindle Edition, 2009).
32 Scott Lash and Celia Lury, *Global Cultural Industry* (London: Polity Press, 2007), 9–10.
33 Wuwei Li, *How Creativity Is Changing China*, ed. Michael Keane, trans. Hui Li and Marina Zhang (London: Bloomsbury, 2010), 49.
34 Nick Couldry and Andreas Hepp, *The Mediated Construction of Reality* (London: Polity Press, 2017), 36.
35 Chengxin Pan, Benjamin Isakhan, and Zim Nwokora, 'Othering as Soft Power Discursive Practice: China Daily's Construction of Trump's America in the 2016 Presidential Election'. *Politics* 40, no. 1 (2019): 54–69.
36 Joseph S. Nye, *Soft Power: The Means to Success in World Politics* (New York: Public Affairs, 2004), 11.
37 See Weihong Zhang, 'China's Cultural Future: From Soft power to Comprehensive National Power'. *International Journal of Cultural Policy* 16, no. 4 (2010): 383–402.
38 Gary D. Rawnsley, 'To Know Us Is to Love Us: Public Diplomacy and International Broadcasting in Contemporary Russia and China'. *Politics* 35 (2015): 273–86 (274).
39 Terry Flew, 'Entertainment Media, Cultural Power, and Post-Globalization: The Case of China's International Media Expansion and the Discourse of Soft power'. *Global Media and China* 1, no. 4 (2014): 278–94.
40 Xiaoling Zhang, 'China's International Broadcasting: A Case Study of CCTV International', in *Soft Power in China: Public Diplomacy through Communication*, ed. J. Wang (New York: Palgrave Macmillan, 2011), 57–71.
41 James Watson and Anne Hill, 'Effects of the Mass Media', in *Dictionary of Media and Communication Studies*, 9th edn, ed. James Watson and Anne Hill (London: Bloomsbury, 2015), 89.
42 Nick Couldry, *Media, Society, World: Social Theory and Digital Media Practice* (London: Polity Press, 2012).
43 Couldry, *Media, Society, World*.
44 Kingsley Edney, Stanley Rosen, and Ying Zhu, *Soft Power with Chinese Characteristics* (London: Taylor and Francis, Kindle Edition, 2019). Locations 671–73.

Chapter 2 Industry +

1 For discussion of Chinese TV formats that have appropriated Western ideas, see Anthony Fung and Xiaoxiao Zhang, 'The Chinese *Ugly Betty*: TV Cloning and Local Modernity'. *International Journal of Cultural Studies* 14, no. 3 (2011): 265–76; and Michael Keane, 'As a Hundred Television Formats Bloom, a Thousand Television Stations Contend'. *Journal of Contemporary China* 10 no. 30 (2002): 5–16.

NOTES

2   See Haiqing Yu, 'Game On: The Rise of the eSports Middle Kingdom'. *Media Industry Journal* 5, no. 1 (2018), doi:http://dx.doi.org/10.3998/mij.15031809.0005.106.
3   For a discussion of social media use among the so-called third age, see Chen Guo, Michael Keane, and Katie Ellis, 'The Emergence of the Third Age in China – Retirees' Use of Mobile Apps in Zhengzhou', in *Impacts of Mobile Use and Experience on Contemporary Society*, ed. Xiaoge Xu (Singapore: IGA, 2019), 20–36.
4   Commercial media production did exist in China and took a surge forward in the early 1990s, but it was 2002 before they were finally embedded as 'industries' within the state's cultural industry policies.
5   Laikwan Pang, *Building a Left-Wing Cinema in China: The Chinese Left-Wing Cinema Movement 1932–1937* (Lanham: Rowman & Littlefield, 2002).
6   Paul N. Edwards, 'Infrastructure and Modernity: Force, Time and Social Organization in the History of Socio-Technical Systems', in *Modernity and Technology*, ed. T. Misa, P. Brey, and A. Feenberg (Cambridge, MA: MIT Press, 2003), 185–226.
7   See Nikhil Anand, Akhil Gupta, and Hannah Appel (eds), *The Promise of Infrastructure* (Durham, NC: Duke University Press, 2018).
8   Richard Kraus, *The Party and the Arty: The New Politics of Culture* (Lanham: Rowman & Littlefield, 2004); Joseph Man Chan, 'Commercialisation without Independence: Trends and Tensions of Media Development in China', in *China Review*, ed. J. Cheng Yu-shek and M. Brosseau (Hong Kong: University of Hong Kong, 1993), 25.2–25.17; Chin-Chuan Lee, 'Administrative Boundaries and Media Marketization', in *Chinese Media, Global Contexts*, ed. Chin-Chuan Lee (London: Routledge, 2003), 156–72; and Michael Keane, *Created in China: The Great New Leap Forward* (London: Routledge, 2007).
9   The Fourth Industrialization Revolution is a term coined by Klaus Schwab. The first revolution was steam power, the second mass production, the third computers, while the fourth is the data revolution. See Klaus Schwab, *The Fourth Industrial Revolution* (London: Currency Books, 2016).
10 Beng-Huat Chua, *Structure, Audience and Soft Power in East Asian Pop Culture* (Hong Kong: Hong Kong University Press, 2012), 14.
11 Ibid.
12 Anthony Fung (ed.), *Asian Popular Culture: The Global (Dis)Continuity* (London: Routledge, 2013), 2.
13 Michael Keane, Brian Yecies, and Terry Flew (eds), *Willing Collaborators: Foreign Partners in China's Media* (London: Rowman & Littlefield, 2018).
14 Yunpeng Ding, 'wei guanggao zhengming' (Restoring the Good Name of Advertising), *Wenhuibao*, 14 January 1979, cited in Randall Stross, 'The Return of Advertising in China: A Survey of the Ideological Reversal'. *China Quarterly* 123 (1990): 485–86.
15 Jinglu Yu, 'The Structure and Function of Chinese Television, 1978–1989', in *Voices of China: The Interplay of Politics and Journalism*, ed. Chin-Chuan Lee (New York: Guildford Press, 1990), 69–87.
16 Ibid., 84.
17 Michael Curtin, *Playing to the World's Biggest Audience: The Globalization of Chinese Film and Television* (Berkeley: University of California Press, 2007).
18 Thomas Gold, 'Go with Your Feelings: Hong Kong and Taiwan Popular Culture in Greater China'. *China Quarterly* 136 (1993): 907–25.
19 Keane, *Created in China*.
20 For a discussion see Yu Hong, 'Between Corporate Development and Public Service: The Cultural System Reform in the Chinese Media Sector'. *Media Culture*

& *Society* 36, no. 5 (2014): 610–27; Yuezhi Zhao, 'The State, the Market and Media Control in China', in *Who Owns the Media?: Global Trends and Local Resistance*, ed. Pradip Thomas, Zaharom Nain, and Sasha Costanza-Chock (London: Zed Book, 2004), 179–212; and Michael Keane and Elaine Jing Zhao, 'The Reform of the Cultural System: Culture Creativity and Innovation in China', in *Cultural Policies in East Asia: Dynamics between the State, Arts and Creative Industries*, ed. Lorraine Lim and Hye-Kyung Lee (London: Palgrave Macmillan, 2014), 155–73.

21   For a discussion see Keane, *Created in China*.

22   Judith Hollows, 'Historical Trajectories of Innovation and Competitiveness: Hong Kong Firms and Their China linkages'. *Creativity and Innovation Management* 8, no. 1 (1999): 57–63.

23   Richard Baldwin, *The Great Convergence: Information Technology and the New Globalization* (Cambridge, MA: Harvard University Press, 2016).

24   Yuefan Xiao, 'Maoism and Disruptive Creativity', in *Boredom, Shanzhai, and Digitisation in the Time of Creative China*, ed. Jeroen de Kloet, Yiu Fai Chow, and Lena Scheen (Amsterdam: Amsterdam University Press, 2019), 186–209.

25   Wenna Zeng and Colin Sparks, 'Localization as Negotiation: Producing a Korean Format in Contemporary China'. *International Journal of Digital Television* 1, no. 8: (2017): 81–98; Arjen Nauta, 'Localizing Korean Television Shows in China: The Practice of Production and Censorship', in *Willing Collaborators: Foreign Partners in Chinese Media*, ed. Michael Keane, Brian Yecies, and Terry Flew (London: Rowman & Littlefield, 2018), 171–86; and Michael Keane, *The Chinese Television Industry* (London: BFI Palgrave, 2015).

26   Lena Scheen, 'Isn't That Funny? The Unsettling Effect of Shanzhai Products', in *Boredom, Shanzhai, and Digitisation in the Time of Creative China*, ed. Jeroen de Kloet, Yiu Fai Chow, and Lena Scheen (Amsterdam: Amsterdam University Press, 2019), 211–16 (212).

27   Winnie Won Ying Wong, *Van Gogh on Demand: China and the Readymade* (Berkeley: University of California Press, 2013).

28   Keane, Yecies, and Flew, *Willing Collaborators*.

29   Weiying Peng, 'Collaborators, Mediators and Processes: Film Coproduction in China', in *Willing Collaborators: Foreign Partners in Chinese Media*, 15 – 30.

30   Sheng Ding, *The Dragon's Hidden Wings: How China Rises with Its Soft Power* (Lanham: Lexington Books, 2008), 66.

31   Terry McGee, George C. S. Lin, Andrew Marton, Mark Wang, and Jiaping Wu, *China's Urban Space: Development under Market Socialism* (London: Routledge, 2007).

32   For a discussion of SE Asian investment in China's tech industries see Douglas Fuller, *Paper Tigers, Hidden Dragons: Firms and the Political Economy of China's Technological Development* (Oxford: Oxford University Press, 2016).

33   Michael Porter, *The Competitive Advantage of Nations* (New York: Free Press, 1990).

34   See Joseph Man Chan, 'Administrative Boundaries and Media Marketization', in *Chinese Media, Global Contexts*, ed. Chin-Chuan Lee (London: Routledge, 2003), 159–76.

35   Jane Zheng, 'A Comparative Perspective on the Industrialization of Art in the Republican Period in Shanghai and today's Creative Industry', in *Handbook of the Cultural and Creative Industries in China*, ed. Michael Keane (Cheltenham: Edward Elgar, 2016), 519–33.

36   Michael Keane, *China's New Creative Clusters: Governance, Human Capital and Investment* (London: Routledge, 2011).

37 Michael Keane and Ying Chen, 'Entrepreneurial Solutionism, Characteristic Cultural Industries and the Chinese Dream'. *International Journal of Cultural Policy* 25, no. 6 (2019): 743–55.
38 Zhejiang Daily, *Zhejiang tese xiaozhen shengzhang ji: benpaoba mengxiang chengzhen* (*The Development of Zhejiang Characteristic Town Running, Dream Town*), *Zhejiang Daily*, accessed 28 March 2017 at http://tsxz.zjol.com.cn/system/2016/07/08/021219849.shtml.
39 New start-ups enjoy rent-free office space for three years, up to one million yuan (US$159 400) in loans from the banking sector, as well as enjoying privileges in sharing cloud computing services, intermediation services such as business and legal advice, and housing subsidies for skilled professionals.
40 Keane and Chen, 'Entrepreneurial Solutionism, Characteristic Cultural Industries and the Chinese Dream'.
41 Ulrich Beck and Elizabeth Beck-Gernsheim, *Individualization* (London: Sage, 2001).
42 Terutomo Ozawa, S. Castello, and Ron Phillips 'The Internet Revolution, the "McLuhan" Stage of Catch-Up, and Institutional Reforms'. *Asia Journal of Economic Issues* 35, no. 2 (2001): 289–98 (297).
43 Kai-fu Lee, *AI Superpowers: China, Silicon Valley and the New World Order* (Boston: Houghton Mifflin Harcourt, 2018).
44 Baldwin, *The Great Convergence*.
45 Yu Zhou, 'Time and Space in China's ICT Industry', in *The Economic Geography of the IT Industry in the Asia-Pacific*, ed. Philip Cooke, G. Searle and Kevin O'Connor (London: Routledge, 2013), 68–85.
46 Xuelin Liu and Jianghua Zhou, 'China's Catch-Up and Innovation Model in the IT Industry', in *The Economic Geography of the IT Industry in the Asia-Pacific*, 144–68 (147).
47 Lee, *AI Superpowers*.
48 Joy Danjing Zhang and Michael Keane, 'Creative Migration, Talent and Celebrity Movements to the Chinese Mainland', in *Willing Collaborators: Foreign Partners in China's Media*, 213–26; also Elaine Jing Zhao, 'Cross-Straits Online Collaboration: Multiple Publics and Intractable Institutions', in *Willing Collaborators: Foreign Partners in China's Media*, 187–98.
49 Eric Harwit, *China's Telecommunications Revolution* (New York: Oxford University Press, 2008).
50 Yu Hong, *Networking China: The Digital Transformation of the Chinese Economy* (Urbana: University of Illinois Press, 2017).
51 Xiao, 'Maoism and Disruptive Creativity'.
52 Xiang Ren, 'Between Sustaining and Disruptive Innovation: China's Digital Publishing Industry in the Age of Mobile Internet', in *Handbook of the Cultural and Creative Industries in China*, 377–95.

Chapter 3 Internet +

1 For a discussion of the two cultures' debates since the 1950s see contributions in *From Two Cultures to No Culture*, ed. Robert Whelan (London: Civitas, 2009).
2 Scott Malcolmson, *Splinternet: How Geopolitics and Commerce Are Fragmenting the World Wide Web* (New York: OR Books, 2016).
3 Scott Lash and Celia Lury, *Global Cultural Industry* (Malden: Polity Press, 2007), 4.
4 For a discussion see Yik Chan Chin, 'Policy Process, Policy Learning and the Role of the Provincial Media in China'. *Media Culture Society* 33, no. 2 (2011): 193–201.

5. Mark McLelland, Haiqing Yu, and Gerard Goggin, 'Alternative Histories of Social Media in Japan and China', in *The Sage Handbook on Social Media*, ed. Jean Burgess, A. Marwick and Thomas Poell (London: Sage, 2017), 53–68.
6. Guobin Yang, 'A Chinese Internet? History, Practice, and Globalization'. *Chinese Journal of Communication* 5, no. 1 (2012): 49–54.
7. Greg Walton, 'China's Golden Shield Corporations and the Development of Surveillance Technology in the People's Republic of China' (Report commissioned by International Centre for Human Rights and Democratic Development, 1 October 2001). Retrieved from https://www.business-humanrights.org/en/full-report-chinas-golden-shield-corporations-and-the-developement-of-surveillance-technology-in-the-peoples-republic-of-china-0.
8. Zixiang Tan, 'Regulating China's Internet: Convergence toward a Coherent Regulatory Regime'. *Telecommunications Policy* 23, nos 3–4 (1999): 261–76.
9. Xiangkui Yao and Richard Suttmeier, 'China's Post-WTO Technology Policy: Standards, Software, and the Changing Nature of Techno-Nationalism' (NBR special report no. 7, Washington, DC: National Bureau of Asian Research, 1 May 2004). Retrieved from https://www.nbr.org/publication/chinas-post-wto-technology-policy-standards-software-and-the-changing-nature-of-techno-nationalism/.
10. E.g. Guoguang Wu, 'In the Name of Good Governance: E-government, Internet Pornography and Political Censorship in China', in *China's Information and Communication Technology Revolution*, ed. Xiaoling Zhang and Yongnian Zheng (London: Routledge, 2009), 68–85. See also Xiaoling Zhang, 'Chinese State Media Going Global', Singapore: East Asia Institute Background Briefing no. 488, 2009. Retrieved from https://research.nus.edu.sg/eai/wp-content/uploads/sites/2/2017/11/Vol2No1_ZhangXiaoling.pdf.
11. Richard Baldwin, *The Great Convergence: Information Technology and the New Globalization* (Cambridge, MA: Harvard University Press, 2016).
12. Yu Hong, *Networking China: The Digital Transformation of the Chinese Economy* (Urbana: University of Illinois Press, 2017).
13. Yuezhi Zhao, 'China's Pursuits of Indigenous Innovations in Information Technology Developments: Hopes, Follies and Uncertainties'. *Chinese Journal of Communication* 3 (2010): 266–89.
14. McLelland, Yu, and Goggin, 'Alternative Histories of Social Media in Japan and China'.
15. Ge Zhang and Gabriel de Seta, 'Being Red on the Internet: The Craft of Popularity on Chinese Social Media Platforms', in *Microcelebrity around the Globe: Approaches to Cultures of Internet Fame*, ed. Crystal Abidin and Megan Brown (Bingley: Emerald, 2019), 57–71.
16. *China Daily*, 'China's Sharing Economy: $501 Billion Market Volume', 17 May, http://www.chinadaily.com.cn/business/tech/2017-05/17/content_29377488.htm (accessed 28 May 2017).
17. Laikwan Pang, *Cultural Control and Globalization in Asia: Copyright, Piracy and Cinema* (London: Routledge, 2006), 104–5.
18. SARFT and MIIT, 'Hulianwang shiting jiemu fuwu guanli guiding (Administrative Provisions on Internet Audio-Visual Program Service)', 29 December 2007. Retrieved from http://www.sarft.gov.cn/articles/2007/12/29/20071229131521450172.html.
19. CNNIC, 'The 30th Survey Report', September 2012. Retrieved from http://www1.cnnic.cn/IDR/ReportDownloads/201209/t20120928_36586.htm.

20 'Chinese Smartphone Maker Rewards Staffers with Stock after Making Fortune 500'. *Wall Street Journal*, 23 July 2019. Retrieved from https://www.wsj.com/articles/chinese-smartphone-maker-rewards-staffers-with-stock-after-making-fortune-500-11563882916.
21 Elaine Jing Zhao, *Digital China's Informal Circuits: Platforms, Labour and Governance* (London: Routledge, 2019).
22 Ibid.
23 'Payment methods in China: How China became a mobile-first nation'. 29 May 2020. https://daxueconsulting.com/payment-methods-in-china/.
24 CNNIC, 'The 45th Statistical Report on Internet Development in China'. April 2020. Retrieved from https://cnnic.com.cn/IDR/ReportDownloads/202008/P020200827549953874912.pdf.
25 Lianrui Jia and Dwayne Winseck, 'The Political Economy of Chinese Internet Companies: Financialization, Concentration, and Capitalization'. *International Communication Gazette* 80, no. 1 (2019): 30–59.
26 Xinhua News, 'Xi Jinping: Build China into a Strong Internet Power', 27 February 2014. Retrieved from http://www.xinhuanet.com/politics/*2014-02*/27/c_119538788.htm.
27 Yu Hong, 'Pivot to Internet Plus: Molding China's Digital Economy for Economic Restructuring?' *International Journal of Communication* 11 (2017): 1486–1506.
28 Ibid.
29 Yu Hong, 'Reading the 13th Five-Year Plan: Reflections on China's ICT Policy'. *International Journal of Communication* 11 (2017): 1755–74 (1756).
30 Jinghan Zeng, Tim Stevens, and Yaru Chen, 'China's Solution to Global Cyber Governance: Unpacking the Domestic Discourse of "Internet Sovereignty"'. *Politics & Policy* 45, no. 3 (2017): 432–64.
31 Xi Jinping, *zai dier jie shijie hulianwang dahui kaimu shi shand de jianghua* (Xi Jinping's talk at the Opening Ceremony in the second World Internet Conference). Xinhua, 16 December 2015. Retrieved from http://news.xinhuanet.com/politics/*2015-12*/16/c_1117481089.htm.
32 Max J Zenglein and Anna Holzmann, 'Evolving Made in China 2025: China's Industrial Policy in the Quest for Global Tech Leadership'. MERICS, 2 July 2019. Retrieved from https://www.merics.org/sites/default/files/2019-07/MPOC_8_MadeinChina_2025_final_3.pdf.
33 'Three-Year Guidance for Internet Plus Artificial Intelligence Plan'. MIIT. 18 May 2016. Retrieved from http://www.miit.gov.cn/n1146290/n1146392/c4808445/part/4808453.pdf..
34 State Council of China, 'New Generation Artificial Intelligence Development Plan', 2017. Retrieved from https://flia.org/notice-state-council-issuing-new-generation-artificial-intelligence-development-plan/
35 AliResearch, 'Internet Plus: from IT to DT *(hulianwang +: cong TT dao DT)*', a report (Beijing: China Machine Press, 2015).
36 The Fourth Industrial Revolution is a term devised by Klaus Schwab, of the Davos Institute to refer to the data revolution: the Second Industrial Revolution was electrical power and mass production; the third was electronics and information technology.
37 Haiqing Yu, *Media and Cultural Transformation in China* (London: Routledge, 2009).

38 Haiqing Yu, 'China's "Social+" Approach to Soft Power'. *East Asia Forum*, 27 June 2019. Retrieved from https://www.eastasiaforum.org/2019/06/27/chinas-social-approach-to-soft-power/.
39 AliResearch, 'From Connection to Empowerment: "Intelligent +" to Power China's High-Quality Economic Growth' (cong lianjie dao funeng: zhineng+ zhuli zhongguo jingji gao zhiliang fazhan), 11 March 2019. Retrieved from https://i.aliresearch.com/img/20190312/20190312110416.pdf.
40 Ibid.
41 Baldwin, *The Great Convergence*.
42 Terutomu Ozama, S. Castello, and Ron Phillips, 'The Internet Revolution, the "McLuhan" Stage of Catch-Up, and Institutional Reforms'. *Asia Journal of Economic Issues* 35, no. 2 (2001): 289–98.
43 SCMP and Abacus (2019) China Internet Report 2019. Retrieved from www.scmp.com/china-internet-report. Also see the next chapter.
44 James Griffith, *The Great Firewall of China: How to Build and Control an Alternative Version of the Internet* (London: Zed Books, Kindle Edition, 2019).
45 Xiuxi Zhu, 'PwC: China Leads OTT Video Revenue Growth in APAC with Heavily Monetized Model', 5 June 2019. Retrieved from https://www.spglobal.com/marketintelligence/en/news-insights/trending/jPkSrpJmuETgphh8hR9acw2.
46 CAC, 'The 2016 (15th) Chinese Internet Conference Opens in Beijing on 21 June', 22 June 2016. Retrieved from http://it.people.com.cn/n1/2016/0622/c1009-28469652.html.
47 Rebecca MacKinnon, 'Liberation Technology: China's "Networked Authoritarianism"'. *Journal of Democracy* 22, no. 2 (2011): 32–46.
48 Tim Oakes, 'Mediating Asia: Information, Democracy, and the State in and Before the Digital Age – Introduction'. *International Journal of Communication* 11 (2017). Retrieved from https://ijoc.org/index.php/ijoc/article/view/5152.
49 Michael Keane and Guanhua Su, 'When Push Comes to Nudge: A Chinese Digital Civilization In-the-Making'. *Media International Australia* 173, no. 1 (2019): 3–16, https://doi.org/10.1177/1329878X19876362.
50 Rogier Creemers, 'The Pivot in Chinese Cybergovernance: Integrating Internet Control in Xi Jinping's China'. *China Perspectives* [Online] 4 (2015): 5–13.
51 Rogier Creemers, 'China's social credit system: an evolving practice of control', 2018. Retrieved from https://ssrn.com/abstract=3175792.
52 Guobin Yang, 'Political Contestation in Chinese Digital Spaces: Deepening the Critical Inquiry'. *China Information* 28, no. 2 (2014): 135–44 (112).
53 Hong Shen, 'China and Global Internet Governance: Toward an Alternative Analytical Framework'. *Chinese Journal of Communication* 9 no. 3 (2016): 304–24.
54 State Council Information Office (SCIO), The Internet in China. Retrieved from http://news.xinhuanet.com/english2010/china/2010-06/08/c_13339232_7.htm.
55 Xi Jinping, *zai dier jie shijie hulianwang dahui kaimu shi shand de jianghua* (Xi Jinping's talk at the Opening Ceremony in the second World Internet Conference).
56 Rogier Creemers, 'Recognizing China's Internet Governance despite Its Foundational Opposition to Western Values', 27 April 2016. Retrieved from https://www.chinausfocus.com/society-culture/recognizing-chinas-internet-governance-despite-its-foundational-opposition-to-western-values.
57 Ibid.
58 Shen, 'China and Global Internet Governance'.

59 Zeng, Stevens, and Chen, 'China's Solution to Global Cyber Governance', 18.
60 Anupam Chander and Uyen P. Le, 'Data Nationalism', *Emory Law Journal* 64, no. 3 (2015): 677–740.
61 Yinan Zhao and Yin Cao, 'China Wants Its Voice Heard in Cyberspace'. *China Daily*, 21 November 2014. Retrieved from http://usa.chinadaily.com.cn/business/2014-11/21/content_18951166.htm.

Chapter 4 Platform +

1 Lianrui Jia and Dwayne Winseck, 'The Political Economy of Chinese Internet Companies: Financialization, Concentration, and Capitalization'. *International Communication Gazette* 80, no. 1 (2018): 30–59 (34).
2 B. Xia and C. Fuchs, 'The Financialization of Digital Capitalism in China'. *Westminster Institute for Advanced Studies* 4 (2016): 1–32.
3 José van Dijck, Thomas Poell, and Martijn de Waal, *The Platform Society: Public Values in a Connective World* (Oxford: Oxford University Press, 2018). For a Chinese discussion of the platform economy see Jin Xu, *Platform Economics (pintai jinjixue)* (Shanghai: Shanghai Jiaotong University Press, 2013).
4 Nick Srnicek, *Platform Capitalism* [Kindle version] (Cambridge: Polity Press, 2017).
5 Yu Hong, *Networking China: The Digital Transformation of the Chinese Economy* (Urbana: University of Illinois Press, 2017).
6 In 2019, a special issue of the *Chinese Journal of Communication* examined the 'platformization of Chinese society'. Critical issues addressed included digital labour, social credit, the cashless society, virtual gifting, Chinese video streaming services and social media use by rural women. See Jeroen de Kloet, Thomas Poell, Guohua Zeng, and Yiu Fai Chow, 'The Platformization of Chinese Society: Infrastructure, Governance, and Practice'. *Chinese Journal of Communication* 12, no. 3 (2019): 249–56.
7 Tarleton Gillespie, 'The Politics of "Platforms"'. *New Media & Society* 12, no. 3 (2010): 347–64 (349–50).
8 Ian Bogost and Nick Montfort, 'Platform Studies: Frequently Questioned Answers'. *Digital Arts and Culture* (December 2009): 12–15.
9 Dan Schiller, *Digital Capitalism: Networking the Global Market System* (Cambridge, MA: MIT Press, 2000); and Hong, *Networking China*.
10 Marshal McLuhan, *Understanding Media: The Extensions of Man* (New York: Signet Books, 1964).
11 Jean-Charles Rochet and Jean Tirole, 'Platform Competition in Two-Sided Markets'. *Journal of the European Economic Association* 1, no. 4 (2003): 990–1029 (990), cited in Anne Helmond, 'The Platformization of the Web: Making Web Data Platform Ready'. *Social Media + Society* 1, no. 2 (2015). Online publication. doi:10.1177/2056305115603080.
12 Jean-Christophe Plantin, Carl Lagoze, Paul N. Edwards, and Christian Sandvig, 'Infrastructure Studies Meet Platform Studies in the Age of Google and Facebook'. *New Media & Society* 20, no. 1 (2018): 293–310.
13 Ibid., 307.
14 Kathleeen N. Hayles, *Unthought: The Power of Conscious Nonconscious* (Chicago: University of Chicago Press, 2017), 35.
15 van Dijck, Poell, and de Waal, *The Platform Society*, 4.
16 Tarlton Gillespie, 'Governance of and by Platforms', in *SAGE Handbook of Social Media*, ed. Jean Burgess, Thomas Poell, and Alice Marwick (London: Sage, 2017).

17 Plantin, Lagoze, Edwards, and Sandvig, 'Infrastructure Studies Meet Platform Studies in the Age of Google and Facebook'.
18 Ibid., 295.
19 Ibid., 301.
20 Ibid., 295.
21 See also van Dijck, Poell, and de Waal, *The Platform Society*.
22 Binbin Wang and Xiaoyan Li, 'Big Data, Platform Economy and Market Competition: A Preliminary Construction of Plan-Oriented Market Economy System in the Information Era'. *World Review of Political Economy* 8, no. 2 (2017): 138–61 (149).
23 van Dijck, Poell, and de Waal, *The Platform Society*.
24 de Kloet, Poell, Zeng, and Chow, 'The Platformization of Chinese Society'.
25 E.g. Hong, *Networking China*.
26 Christian Fuchs, 'Baidu, Weibo and Renren: The Global Political Economy of Social Media in China'. *Asian Journal of Communication* 26, no. 1 (2016): 14–41. See also Shoshana Zuboff, *The Age of Surveillance Capitalism: The Fight for a Human Future at the New Frontier of Power* (London: Profile Books, 2019).
27 For a discussion of Chinese enterprises going global see Huiyao Wang and Miao Lu, *China Goes Global: How China's Overseas Investment on Its Business Enterprises* (London: Palgrave Macmillan, 2016).
28 Yong Zhong, 'The Chinese Internet: A Separate Closed Monopoly Board'. *Journal of International Communication* 18, no. 1 (2012): 19–31.
29 David Evans, Vanessa Yanhua Zhang and Howard Chang, 'Analyzing Competition among Internet Players: Qihoo 360 v. Tencent'. *Antitrust Chronicle, Competition Policy International* 12 (2013). Retrieved from https://www.competitionpolicyinternational.com/analyzing-competition-among-internet-players-qihoo-360-v-tencent/.
30 Ryan McMorrow and Nian Liu, 'Sellers Asked to Choose in Battle between Alibaba and Pinduoduo', *FT.com*, 14 January 2020. Retrieved from https://www.ft.com/content/b55d0e0a-33a1-11ea-9703-eea0cae3f0de.
31 Kai-fu Lee, *AI Superpowers: China, Silicon Valley and the New World Order* (Boston: Houghton Mifflin Harcourt, 2018).
32 Yujie Chen, Zhifei Mao, and Jack Linchuan Qiu, *Super-Sticky WeChat and Chinese Society* (Bingley: Emerald, 2018).
33 See number of monthly active WeChat users from 3rd quarter 2011 to 3rd quarter 2018 (in millions). Available at Statistica: www.statista.com/statistics/255778/number-of-active-wechat-messenger-accounts.
34 Tim Culpan, 'The World's Most Powerful App Is Squandering Its Lead', *Bloomberg Opinion*, 23 July 2018. Retrieved from www.bloomberg.com/opinion/articles/2018-07-22/world-s-most-powerful-app-is-squandering-its-lead.
35 Connie Chan, 'Money as Message', *Andreesen Horoqwitz*. Retrieved from https://a16z.com/2016/07/24/money-as-message/.
36 Jean-Christophe Plantin and Gabriele De Seta, 'WeChat as Infrastructure: The Techno-Nationalist Shaping of Chinese Digital Platforms'. *Chinese Journal of Communication* 12, no. 3 (2019): 257–73.
37 'Top 10 Companies Behind the 2019 Midas List: Exits and Unicorns That Helped Their Investors the Most', *Forbes*, 2 April 2019. Retrieved from http://bit.ly/2PoxF6Z.
38 Florian Schneider, *China's Digital Nationalism* (Oxford: Oxford University Press, 2019), 225.

39 Viktor Mayer-Schönberger and Thomas Ramage, *Reinventing Capitalism in the Age of Big Data* (New York: Basic Books, 2018).
40 See Thomas Reinbacher, 'China's Digital Empire', 2018. Retrieved from http://dr-reinbacher.com/china-digitalempire/
41 Michael Keane and Haiqing Yu, 'China's Emerging Platform Capitalists in the Asia Pacific'. *International Journal of Communication* 13 (2019): 4624–41.
42 Cave, Danielle; Samantha Hoffman, Alex Joske, Fergus Ryan, and Elise, Mapping China's technology giants. International Cyber Policy Centre, Australian strategic Policy Institute, Issue paper report no. 15, 18 April 2019. Retrieved from https://www.aspi.org.au/report/mapping-chinas-tech-giants.
43 Ibid.
44 Wang and Lu, *China Goes Global*, 4.
45 Kalina S. Staykova and Jan Damsgaard, 'Platform Expansion Design as Strategic Choice: The Case of WeChat and Kakaotalk'. *Research Papers* 78 (2016). Retrieved from http://aisel.aisnet.org/ecis2016_rp/78.
46 Chung-yan Chow, 'Alibaba Buys the South China Morning Post: Full Q&A with Executive Vice Chairman Joseph Tsai'. *South China Morning Post*, 11 December, 2015. Retrieved from https://www.scmp.com/news/hong-kong/article/1890057/alibaba-buys-south-china-morning-post-full-qa-executive-vice-chairman.
47 Keane and Yu, 'China's Emerging Platform Capitalists in the Asia Pacific'.
48 Kai Jia, Martin Kenney and John Zysman, 'Global Competitors? Mapping the Internationalization Strategies of Chinese Digital Platform Firms', in *International Business in the Information and Digital Age (Progress in International Business Research, Vol. 13)*, ed. R. van Tulder, A. Verbeke, and L Piscitello (Bingley: Emerald Insight, 2018) 187–215 (201).
49 Jane Li, 'How China's Alibaba and Tencent Are Divvying up India's Unicorns', Quartz India. 17 December 2019. Retrieved from https://qz.com/india/1767741/how-chinas-alibaba-and-tencent-are-divvying-up-indias-unicorns/.
50 Jia, Kenney, and Zysman, 'Global Competitors?'
51 Aditi Shrivastava, 'After Merger with Didi Chuxing, India to Become Uber's Main Battleground', 2 August 2016. https://economictimes.indiatimes.com/small-biz/startups/after-merger-with-didi-chuxing-india-to-become-ubers-main-battleground/articleshow/53488514.cms.
52 Luzhou Li, *Zoning China: Online Video, Popular Culture, and the State* (Cambridge, MA: MIT Press, 2019).
53 Jason Davis, 'The TikTok Strategy: Using AI Platforms to Take over the World', https://knowledge.insead.edu/entrepreneurship/the-tiktok-strategy-using-ai-platforms-to-take-over-theworld-11776.
54 Zuboff, *The Age of Surveillance Capitalism*.
55 Emma Lee, 'Bytedance Eroding Ad Revenue Share from BAT: Report. *Technode*, 12 February 2020. Retrieved from https://technode.com/2020/02/12/bytedance-eroding-ad-revenue-share-from-bat-report/.
56 Maryam Mohsin, '10 TikTok Statistics That You Need to Know in 2020 [Infographic]'. 22 November 2019. Retrieved from https://au.oberlo.com/blog/tiktok-statistics.
57 Ibid.
58 Yi Hong Poo, 'Can Grab Succeed as the Southeast Asia Super App?' *Medium*, 16 November 2019. https://medium.com/swlh/can-grab-succeed-as-the-southeast-asia-super-app-7b4cd2a58384.

59 Ibid.
60 John Thornhill, 'China's Digital Economy Is a Global Trailblazer: Financial Times', 20 May 2017. Retrieved from https://www.ft.com/content/86cbda82-0d55-11e7-b030-768954394623.
61 Dal Yong Jin, 'Digital Platform as a Double-Edged Sword: How to Interpret Cultural Flows in the Platform Era'. *International Journal of Communication* 11 (2017): 3880–98.

Chapter 5 Assessing the Evidence

1 For countries with the most Nobel Prize recipients in literature see Statistica.com https://www.statista.com/statistics/262898/literature-nobel-prizes-awarded-by-nationality/.
2 'Jackie Chan Presented with Honorary Oscar', *NME*, 13 November 2016. Retrieved from https://www.nme.com/news/jackie-chan-presented-honorary-oscar-1851229.
3 We use the term 'cultural discount' to refer to the difficulty of achieving success in large markets when the product has a foreign accent or cultural nuances that hinder recognition.
4 Christine Borgman, *Big Data, Littler Data, No Data. Scholarship in the Networked World* (Cambridge, MA: MIT Press, 2015), 6.
5 For a critical argument about how metrics have become dysfunctional, see Jerry Z. Muller, *The Tyranny of Metrics* (Princeton, NJ: Princeton University Press, 2018).
6 The term 'attention economy' is often used to indicate the battles for the eyeballs of consumers in an age of information overload.
7 The question of assessing cultural value online is now more important to resolve. See Dave O'Brien and Pat Lockley, 'The Social Life of Cultural Value', in *Making Culture Count: The Politics of Cultural Measurement*, ed. Lachlan MacDowall, Marnie Badham, Emma Blomkamp, and Kim Dumphry (London: Palgrave, 2015), 87–106.
8 For a discussion see Bobby Duffy, *The Perils of Perception: Why We're Wrong About Nearly Everything* (London: Atlantic Book, 2019), 67.
9 Social media can be used as a marketing tool in the audiovisual industries. For a discussion of how UK content has used this strategy in China, see Filippo Gilardi, Celia Lam, Cohen Tan, Andrew White, Shuxin Cheng, and Yifan Zhao, 'International TV Series Distribution on Chinese Digital Platforms: Marketing Strategies and Audience Engagement'. *Global Media and China* 3 no. 3 (2018): 213–30.
10 Kingsley Edney, Stanley Rosen, and Ying Zhu, 'Introduction', in *Soft Power with Chinese Characteristics*, ed. Kingsley Edney, Stanley Rosen and Ying Zhu (London: Routledge, Kindle Edition, 2019), Locations 619–21.
11 For a longer discussion of metric and big data, see Brian Yecies, Michael Keane, Haiqing Yu, Elaine Zhao, Susan Leong, and Huan Wu, 'The Cultural Power Metric: Toward a Reputational Analysis of China's Soft Power in the Asia-Pacific'. *Global Media and China* 4, no. 2 (2019), 203–19. https://doi.org/10.1177/2059436419849724.
12 Alberto C. Portugal, 'The Role of City Rankings in Local Public Policy Design: Urban Competitiveness and Economic Press'. *Global Media & China* 4, no. 2 (2019): 162–78.
13 Richard Florida, *The Rise of the Creative Class* (New York: Basic Books, 2002).
14 Richard Florida, C. Mellander, and H. Qian, 'China's Development Disconnect'. *Environment and Planning A: Economy and Space* 44, no. 3 (2012): 628–48.

For a critique of this position, see Juncheng Dai, Shangyi Zhou, Michael Keane, and Qian Huang, 'Mobility of the Creative Class and City Attractiveness: A Case

Study of Chinese Animation Workers'. *Eurasian Geography and Economics* 53, no. 5 (2012): 649–70.
15 China's soft power has to compete with an unfair Western playing field according to Chang Zhang and Ruiqing Wu, 'Battlefield of Global Ranking: How Do Power Rivalries Shape Soft Power Index Building?' *Global Media & China* 4, no. 2 (2019): 179–202.
16 For a discussion of Quora see Lan He, Rongdang Wang, and Mingsheng Jiang, 'Evaluating the Effectiveness of China's National Branding with Data from Social Media'. *Global Media and China*, 2019. Retrieved from https://doi.org/10.1177/2059436419885539.
17 Julian Baggini, *How the World Thinks* (London: Granta, 2019, Kindle Edition), Location 1478.
18 Stanley Rosen, 'Ironies of Soft Power Projection: The United States and China in the Age of Donald Trump and Xi Jinping', in *Soft Power with Chinese Characteristics*, Location 855.
19 For another argument about the unfair playing field of soft power metrics, see Huailiang Li, 'Qianxi zhongguo wenhua zouchuqu xiaoguo pinggu tixi de jiangou [Constructing an Evaluation System on Effect of Chinese Culture Going Out]', *Nankai Xuebao [Nankai Journal] (Philosophy, Literature and Social Science Edition)*, no. 3 (2018): 68–75.
20 See Yingchi Chu, 'The Politics of Reception: Made in China and Western Critique'. *International Journal of Cultural Studies* 17, no. 2 (2014): 159–73 (160).
21 Beng-Huat Chua, *Structure, Audience and Soft Power in East Asian Pop Culture* (Hong Kong: Hong Kong University Press, 2012), 81.
22 For a study of China's media in Africa see Vivian Marsh, 'Tiangao or tianxia: The Ambiguities of CCTV's English Language News for Africa', in *China's Media Goes Global*, ed. Daya Thussu, Hugo de Burgh, and Anbin Shi (London: Routledge, 2018), 103–21.
23 Hugo de Burgh, *China's Media in the Emerging World Order* (Buckingham: University of Buckingham Press, 2017), 11.
24 See BBC News https://www.bbc.com/news/world-asia-china-46630781.
25 See Thomas Claburn, 'Facebook Flat-Out "Lies" about How Many People Can See Its Ads – Lawsuit'. *The Register*, 17 August, 2019. Retrieved from https://www.theregister.com/2018/08/17/facebook_ad_reach_lawsuit/?source=techstories.org.
26 Xiaoling Zhang, 'China's International Broadcasting: A Case Study of CCTV International', in *Soft Power in China: Public Diplomacy through Communication*, ed. J. Wang (New York: Palgrave Macmillan, 2011), 57–71.
27 For a review of *The Wandering Earth*, see https://www.indiewire.com/2019/05/wandering-earth-review-netflix-1202132477/; however, a more positive spin comes from Bruno Macaes. Retrieved from https://www.lowyinstitute.org/the-interpreter/film-review-wandering-earth.
28 For a discussion see Pamela McClintock and Steve Galloway, 'Matt Damon's "The Great Wall" to Lose $75 Million: U.S.-China Productions in Doubt'. *Hollywood Reporter*. Retrieved from https://www.hollywoodreporter.com/news/what-great-walls-box-office-flop-will-cost-studios-981602.
29 McClinock and Galloway, *The Great Wall* received ratings of 6/10 on IMDB, 35 per cent on the Rotten Tomatoes site and 5.4/10 on Douban, the Chinese online rating site. For a critical discussion of the history of Sino-Hollywood co-productions see

Aynne Kokas, *Hollywood Made in China* (Berkeley: University of California Press, 2017). For a review see Amy Qin, 'The Great Wall: What Critics and Filmgoers Are Saying in China'. *New York Times*, 22 December 2016. Retrieved from https://www.nytimes.com/2016/12/22/movies/the-great-wall-what-critics-and-filmgoers-are-saying-in-china.html; for a discussion of *The Great Wall and Wolf Warrior 2* see Ying Zhu and Michael Keane, 'China's Cultural Power Reconnects with the World', in *BRICS Framing a New Global Communication Order?* ed. Daya Thussu and Karle Nordenstraang (London: Routledge, 2020).

30 H. Huang, Z. Sun, C. Wang, and Z. Yang, *Zhongguo dianying yu guojia yingxiang chuanbo* [*Chinese film and the communication of national image*], *Xiandai chuanbo* [*Modern Communication*] 1: 22–28.

Chapter 6 East Asia: Hong Kong and Taiwan

1   The term 'China Circle' is used by Barry Naughton in a book of the same name. In this model Hong Kong had the smallest circle by area but the largest influence. Barry Naughton (ed.), *The China Circle: Economics and Technology in the PRC, Taiwan, and Hong Kong* (Washington, DC: Brookings Institute Press, 1997).
2   For a discussion of the halcyon years of Hong Kong as well as Taiwan, see Michael Curtin, *Playing to the World's Biggest Audience: The Globalization of Chinese Film and Television* (Berkeley: University of California Press, 2007).
3   Joseph Chan, 'Television in Greater China: Structure, Exports, and Market Formation', in *New Patterns in Global Television: Peripheral Vision*, ed. John Sinclair, Elizabeth Jacka, and Stuart Cunningham (Oxford: Oxford University Press, 1996), 126–60.
4   Rou-Lan Chen, 'Taiwan's Identity in Formation: in Reaction to a Democratizing Taiwan and a Rising China'. *Asian Ethnicity*, 14, no. 2 (2013): 229–50; Frank C. S. Liu and Francis L. F. Lee, 'Country, National, and Pan-National Identification in Taiwan and Hong Kong: Standing together as Chinese?' *Asian Survey* 53, no. 6 (2013): 1112–34.
5   Ien Ang, *On Not Speaking Chinese: Living between Asia and the West* (London: Routledge, 2001), 36, original emphasis.
6   Chi Kit Chan, 'China as "Other"': Resistance and Ambivalence toward National Identity in Hong Kong'. *China Perspectives* no. 1 (2014): 25–34.
7   See Ackbar Abbas, *Hong Kong: Culture and the Politics of Disappearance* (Minnesota: University of Minnesota Press, 1997) for an in-depth analysis of how Hong Kong's culture and identity appeared at the time of imminent disappearance on the cusp of the handover to Beijing.
8   For a discussion of new forms of artistic expression inspired by competing ideas of identity and culture, see Antony Dapiran, 'Culture of Reappearance: The Search for Hong Kong Identity, 20 Years After the Handover, Fuels the City's Creativity'. *ArtAsiaPacific* no. 104 (2017): 45–48.
9   Ibid., 48.
10 Kyung-Sup Chang, 'The Second Modern Condition? Compressed Modernity as Internalized Reflexive Cosmopolitization'. *British Journal of Sociology* 61, no. 3 (2010): 444–64 (446).
11 Chen, 'Taiwan's Identity in Formation'.
12 Thomas Gold, 'Go with Your Feelings: Hong Kong and Taiwan Popular Culture in Greater China'. *China Quarterly* no. 136 (1993): 907–25.

13 See Laikwan Pang, 'Postcolonial Hong Kong Cinema: Utilitarianism and (Trans)local'. *Postcolonial Studies* 10, no. 4 (2007): 413–30; Shujen Wang *Framing Piracy: Globalization and Film Distribution in Greater China* (Lanham, MD: Rowman & Littlefield, 2003); and Elaine Jing Zhao and Michael Keane, 'Between Formal and Informal: The Shakeout in China's Online Video Industry'. *Media, Culture and Society* 35, no. 6 (2013): 724–41.
14 See Curtin, *Playing to the World's Biggest Audience*.
15 See Yiu Fai Chow, 'Exploring Creative Class Mobility: Hong Kong Creative Workers in Shanghai and Beijing'. *Eurasian Geography & Economics* 58, no. 4 (2017): 361–85; and Elaine Jing Zhao, 'Collaboration Reconfigured: The Evolving Landscape of Entertainment TV Markets between Taiwan and Mainland China'. *Media International Australia* 159, no. 1 (2016): 53–62.
16 Pang, 'Postcolonial Hong Kong Cinema'; Mirana M. Szeto and Yun-Chung Chen, 'Mainlandization or Sinophone Translocality? Challenges for Hong Kong SAR New Wave Cinema'. *Journal of Chinese Cinemas* 6, no. 2 (2012): 115–34; and Ruby Cheung, *New Hong Kong Cinema: Transitions to Becoming Chinese in 21st-Century East Asia* (Oxford: Berghahn Books, 2016).
17 See Darrell Davis, 'Two Systems Differential: Informal Media and Decolonization in Hong Kong', in *Willing Collaborators: Foreign Partners in China's Media*, ed. Michael Keane, Brian Yecies, and Terry Flew (London: Rowman & Littlefield, 2018), 63–78.
18 Elaine Jing Zhao, 'Professionalization of Amateur Production in Online Screen Entertainment in China: Hopes, Frustrations and Uncertainties'. *International Journal of Communication*, no. 10 (2016): 5444–62.
19 See Lauly Li, 'Investment Commission rejects iQiyi's application', Taipei News, 29 November 2016, http://www.taipeitimes.com/News/biz/archives/2016/11/29/2003660181 (accessed 6 August 2018).
20 Tarleton Gillespie, 'The Politics of "Platforms"'. *New Media & Society* 12, no. 3 (2010): 347–64.
21 For an in-depth discussion of transformations and consequences brought by internet-distributed television portals in the US context, see Amanda D. Lotz, *Portals: A Treatise On Internet-Distributed Television* (Ann Arbor, MI: Maize Books, 2017).
22 Wilfred Yang Wang and Ramon Lobato, 'Chinese Video Streaming Services in the Context of Global Platform Studies'. *Chinese Journal of Communication* 12, no. 3 (2019): 356–71 (367).
23 See Liberty Times Net, 'Video Streaming Platforms Land in Taiwan', 14 March, 2019, https://news.ltn.com.tw/news/focus/paper/1274023 (accessed 6 July 2019).
24 See Variety, 'Taiwan Rejects License Application by China's iQiyi', 30 November 2016, https://variety.com/2016/digital/asia/taiwan-rejects-licence-for-china-iqiyi-1201930049/ (accessed 8 July 2019).
25 Lianrui Jia and Dwayne Winseck, 'The Political Economy of Chinese Internet Companies: Financialization, Concentration, and Capitalization'. *International Communication Gazette* 80, no. 1 (2019): 30–59.
26 Zhao, 'Collaboration Reconfigured'; Yiu Fai Chow, 'Exploring Creative Class Mobility: Hong Kong Creative Workers in Shanghai and Beijing'; Danjing Joy Zhang and Michael Keane, 'Creative Migration: Talent and Celebrity Movements to the Chinese Mainland', in *Willing Collaborators: Foreign partners in Chinese Media*, ed. Michael Keane, Brian Yecies, and Terry Flew (London: Rowman & Littlefield, 2018), 213–25.

27 See Hanshu Zhang, 'LeTV Plans to Enter Hong Kong Market with 300 Million Yuan Investment in Local Content Acquisition', 19 August 2014, https://m.21jingji.com/article/20140819/herald/eff3974009101286402abb9466c857fd.html (accessed 6 August 2018).
28 For discussions on TV formats, see Jean K. Chalaby, 'Drama without Drama: The Late Rise of Scripted TV Formats'. *Television and New Media* 17, no. 1 (2015): 3–20; Albert Moran, *Copycat TV: Globalisation, Program Formats and Cultural Identity* (Luton: University of Luton Press, 1997); Michael Keane, Anthony Y. H. Fung, and Albert Moran, *New Television, Globalisation, and the East Asian Cultural Imagination* (Hong Kong: Hong Kong University Press, 2007).
29 Zhao, 'Collaboration Reconfigured'.
30 Beng-Huat Chua and Koichi Iwabuchi, 'Introduction: East Asian TV Dramas: Identifications, Sentiments and Effects', in *East Asian Pop Culture: Analysing the Korean Wave*, ed. Beng-Huat Chua and Koichi Iwabuchi (Hong Kong: Hong Kong University Press, 2008), 1–12; and Dooho Shim, 'Hybridity and the Rise of Korean Popular Culture in Asia'. *Media, Culture & Society* 28, no. 1 (2006): 25–44.
31 See China Daily, 'LeTV Sports Gets EPL Rights for Hong Kong', 23 September 2015, http://www.chinadaily.com.cn/business/2015-09/23/content_21955603.htm (accessed 1 July 2018).
32 Peter Millward, *The Global Football League: Transnational Networks, Social Movements and Sport in the New Media Age* (Basingstoke: Palgrave, 2011).
33 Elaine Jing Zhao, *Digital China's Informal Circuits: Platforms, Labour and Governance* (London: Routledge, 2019), 72–73.
34 Michele Hockx, *Internet Literature in China* (New York: Columbia University Press, 2015); and Elaine Jing Zhao, 'Social Network Market: Storytelling on a Web 2.0 Original Literature Site'. *Convergence* 17, no. 1 (2011): 85–99.
35 Zhao, *Digital China's Informal Circuits*, 85–107.
36 See Taipei Times, 'Chinese Platform Panned For Axing Taiwan Drama', 7 August 2017, http://www.taipeitimes.com/News/taiwan/archives/2017/08/07/2003676085 (accessed 8 July 2018).
37 Eva Tsai, 'Caught in the Terrains: An Inter-referential Inquiry of Trans-border Stardom and Fandom'. *Inter-Asia Cultural Studies* 8, no. 1 (2007): 137–56.
38 Florian Schneider, *China's Digital Nationalism* (Oxford: Oxford University Press, 2019).
39 See United Daily News, 'On the Popularity of *The Rap of China* across the Strait', 28 September 2017, https://opinion.udn.com/opinion/story/11517/2726019 (accessed 8 August 2018).
40 See Xinhua News, 'MOC Publishes a Black List of Internet-distributed Songs', 10 August 2015, http://www.xinhuanet.com//politics/2015-08/10/c_1116205562.htm (accessed 8 August 2018).
41 Zhao, *Digital China's Informal Circuits*, 64–68.
42 See Washington Post, 'TikTok's Beijing Roots Fuel Censorship Suspicion As It Builds a Huge U.S. Audience', 15 September 2019. https://www.washingtonpost.com/technology/2019/09/15/tiktoks-beijing-roots-fuel-censorship-suspicion-it-builds-huge-us-audience/ (accessed 16 October 2019).
43 China Times, 'TikTok is Rising in Taiwan with Monthly Active Users Reaching 3 Million', 28 December 2018, https://www.chinatimes.com/newspapers/20181228000464-260204?chdtv (accessed 16 October 2019).

Chapter 7 South East Asia: Singapore and Malaysia

1. The interviewees were initially contacted through our personal networks and their numbers increased by snowballing. Interviewees included individuals from 18 to 70 years.
2. Thomas Smale, 'The Best Countries to Start a Business are [...]', Entrepreneur Asia Pacific, 18 January, 2017. Retrieved from https://www.entrepreneur.com/article/287908.
3. In Singapore, 'other' is one of the four ethnic classifications: Chinese, Malay, Indian and Other.
4. Amy Chew, 'Malaysia's Economy Just Got a US$33 Billion Boost from China [...] So Why the Unhappiness?' South China Morning Post, 21 November 2016. Retrieved from https://www.scmp.com/week-asia/geopolitics/article/2047345/malaysias-economy-just-got-us33-billion-dollar-boost-china-so.
5. Rozana Latiff and Norihikou Shirouzu, 'China's Geely Buys 49.9 Percent of Malaysian Automaker Proton'. Reuters, 24 May 2017. Retrieved from https://www.reuters.com/article/us-proton-m-a-geely-idUSKBN18K0HE.
6. Xin Yi Tho, 'The Jack Ma Factor', The Star Online, 26 March 2017. Retrieved from https://www.thestar.com.my/news/nation/2017/03/26/the-jack-ma-factor.
7. See, for example, Dan Price, '5 Tips to Buy Safely on AliExpress and Avoid Frauds or Scams', MUO (Make Use Of), 7 February, 2020. Retrieved from https://www.makeuseof.com/tag/buy-safely-aliexpress-scams/.
8. Susan Leong, 'Provisional Business Migrants to Western Australia, Social Media and Conditional Belonging', in *Media and Communication in the Chinese Diaspora: Rethinking Transnationalism*, ed. Wanning Sun and John Sinclair (London: Routledge, 2016), 189–207.
9. Susan Leong, 'Prophets of Mass Innovation: The Gospel According to BAT', *Media Industries Journal* 5, no. 1 (2018). doi:10.3998/mij.15031809.0005.105.
10. Pooja Singh, 'Southeast Asia's Latest Billionaire Is a Gaming Guru'. Retrieved from https://www.entrepreneur.com/article/331114.
11. Jeanette Tan, 'Former SMRT Bus Driver: Why We Went on Strike (Part 1)', 5 April 2013. Retrieved from https://sg.news.yahoo.com/former-smrt-bus-driver—why-we-went-on-strike—part-1—135100687.html.
12. https://youtu.be/UF8uR6Z6KLc.
13. Jessica Tan, 'Game for Garena: Singapore's Answer to Tencent and Alibaba', Forbes n/d. Retrieved from https://www.forbes.com/sites/forbesasia/2015/06/23/game-for-garena-singapores-answer-to-tencent-and-alibaba/#9c9389b41000.
14. 'Forrest Li', Forbes. Retrieved from https://www.forbes.com/profile/forrest-li/#5a094563b60b.
15. Jessica Tan, 'Game for Garena: Singapore's Answer to Tencent and Alibaba', Forbes n/d.
16. Susan Leong, 'Sinophone, Chinese, and PRC Internet: Chinese Overseas in Australia and the PRC Internet'. *Digital Asia* 3 (2016): 117–37.
17. Parag Khanna, *The Future Is Asian: Global Order in the Twenty-First Century* (London: Weidenfeld & Nicolson, 2019), 19.
18. Ibid., 23.

Chapter 8 Oceania: Australia and New Zealand

1. In 1996, for example, 1.2 per cent of the population in Australia spoke Cantonese at home and 0.5 per cent were Mandarin speakers; Australia Bureau of Statistics. 1999. Australian Social Trends. Available at https://www.abs.gov.au/AUSSTATS/abs@.nsf/2f762f95845417aeca25706c00834efa/d67b7c95e0e8a733ca2570ec00111 7a2!OpenDocument. The number of Mandarin speakers has risen significantly in the past decade. By 2016 the number had more than doubled Cantonese speakers. Retrieved from https://identitycomms.com.au/2017/06/top-10-languages-spoken-in-australia-2016-census/.
2. Susan Leong, 'Provisional Business Migrants to Western Australia, Social Media and Conditional Belonging', in *Media and Communication in the Chinese Diaspora: Rethinking Transnationalism*, ed. Wanning Sun and John Sinclair (London: Routledge, 2016), 189–207.
3. For 'filter bubbles', see Axel Bruns, *Are Filter Bubbles Real?* (London: Policy Press, 2019). Bruns argues for shifting our focus away from platforms or algorithms for political hyperpolarisation in echo chambers and filter bubbles, toward issues in our societies and democracies. The 'cultural filter bubbles' is a specific type of personalized searches and feedback loops for linguistically, racially, and culturally specific groups.
4. See David Walker and Agnieszka Sobocinska, 'Australia's Asia', in *Australia's Asia: From Yellow Peril to Asian Century*, ed. David Walker and Agnieszka Sobocinska (Crawley, WA: UWA, 2012), 1–23.
5. Pauline Hanson's maiden political speech, 14 September 2016. Available from https://www.theguardian.com/australia-news/2016/sep/14/pauline-hanson-first-speech-senate-calls-for-immigration-ban.
6. For New Zealand's early history of restrictions on immigration, see https://teara.govt.nz/en/immigration-regulation/page-2 (accessed 18 February 2020).
7. This is also known as the high net worth population, with individual liquid financial assets of around USD one million.
8. See Statistica.com, 'Number of Chinese students in Australia', 28 July 2020. Available at https://www.statista.com/statistics/430276/number-of-chinese-students-in-australia-by-education-sector/#:~:text=There%20were%20more%20than%20 260%2C000,the%20higher%20education%20sector%20alone.
9. 'Tertiary education enrolments by international students', November 2018. Retrieved from https://www.educationcounts.govt.nz/statistics/indicators/main/student-engagement-participation/international_students_enrolled_in_formal_tertiary_education.
10. See Anne-Marie Brady, 'China 2.0, and the Challenges It Poses to New Zealand', *Noted*, 19 November 2018. Available at https://www.noted.co.nz/currently/politics/anne-marie-brady-xi-jinping-china-challenge-to-nz/.
11. Clive Hamilton, *Silent Invasion: China's Influence in Australia* (Sydney: Hardie Grant, 2018).
12. ASPI has produced a series of reports on China, as represented by those written by executive director Peter Jennings, such as https://www.aspi.org.au/opinion/better-safe-sorry-china (accessed 11 May 2020).
13. Latika Bourke, 'Why Are Huawei and 5G Such a Big Deal around the World?' *Sydney Morning Herald*, 14 February 2020. Available at Why are Huawei and 5G such a big deal https://www.smh.com.au/world/europe/why-are-huawei-and-5g-such-a-big-deal-around-the-world-20200131-p53wf0.html.

14 'How a visit to Australia helped Jack Ma become an internet tycoon', SBS News, 8 September 2018. Available at https://www.sbs.com.au/news/how-a-visit-to-australia-helped-jack-ma-become-an-internet-tycoon.
15 Jaivin's account is detailed in a special issue of *Australian Foreign Affairs*. See Linda Jaivin, 'Red Detachment: Is Chinese Culture beyond Reach?' *Australian Foreign Affairs* 5, February 2019: 29–54.
16 Yingchi Chu, 'The Politics of Reception: Made in China and Western Critique'. *International Journal of Cultural Studies* 17, no. 2 (2014): 159–73.
17 Linda Jakobson and Bates Gill, *China Matters: Getting It Right for Australia* (Melbourne: Black Books, 2017).
18 Sarah Teo, 'Can Australia Be One of Us?' *Australian Foreign Affairs*, no. 5 (2019): 77–93 (92).
19 The report written by Wanning Sun finds that the content of China's state media has found its way into the space of some of Australia's ethnic Chinese-language media and that, in contrast to the mostly anti-communist stance of a few decades ago, the majority of these media report on China favourably or refrain from criticizing China openly. See Australian China Relations Institute (ACRI) (2016), Chinese-Language Media in Australia: Developments, Challenges, and Opportunities. Available at www.australiachinarelations.org/content/chinese-language-media-australia-developments-challenges-and-opportunities-2.
20 Wanning Sun and Haiqing Yu, 'WeChatting the Australian Election: Mandarin-Speaking Migrants and the Teaching of New Citizenship Practices'. *Social Media + Society* [online], (January 2020). doi:10.1177/2056305120903441.
21 Wanning Sun, 'Is There a Problem with … WeChat?' *China Matters Policy Brief*, April 2019. Available at chinamatters.org.au/policy-brief/policy-brief-april-edition.
22 Luke Russo, 'What is TikTok?', 12 July 2020. Available at https://www.smperth.com/resources/tiktok/what-is-tiktok/.
23 See 'Power and Influence', Australian Broadcasting Commission, 5 June 2017. https://www.abc.net.au/4corners/power-and-influence-promo/8579844.
24 For a discussion of Murdoch's so-called adventures in China see Bruce Dover, *Rupert's Adventures in China: How Murdoch Lost a Fortune and Found a Wife* (London: Viking Books, 2008); also Michael Keane, *The Chinese Television Industry* (London: BRFI Palgrave, 2015); for a discussion of satellite TV in Guangdong see Yik Chan Chin, *Television Regulation and Media Policy in China* (London: Routledge).
25 Keane, *The Chinese Television Industry*.
26 See Ian Huffer, 'The Circulation of Chinese Film in New Zealand as a Potential Platform for Soft Power'. *Media International Australia* 176, no. 1 (2020): 78–92, https://doi.org/10.1177/1329878X20921570
27 See *Common Ground: Opportunities for Australian Screen Partnerships in Asia*. Available at Screen Australia, http://www.screenaustralia.gov.au/getmedia/044d734f-545e-4b58-bfee-d2980402e76b/CommonGround_Report2013.pdf.
28 Stan Rosen, *The Use of Film for Public Diplomacy: Why Hollywood Makes a Stronger Case for China*, 2011. Available at USC Annenberg, http://uscpublicdiplomacy.org/pdin_monitor_article/the_use_of_film_for_public_diplomacy_why_hollywood_makes_a_stronger_case_fo.
29 Don Groves, 'Bait 2 Morphs into Deep Water', 2013. Available at http://if.com.au/2013/07/31/article/Bait-2-morphs-into-Deep-Water/FPECJYBIII.html.

30. John Sinclair and Stuart Cunningham, 'Go with the Flow: Diasporas and the Media'. *Television & New Media* 1, no. 1 (February 2000): 11–31. doi:10.1177/152747640000100102.
31. Keane, *The Chinese Television Industry*.
32. Wanning Sun and Jing Han, 'If You Are the One and SBS: The Cultural Economy of Difference'. *Media International Australia* 175, no. 1 (2020): 6–19.
33. Ibid., 10.
34. Ibid.
35. Nicole Talmacs, 'Chinese Cinema and Australian Audiences: An Exploratory Study'. *Media International Australia* 175, no. 1 (2020): 50–64.
36. For a discussion of how priming works see David McRaney, *You Are Not so Smart* (Oxford: Oneworld, 2012).
37. For a discussion see Bobby Duffy, *The Perils of Perception: Why We're Wrong about Nearly Everything* (London: Atlantic Book, 2019), 67.
38. See Huffer, 'The Circulation of Chinese Film in New Zealand as a Potential Platform for Soft Power'.
39. For a discussion see Duffy, *The Perils of Perception*, 67.
40. See Huffer, 'The Circulation of Chinese Film in New Zealand as a Potential Platform for Soft Power'.
41. This image we used referred to the animated version of Mulan released in 1998, not Disney's controversial 2020 movie.
42. Meng Yang, 'An American Panda in Chinese Clothing – the Interpretation of Paul's Cultural Identity in Kungfu Panda'. *Journal of Gansu Lianhe University* (Social Science edition) 27, no. 1672–707X (2011): 85–88.
43. Georgette Wang and Emilie Yueh-yu Yeh, 'Globalization and Hybridization in Cultural Products: The Cases of Mulan and Crouching Tiger, Hidden Dragon'. *International Journal of Cultural Studies* 8, no. 2 (June 2005): 175–93. doi:10.1177/1367877905052416.
44. We received 156 responses from people with Australian nationality, that is, they were holders of Australian passports. Ages ranged from 18 to more than 60, with the majority falling in the 18–28 demographic; 45.9 per cent of respondents said they couldn't speak or read Chinese.
45. For research on the Chinese diaspora and their media consumption habits in Australia, see Wanning Sun and Haiqing Yu's research at https://ozchinamedia.org/.

Chapter 9 From Cultural Presence to Innovative Nation

1. See, for example, Peter MacCawley, 'China's Belt and Road Initiative: Status Report', The Interpreter, 10 July 2019. Retrieved from https://www.lowyinstitute.org/the-interpreter/china-s-belt-and-road-initiative-status-report.
2. For a report on Huawei in Australia, see: Danielle Cave, et al., 'Huawei and Australia's 5G Network', Australia Strategic Policy Institute, 10 October 2018. https://www.aspi.org.au/report/huawei-and-australias-5g-network.
3. Peter Nolan, *China and the West: Crossroads of Civilization* (London: Routledge, 2018).
4. Martin Jacques, *When China Rules the World: The End of the Western World and the Birth of a New Global Order*, 2nd edn (London: Penguin Books, 2012).
5. Weiwei Zhang, *China Horizon, the: Glory and Dream of a Civilizational State* (Beijing: World Scientific Press, 2016), 2.

6 Hugo de Burgh, *China's Media in the Emerging World Order* (Buckingham: University of Buckingham Press, 2017), 31.
7 E.g. Juan Pablo Cardenal and Heriberto Araujo, *China's Silent Army: The Pioneers, Traders, Fixers and Workers Who Are Remaking the World in Beijing's Image* (London: Penguin Books, 2014, Kindle Edition); Huiyao Wang and Miao Lu, *China Goes Global: How China's Overseas Investment on Its Business Enterprises* (London: Palgrave Macmillan, 2016); and Lourdes Casanova and Anne Miroux, *The Era of Chinese Multinationals: Competing for Global Dominance* (London: Academic Press, 2020).
8 Sheng Ding, *The Dragon's Hidden Wings: How China Rises with Its Soft Power* (Lanham: Lexington Books, 2008), 66–67.
9 Gregory Lee, *China Imagined* (London: Hurst, 2019), Kindle edition, 253.
10 Vicky Xiuzhong Xu, 'China's Youth Are Trapped in the Cult of Nationalism', *Foreign Policy*, 1 October 2019. Retrieved from https://foreignpolicy.com/2019/10/01/chinas-angry-young-nationalists/.
11 The idea of national humiliation resonates deeply with the Chinese population and dates back to the Opium Wars in the mid-nineteenth century. The theme figures in a great many audiovisual works, from movies, TV serials to games.
12 See Xi Jinping's Keynote Speech at the Opening Ceremony of the International Horticultural Exhibition 2019 – *Beijing Review* Edited Excerpt. Available at http://www.bjreview.com/Beijing_Review_and_Kings_College_London_Joint_Translation_Project/2019/201909/t20190903_800177587.html.
13 Rebecca A. Fannin, *Tech Titans of China: How China's Tech Sector Is Challenging the World by Innovating Faster, Working Harder and Going Global* (Boston: Nicholas Brearley, 2019).
14 See WISE, The Future Think Tank. Available at https://www.wisenotwise.com/
15 Benjamin Pimentel, 'As a tech Cold War looms, this veteran Silicon Valley Patent Attorney Says That China's Push to Win the AI Processor Market Is a Serious Threat to American Tech', Business Insider, 19 May 2019. Retrieved from https://bit.ly/3dHDbfi.
16 In an interview with the BBC's Karishma Vaswani on 18 February 2019, Ren Zhengfei made these comments; this interview is included in full in the Huawei book, *In His Own Words: Dialogues with Ren*, Huawei Internal, 129.
17 John Fitzgerald, 'Mind Your Tongue', *Australian Strategic Policy Institute*, 2 October 2019. Retrieved from https://www.aspi.org.au/report/mind-your-tongue.
18 Alexie Drew, John Gerson, Charles Parton, and Benedict Wilkinson, 'Rising to the China Challenge', The Policy Institute, King's College, 7 January 2020. Retrieved from https://www.kcl.ac.uk/news/rising-to-the-china-challenge.
19 Clive Hamilton, *Silent Invasion: China's Influence in Australia* (Sydney: Hardie Grant, 2018).
20 See Tom Huddleston, 'Carly Fiorina Says the Chinese "Don't Innovate"', *Time*. 26 May 2015. Retrieved from https://time.com/3897081/carly-fiorina-china-innovation/.
21 E.g. Yu Hong and Jian Xu, 'Toward Fragmented Platform Governance in China: Through the Lens of Alibaba and the Legal-Judicial System'. *International Journal of Communication* 13 (2019): 4642–62.
22 For a comprehensive discussion of the trade war, see Bob Davis and Lingling Wei, *Superpower Showdown: How the Battle between Trump and Xi Threatens a new Cold War* (New York: Harper Collins, 2020).

23   Grzegorz Stec, 'Beyond Tech Transfer: The Challenge of Chinese Tech Expanding Abroad'. *The Diplomat*, 25 May 2018. Retrieved from https://thediplomat.com/2018/05/beyond-tech-transfer-the-challenge-of-chinese-tech-expanding-abroad/.

24   Danielle Cave, Samantha Hoffman, Alex Joske, Fergus Ryan, and Elise, 'Mapping China's Technology Giants', International cyber Policy Centre, Australian Strategic Policy Institute (ASPI), Issue paper report no. 15, 17 April 2019. Retrieved from https://www.aspi.org.au/report/mapping-chinas-tech-giants.

25   Fergus Ryan, Danielle Cave, and Vicky Xiuzhong Xu, 'Mapping More of Chinese Technology Giants: AI and Surveillance', ASPI, 28 November 2019. Retrieved from https://www.aspi.org.au/report/mapping-more-chinas-tech-giants.

26   Greg Roumeliotis, Yingzhi Yang, Echo Wang, and Alexandra Alper, 'Exclusive: U.S. Opens National Security Investigation into TikTok'. *Reuters*, 2 November 2019. Retrieved from https://yhoo.it/3c7cv7i.

27   Grace Tobin, 'It's Time to Talk about TikTok and What It's Doing with Our Kids' Data', *ABC*, 19 February 2020. Retrieved from https://www.abc.net.au/news/2020-02-19/should-we-trust-chinese-owned-tiktok-personal-data/11962086.

28   'Mark Zuckerberg Stands for Voice and Free Expression', Facebook News. 1 October 2019. Retrieved from https://about.fb.com/news/2019/10/mark-zuckerberg-stands-for-voice-and-free-expression/.

29   Nicolas Bega, 'TikTok's Headquarters Could Move Outside China', *New York Post*, 23 December 2019. Retrieved from https://nypost.com/2019/12/23/tiktoks-headquarters-could-move-outside-china/.

30   Luzhou Li, *Zoning China: Online Video, Popular Culture, and the State* (Cambridge, MA: MIT Press, 2019).

31   Koichi Iwabuchi, *Recentering Globalization: Popular Culture and Japanese Transnationalism* (Durham, NC: Duke University Press, 2002).

32   Robert D. Kaplan, 'A New Cold War Has Begun', *Foreign Policy*, 7 January 2019. Retrieved from https://foreignpolicy.com/2019/01/07/a-new-cold-war-has-begun/.

INDEX

Abbas, Ackbar 103
ABC (Australian Broadcasting Commission) 141, 145
Academy Awards 38, 85
AI (Artificial Intelligence) 4, 55, 160
algorithms, algorithmic 7, 10, 23, 45, 48, 60, 68, 71, 87, 114
Alibaba, Alibaba.com 7, 23, 51, 52, 57–60, 63, 67, 71–79, 96, 105, 111, 121–23, 129, 131, 132, 139, 148–50, 159–60
Alibaba Research Centre 58
AliExpress 122, 124, 150
Alipay 24, 53, 72, 73, 77, 147, 148–50
Alley, Rewi 137
Amazon 71, 81, 121, 131, 150
Ang, Lee (Li An) 18, 145
Ang, Ien 145
animation 36, 38, 86, 94, 106, 146
anime 19
Ant Financial 77–78, 121, 147
ASPI (Australian Strategic Policy Institute) 138
automation 42

Baidu 7, 51–53, 58, 67, 71, 73, 77–78, 96, 101, 105–6, 128–29, 147
Baggini, Julian 91
Baldwin, Richard 36, 41, 60
big data 3, 7, 22, 54–58, 60, 68, 71–72, 81, 85–86, 88
Belt and Road Initiative (BRI) 2, 31, 43, 138, 155
Bilibili 98, 135, 152
BitTorrent sites: BT sites 20
blockbusters 19, 95, 146
Blue Books (*lanpi shu*) 8, 34, 94

Borgman, Christine 86
Brady, Anne-Marie 138
Bytedance 24, 46, 54, 68, 71, 74–75, 79–80, 160. *See also* TikTok, Douyin

capitalism 2, 44–45, 68, 71, 89
    platform capitalism 75
    surveillance capitalism 76, 79
    digital capitalism 5, 59, 69
Carousell 123–24
celebrity, celebrities 5, 14, 22–23, 28, 51, 85, 102, 110, 151
censorship 18, 33, 48, 63–64, 102, 113, 127, 140, 151, 160–61
Central Cyber Security and Informatization Leading Group 64
Chang, Kyung-Sup 103
Chan, Jackie 85, 151
Chan, Joseph Man 39
China Central Television (CCTV) 22, 27, 31, 34, 93, 95, 135, 143
China Global TV Network (CGTN) 27, 95, 140
China Mobile 43, 50
China threat 94, 138
Chinese Dream 1, 4, 56, 58, 67, 103, 158
Chu, Yingchi 20, 93
Chua, Beng-Huat 32–33, 93
City Brain (Alibaba) 121
Civilization 6, 13–15, 45, 49, 103, 151, 155, 157–58
CEPA (the Closer Economic Partnership Agreement) 102, 105
convergence 2, 20, 25, 35, 41, 43, 47, 50–51, 60, 62
coproduction 95, 145

INDEX

copyright 20, 52, 96. *See also* intellectual property
Couldry, Nick 26
COVID-19 24, 59, 138
clusters, clustering 4–5, 36, 39, 46, 60
Crouching Tiger, Hidden Dragon 18, 93, 145
culture
    culture as civilization 13
    New Culture Movement 15
    traditional 14, 90, 151
cultural discount 85
cultural industry/industries 16, 19, 22, 25, 32, 34–35, 45, 47, 92, 105, 109, 156
cultural and creative industries 7–8, 25–26, 29, 32, 42, 47, 62, 104
cultural innovation 35–36, 38
cultural exports 13, 91. *See also* going out
cultural power 24–25, 27, 32, 38, 45, 88, 117, 155, 162
Cultural Revolution 16, 139, 149, 157
cultural soft power 6, 13–14, 27–28, 88, 92
cultural security 26
cultural services 17–18
cultural trade deficit 6
Curtin, Michael 21, 34
Cyberport 104
cybersecurity 54, 64–65
Cyberspace Administration of China 4, 62

data analytics 42, 92
Davis, Darrell 105
De Burgh, Hugo 156
De Kloet, Jeroen 70
Deng Xiaoping 31–32, 34, 44
Didi Chuxing 24, 51, 54, 68, 72, 74, 78–79, 130, 157
digital
    digital champions 7, 13, 58, 67, 116, 161–62
    Digital China 6, 60, 67, 96, 121, 129, 163
    digital empire 2, 7, 68, 72–73, 75
    See also digital capitalism; digital economy
Digital Free Trade Zone (DFTZ) 121
Ding, Sheng 38
discourse war 13, 88, 155

Douyin 71, 74, 79, 135, 148, 153. *See also* ByteDance and TikTok
Dream Town 40

East Asian pop culture 13, 27, 93
ECFA (the Economic Cooperation Framework Agreement 102, 105
economy
    platform economy 7, 67, 68, 70
    sharing economy 22, 51–52, 157
E-commerce 3, 5, 23, 51, 53, 59, 71–73, 77–78, 121–24, 131, 139, 149–50, 158–59
electronic world trade platform 77

Facebook 49, 62, 69–71, 73, 79–81, 90, 95, 97, 102, 130, 150, 152–53, 161, 167
Fan Bingbing 31
Fan Zhou 25
Feng Xiaogang 16, 31, 149
Five G (5G) 43, 45, 51, 57, 59, 60, 130, 139, 151, 155
Florida, Richard 89
Fuchs, Christian 71
Fung, Anthony 33, 104

gangtai culture 34
Garena 131
Gillespie, Tarleton 68–69, 107
going out (*zou chuqu*) 7, 21, 24, 32, 38, 48, 66–68, 74–75, 93–94, 101, 116, 131, 155–56
Gold, Thomas 34
Google 4, 23, 49, 52, 62, 69–71, 79, 91, 108, 128–29, 153
governance
    internet governance 50, 61–66
    platform governance 71
    social governance 54, 59, 63
Grab, GrabPay 74, 79, 80, 125
Great Firewall of China (GFC) 47, 63
Greater Bay Area Plan 102
Greater China 102, 117, 120

Hamilton, Clive 138, 160
Han, Jing 143

INDEX

Harwit, Eric. 43
Hepp, Andreas 26
Hill, Anne 28
historical dramas 19
Hollywood 52, 85, 93, 95, 97, 148, 151, 157
Hong, Yu 43, 55
Huawei 42, 52, 57, 63, 76, 81, 91, 121, 125, 138–39, 148–51, 155, 158–60
Hu Jintao 62, 86, 88

I am a Singer (woshi geshou) 110
If You are the One (feicheng wurao) 21, 37, 94, 143–44, 151
intellectual property 5, 23, 37, 61, 66, 156, 160
Intelligent + 7, 24, 56, 58, 60
Internet of Things (IoT) 3, 22, 38, 54, 68
intelligent technology 23, 60
iQiyi 8, 24, 52, 77, 87, 94, 96, 98, 101, 105–13, 115, 117, 152, 156–66

Jacques, Martin 155
Jaivin, Linda 16, 139
Jia, Lianrui 71
Jia, Zhangke 146
Jobs, Steve 123, 131

Korean Wave 110, 116. *See also* Hallyu
Kung fu 85, 95, 104, 147–48, 151
Kung Fu Panda (gongfu xiongmao) 147–48, 151

Lash, Scott 25–26, 47
Lazada 77, 121
Lee, Kai-fu 23, 41–42
LeTV/LeEco 8, 52, 101–2, 105, 108, 111–12
Li, Bingbing 85
Li, Huailiang 92
Li, Keqiang 3, 22–23, 40, 55–56
Li, Robin 129, 147
Li, Wuwei 17, 26
Li, Xiaodong 131
Lowy Asia Power Index 88, 90
Lu, Xun 15
Lury, Celia 25–26, 47

Ma, Jack (Ma Yun) 23, 28, 77, 121, 123, 139, 147–49, 151, 157
Ma, Pony (Ma Huateng) 129, 147
McLuhan, Marshall 27, 69
Made in China 20, 25, 22, 54, 56
maker spaces 3–6, 40, 158
Marsh, Vivien 94
mass innovation 3, 22, 35, 40, 42, 55, 56, 59
Meituan-Dianping 54, 68, 72, 74
Morrison, George 137
Mulan 147–48
Muller, Jerry 86
Murdoch, Rupert 141

National People's Congress 56, 58
NetEase 51, 124
Nirvana in Fire 94, 110
Nolan, Peter 155
Nye, Joseph 27, 88

Oppo 150
original design manufacturing (ODM) 104
original equipment manufacturing (OEM) 36, 104
over-the-top (OTT) content providers 107
Ozawa, Terutomo 41, 60

People's Daily 34, 140
Pew Research Centre 91
Plantin, Jean-Christophe 69–70
platform
platform society 70–71
  See also platform economy; platform capitalism
platformization 5, 70–71
popular culture 13, 19, 29, 110, 113. *See also* East Asian pop culture
Porter, Michael 39
Portland Soft Power 30 Index 86, 89, 92
propaganda 15, 18–19, 26, 28, 32–33, 44–45, 94, 140, 146, 155, 158, 160

QQ 51, 53, 67, 72, 124, 135, 149, 167
Quora.com 90

reality TV 21, 37, 94, 141
reform of the cultural system 34
robots, robotics 7, 40, 42, 56, 59, 68, 74, 81, 158
Rosen, Stanley 92, 142

Scheen, Lena 37
Schneider, Florian 75, 113
SEA 131
Shanzhai 5, 23, 37
Shen, Hong 63
Shenzhen 3–4, 8, 23, 37, 39, 53, 158–59
Shopee 121, 124, 131, 167
Silk Roads 15. *See also* Belt and Road (BRI)
Silicon Valley 23, 32, 49, 54, 62, 131, 133
Sina Weibo 63, 71, 130, 147–49
Social + 7, 48, 59, 72, 131
South China Sea 24, 119
Su, Wendy 19
Sun, Wanning 140, 143–44
superstructure 15, 25, 31, 47, 60, 162
surveillance 5, 24, 47, 57, 62–65, 71, 76, 79, 138, 150, 158, 160

technology parks 39, 44
telecom operators, telecommunications 7, 20, 43, 50, 53, 59, 108, 159
Tencent (tengxun) 7, 24, 39, 51–52, 56, 58–59, 67, 71–73, 78–79, 96, 98, 105, 107, 115, 117, 132, 131, 129, 140, 147, 149, 152, 156, 158–60, 166
Tencent Video 24, 52, 96, 98, 105, 107, 115, 117, 152, 156, 166
Teo, Sarah 139
The Farewell 93, 146
The Flowers of War 20
The Great Wall 20, 85, 95, 145–46
The Parasite 29, 85
The Rap of China (*zhongguo you xihua*)
The Wandering Earth 95, 99, 146
TikTok 1–3, 7, 8–9, 46, 71, 74, 79–80, 96, 101, 106, 112, 114–15, 130, 135, 140, 147, 152, 157, 160, 166. *See also* Douyin, ByteDance
Toutiao 71, 74, 79, 135
Tudou (also Youku Tudou) 24, 52, 72, 105

User Generated Content (UGC) 20, 25, 40, 96, 114, 161

venture capital 4, 23, 41, 44, 67, 74, 80
video-on-demand (VOD) 96
video streaming 105, 106, 108
Virtual Reality (VR) 6, 22, 158–59

Wanda Group 21, 111
Wanghong 25
Wang, Jianlin 21
Watson, James 28
WeChat 24, 53, 63, 71–73, 77, 97–98, 114–15, 125, 130, 135, 140, 147, 149, 152–53, 160–61, 167
Winseck, Dwayne 71
Wolf Warrior 2, 93, 95, 147
Wong, Winnie 37
Wu, Ruiqing 90

Xiao, Xuefan 37, 44
Xiaomi 38, 53, 150–51
Xi, Jinping 2, 10, 13, 19, 27, 28–29, 54, 56, 62, 64, 151, 155

Youku; Youku Tudou 23–24, 52, 72, 96, 105, 115, 152, 166
YouTube 62, 70, 98, 102, 106, 115, 156, 166. *See also* Tudou

Zhang, Chang 90
Zhang, Weiwei 155–56
Zhang, Yimou 145
ZTE 42, 57, 81, 158
Zuckerberg, Mark 161
Zuboff, Shoshana 79

www.ingramcontent.com/pod-product-compliance
Lightning Source LLC
Chambersburg PA
CBHW021828300426
44114CB00009BA/364